The
Ethical

Use of Touch
in Psychotherapy

We dedicate this book to

Peter Dimock,

who has touched our lives

and the lives of so many others,

and to Jeff and Kate An, whose touch we cherish.

The
Ethical

Use of Touch
in Psychotherapy

Mic Hunter
Jim Struve

SAGE Publications
International Educational and Professional Publisher
Thousand Oaks   London   New Delhi

For information:

SAGE Publications, Inc.
2455 Teller Road
Thousand Oaks, California 91320
E-mail: order@sagepub.com

SAGE Publications Ltd.
6 Bonhill Street
London EC2A 4PU
United Kingdom

SAGE Publications India Pvt. Ltd.
M-32 Market
Greater Kailash I
New Delhi 110 048 India

Printed in the United States of America

Library of Congress Cataloging-in-Publication Data

Hunter, Mic.
    The ethical use of touch in psychotherapy /by Mic Hunter and
Jim Struve.
        p.   cm.
    Includes bibliographical references and index.
    ISBN 0-7619-0360-7 (cloth). — ISBN 0-7619-0361-5 (pbk.)
    1. Touch—Therapeutic use. 2. Psychotherapy. I. Struve, Jim
II. Title.
    RC489.T69H86   1997
    616.89′14—dc21   97-4799

    99 00 01 02 03 10 9 8 7 6 5 4 3 2

Acquiring Editor:	C. Terry Hendrix
Editorial Assistant:	Dale Mary Grenfell
Production Editor:	Diana E. Axelsen
Production Assistant:	Karen Wiley
Typesetter/Designer:	Marion Warren
Indexer:	Mary Mortensen
Cover Designer:	Candice Harman

Contents

Preface

Although physical contact between those who seek to heal and those who search for relief has a long history, the use of touch within the psychotherapeutic relationship has not yet received widespread acceptance. An ever-growing body of research does indicate that when applied appropriately, touch between psychotherapist and client can benefit the client. Despite such findings, even discussing the topic of touch is anxiety producing for many clinicians. The primary objection to the use of touch has been the fear that any form of touch will eventually lead to sexual contact. Ironically, in an attempt to develop and maintain high ethical standards for the profession of psychotherapy, something that has been proved to be an effective treatment technique has been all but forbidden.

The primary objection to therapist-client contact results from extreme cases in which a therapist has violated professional standards and has, consequently, become sexual with clients. Any psychological technique—touch, talk, testing, research—can be done in an unethical manner by a particular therapist. The unethical use of any technique ought to be the cause for an indictment not of the technique but rather of the clinician who misused it. Touch is too valuable a tool in the service of human healing to deny its use to the psychotherapist.

As interest and debate on the use of touch continue, it will become increasingly important that the topic be addressed in degree-granting training programs and that those with the awesome responsibility of responding to ethical complaints made against colleagues become better informed about the clinical dimensions regarding the ethical use of touch in psychotherapy. We hope that this book, and the ones to follow it, will provide the field with a method of determining ethical standards for the use of touch, rather than merely banning it or pretending that it does not take place.

This book is the result of a long process that began several years ago when a participant in a workshop on the treatment of males sexually abused in childhood asked us our policy on touching these clients. In an attempt to respond to the question, we found ourselves involved in a lively discussion of clinical technique, ethics, and therapeutic philosophy. This experience led one of us (Hunter) to explore the topic further in a series of papers as a part of studies toward a doctoral degree. We began to incorporate this material into our presentations, eventually leading to workshops focusing entirely on the use of touch in psychotherapy at two national conferences on male sexual abuse survivors.

During these numerous presentations, three things rapidly became apparent. First, participants had strong emotional reactions to the mere mention of the subject of touch within psychotherapy. Second, although people had strong opinions on the topic, their stands, pro or con, were based on little or no exposure to the professional literature. Third, because many clinicians were already using touch as a part of their treatment, they were hungry for information and guidance on how to use touch. We heard frequent expressions of relief and gratitude that the topic of touch was finally being openly addressed. It appears that Wilson (1982) was correct when she wrote, "It may be that the touch taboo is not deterring many therapists from using touch, but is strong enough to keep them from admitting it to one another" (pp. 66-67). Eventually, it became apparent to us that there was enough interest in the topic to warrant a book.

As we wrote, we kept in mind three different groups of readers: those already practicing verbally based psychotherapy; students and faculty in clinical training programs who are searching for a textbook to use in their courses on counseling techniques and professional ethics; and members of licensing or professional conduct boards. As word of this project spread, consumers of psychotherapy contacted us to ask, "Is your book something I could read?" These people were interested in having touch be a component of their verbal psychotherapy, and they wanted to be sure it was provided in an ethical manner. We hope our style of writing is accessible to those clients who wish to learn more about the possible role that touch might play in their personal growth.

Our original manuscript proved to be overly ambitious. In attempting to be thorough, we created a document that would have been cost prohibitive for one of the primary groups of readers we sought to influence, those in training programs. Therefore, we reluctantly eliminated over 200 pages. The material removed came largely from the chapters on the historical aspects of the touch. We hope that those readers who desire more detail in this area will obtain the articles and books cited.

This book is not intended to promote a new form of psychotherapy, nor is it written to promote body-centered forms of therapy. Rather, we promote the ethical use of touch as an adjunct to talk therapy. We believe that touch can be a useful technique as a part of psychotherapy regardless of the theoretical orientation of the treatment provider. Therefore, this book is written for practitioners from all disciplines.

After observing ourselves and other psychotherapists for many years, it became clear to us that much of the touch exhibited by most psychotherapists is best described using Watson's (1975) term *expressive* touch—that is, physical contact that is relatively spontaneous in nature but is not necessarily a component of a physical task. One of our intentions in writing this book is to encourage psychotherapists to view the touch in which they engage as *instrumental* touch—Watson's term for deliberate physical contact to perform a specific task. Some people may not appreciate our intent. For example, Peloquin (1989), in her article titled "Helping Through Touch: The Embodiment of Caring," wrote, "There is a power to touch, and a magic. Some call it mystery" (p. 299). In her conclusion, she noted, "There has been no attempt to reduce the act of 'touching another' to a procedure, to formulate a protocol for touch, or lay claim to one definitive mean for touch" (p. 318).

We, on the other hand, will attempt to suggest specific procedures (we do not think it reduces the meaning of touch for it to be done thoughtfully), and we will recommend protocols for the ethical and effective use of touch in psychotherapy. Our goal is to provide not a "cookbook" of techniques to be thoughtlessly applied but rather a way of thinking about touch so that clinicians will have a foundation on which to make ethically sound determinations about whether, and how, to use touch with particular individuals within their own clinical setting. As Gabbard wisely noted, "Flexibility is one hallmark of effective psychotherapy" (1994, p. 283).

In the process of our research and writing, we found that psychotherapists have much yet to learn about touch. Wilison and Masson (1986) pointed out several aspects that ought to be studied. They identified the development of baselines based on nonclinical populations; response to touch as affected by socioeconomic level, cultural background, education level, personality, and age; the effects of touch in the therapeutic relationship through time; critical junctures that can be affected positively or negatively by the use of touch; how various diagnostic groups are affected by touch; and the origins and usefulness of therapist beliefs about touch. Although they provided this list more than 10 years ago, little has been done to address their concerns.

To the list of areas that call for additional research, we will add the effect of the therapist's and client's sexual orientation on the impact of touch; the effects of verbally processing each experience of touch compared with not discussing it; the effects of specific types of touch, such as hugging, rocking, and hand-holding; and the effects of movement during touch versus static touch (i.e., stroking or patting versus the hand merely resting on the client). Finally, the existing literature on the use of touch focuses almost entirely on the dyadic therapeutic relationship, ignoring the use of touch with couples, with families, and within the setting of group psychotherapy. There is considerable need to expand our attention to address this issue within the variety of venues that constitute psychotherapy.

We have approached this project as clinicians, rather than as researchers. We view this book as only a beginning. No doubt it will raise as many questions as it seeks to answer. We will consider it successful if it stimulates further empirical research and clinical discussion on the ethical use of touch. In the process of preparing this manuscript, we engaged in many hours of debate with one another and with colleagues throughout the country. We have learned much about ourselves as people and as psychotherapists. It is our sincere hope that our work will be of value to you as you engage in your own self-examination. As you begin your exploration of the ethical uses of touch by psychotherapists, we encourage you to keep in mind the words of Arnold Lazarus and Harry Guntrip:

> When taken too far, certain well-intentioned ethical guidelines can become transformed into artificial boundaries that serve as destructive prohibitions and thereby undermine clinical effectiveness. Rigid roles and strict codified rules of conduct between therapist and client can obstruct a clinician's artistry. Those anxious conformists who go entirely by the book and live in constant fear of malpractice suits are unlikely to prove significantly helpful to a broad array of clients. It is my contention that one of the worst professional/ethical violations is to permit current risk-management principles to take precedence over human interventions. (Lazarus, 1994, p. 255)

> But it seems to me that, once grounded in the fundamentals of theory, the important thing is to be constantly testing ideas by the evidence that patients bring. To care for people is more important than to care for ideas, which can be good servants but bad masters, and my interests have always been primarily in clinical work rather than in theory as such. The survey of theory that follows no doubt omits much that is important but it is close to, and primarily reflects what I am able to see actually going on in disturbed human beings seeking help. (Guntrip, 1971, p. 27)

Acknowledgments

We take this opportunity to acknowledge those persons whose names do not appear on the title page but who have made significant contributions to this project. Our thanks go to Peter Dimock for his contributions to the early drafts, including the clinical examples he provided to illustrate some of the theoretical material; to Terry Hendrix, for enthusiastically agreeing to publish this book when other publishers were so frightened by the topic; to Joanna Colrain, Kathy Steele, Jesse Harris-Bathrick, Gary Schoener, Drs. Charm Davidson, William Percy, Paul Linden, Judith Horton, Larry Morris and the anonymous reviewers contacted by Sage Publications for reviewing the manuscript; to Dr. Paul Olson for his encouragement when this book was merely a position paper for his ethics course; to Kate An, Jeff, Jerri, and Graham for their understanding and support during those long hours as we conceived and developed this book; to our friends and colleagues from the National Organization on Male Sexual Victimization; to our clients, from whom we have learned so much about this issue; and to all those who allowed us to present and refine this material at workshops and conferences through the years.

Part I

Foundations and Historical Background

A s we undertake our venture into the realm of exploring the ethical use of touch in psychotherapy, we begin by examining the foundations and historical background of this issue. For the use of touch to be truly ethical, its application must be grounded in a solid philosophical and theoretical framework. In addition, it is important to learn from those who have preceded us. Therefore, it is helpful to take the time to understand the historical roots that have created the current context in which we will attempt to employ touch within our own clinical settings.

We have included this section of the book because we believe that theory and context are essential to determining when the use of touch is ethical. Although much of the material contained in Part I is not inherently clinical in nature, we believe that a solid understanding of the issues surveyed in this part will directly affect the degree to which any clinician is effective in employing therapeutic techniques of touch.

Much of the information in this part provides an underpinning that determines the validity and effectiveness of using touch within therapeutic settings. We encourage readers to take their time with these

1

chapters in Part I before rushing on to Part II, which will address issues more directly related to the clinical application of touch within the setting of psychotherapy. We have synthesized highly technical and research-oriented material to make it more readable for those who may approach this issue from more clinical than scientific interest. Adequate references have been included to guide those readers who seek more detailed exploration of specific issues related to the foundations and historical background of touch.

Chapter 1

The Physiology of Touch

As Peloquin (1989) noted, "If length of entry in the dictionary communicates the importance of a word's function, then the fourteen full columns on 'touch' in the Oxford English Dictionary affirms the significance ascribed to touch" (p. 299). Touch is a primary process by which humans gather information about the world.

It may seem odd for a book that is written primarily for psychotherapists about psychotherapy to begin with a nonclinical discussion of the physiology of touch. We believe, however, that the information about physiology is important—and worthy of consideration. One of our intentions in writing this book is to offer an overview of the various dimensions of the ethical use of touch in psychotherapy. Therefore, any comprehensive presentation needs to include a discussion of physiology. More important, however, much of the impact of touch on people occurs at the physiological level.

AUTHORS' NOTE: We have intentionally varied our use of the pronouns *she* and *he* from chapter to chapter.

In many respects, touch is primarily a visceral experience, especially when it is paired with intense emotions. Within this context, practitioners who choose to use touch as a therapeutic tool should have at least an overall working knowledge of how physical contact affects people's bodies. We hope that awareness of the basic physiological dimensions of touch will provide a more solid foundation to explore ways to apply touch within individual frameworks of psychotherapy.

▓ The Evolution and Mechanics of Skin Sensitivity

The principal sensations of touch, pressure, temperature, and pain are realized through the skin. Most knowledge about how the skin functions has been learned relatively recently, since the 1940s. The skin is the largest sensory organ and may actually be regarded as the largest organ of the body. We can easily suggest that the skin is the second most significant human organ system, surpassed in importance only by the brain.

Montagu (1971), in his landmark book, *Touching*, noted that "the sense most closely associated with the skin, the sense of touch, 'the mother of the senses,' is the earliest to develop in the human embryo" (p. 1). The skin is already highly developed even before the embryo has either eyes or ears. Although the fetus is less than 1 inch long during the 8th week of gestation, it is already capable of responding to touch. Montagu noted that a light stroking on the face of the fetus even at this early stage of development could cause a reflexive turning away from the source of the stimulation.

In utero, the skin is continually stimulated by the amniotic fluid as well as by the touch and pressure of the womb. Responsiveness and sensitivity to touch can be seen during the earliest stages of infancy. Even before an infant can demonstrate active gestures of alertness, he[1] is highly responsive to touch. With ever-increasing speed, the newborn infant exhibits a number of reflexes that indicate a growing sensitivity to touch. For example, early in the developmental process, a gentle stroke on the cheek alerts the baby to turn his head in the direction of the stroke. When a finger is placed on a baby's lips, he responds instinctively with a sucking motion. Even before it is clear that a child can visually discern a mother's breast, physical contact with a breast prompts an automatic sucking response. Holding a young child firmly or wrapping him in a soft blanket tends to reduce crying and fussing.

Touch can be active or passive. Brown (1984) clarified some of the important features of passive and active touch. *Passive touch* (being the recipient of touch) functions in several ways, including (a) to stimulate an organism to an alert state to allow for responsiveness, (b) to facilitate the control of excessive input and hyperresponsiveness, (c) to experience pain, (d) to communicate emotional responses, and (e) to warn an organism to protect itself. *Active touch* (being the initiator of touch) also functions in distinct ways, including (a) to facilitate communication with another; (b) to divert, calm, or modify the response of another; (c) to alert another; (d) to facilitate exploration; and (e) to enhance or solidify a word or a communication.

Another type of touch is *self-touch*. Self-touch has several important functions, including to support self-control, to assist exploration, and to facilitate self-stimulation.

▦ The Structure of the Skin

The skin constitutes almost 20% of the total body weight in humans, and skin contains more than a half million receptors scattered across all regions of the body (Collier, 1985). Skin serves as the interface between the body's internal structures and the external environment, functioning as a protective armor against mechanical injury. The thickness of the skin varies throughout different regions of the body, with its thickness ranging from $\frac{1}{50}$ of an inch on the eyelid to $\frac{1}{3}$ of an inch on the palms of the hand and the soles of the feet. Despite these variations in thickness, most areas of skin are inhabited by a cumulative total of about 15 feet of blood vessels and about 72 feet of nerves (Cohen, 1987).

From an evolutionary perspective, the skin and the nervous system both develop from the same layer of embryonic tissue, the ectoderm. This shared lineage provides a critical link between the skin and the nervous system. As the fetus develops, the nervous system folds into the body's interior and fastens itself shut, and the skin continues to function as a type of external nervous system. The skin forms a myelin sheath that provides the necessary protective encasement for nerve fibers, which communicate sensory messages along the spinal cord to the brain.

The skin maintains a constant state of readiness to receive messages. Five sensations can arise from stimulation to the nerve endings in the skin: touch, pain, heat, cold, and pressure. The human body is especially sensitive to stimulation that is activated by tactile contact.

Conscious sensations of specific stimuli depend on the functioning of certain brain areas. Physiological damage to particular regions of the brain that result from a stroke, infection, injury, or a tumor may contribute to selective loss in the ability to process certain types of sensory data. Similarly, injuries to receptor areas in the skin may cause difficulties in receiving or transmitting certain sensory experiences. Through accumulated life experiences, humans also have the capacity to learn skills that allow them to dissociate or distort perceptions of sensory stimuli as they are processed.

For example, it is common for athletes to dissociate certain distracting physical stimuli as they pursue specific training regimens to promote their abilities, thereby increasing their pain threshold and enhancing their performance. Elite athletes may even accomplish phenomenal feats while "ignoring" an otherwise debilitating injury. Likewise, many victims of prolonged trauma, such as political torture or physical/sexual abuse, are able to survive overwhelming and seemingly intolerable pain because of their ability to dissociate from physical and/or emotional aspects of their experience. Unfortunately, survivors may often continue such dissociative coping responses well beyond the actual circumstances of their trauma.

▧ Physiological Responses to Touch

A wide array of research demonstrates that measurable physiological changes may be produced when touch is applied under the proper circumstances. Krieger (1975) reported a significant change in hemoglobin values after patients on a medical unit were touched by health care staff. Knable (1981) documented identifiable changes in blood pressure, heart rate, and respiratory rate in severely ill patients when nurses held their hands for up to 3 minutes. Lynch, Thomas, Mills, Malinow, and Katcher (1974) found similar results, documenting significant changes in heart rate during hand-holding or pulse taking for a sample of patients in a shock-trauma unit.

Smith (1989) reported that premature infants who were massaged for 15 minutes three times a day gained weight 45% more rapidly than those infants who were left alone in their incubators. Smith noted that "the massaged infants did not eat more than the others. Their weight gain seemed to be related to effects of touch on their metabolism" (p. 199). Montagu (1971) noted research studies that demonstrated positive effects on a person's immunological system, including enhanced resistance to infections and other diseases, when that person had received stimulation of the skin during early childhood.

Distinct and measurable physiological responses can be noted following physical contact with the skin (Collier, 1985). These responses tend to be expressed through changes in one or a combination of three related phenomena: changes in temperature, changes in the amount of perspiration on the skin (usually seen as sweating), and changes in muscular tension. These physiological changes are essentially involuntary in their nature and, therefore, beyond conscious control.

▦ Variations in Touch Perception

Like most nonverbal behaviors, touch rarely has a definitive or singular implication. Rather, a variety of qualitative factors influence the variability and meaning of touch, including duration, frequency, intensity, scope of contact, sequence of action, degree of reciprocity, body parts involved, context or setting, relationship or roles of the individuals involved, and relationship of touch to other stimuli (Thayer, 1982).

▦ Touch as Validation of Reality Through Integration With Other Senses

Adults, as well as children, use touch to corroborate information that is gathered by our other senses, facilitating the process by which we validate the accuracy of what we hear, smell, see, or taste. Generally, in those situations in which we doubt the reliability of touch, most sighted persons call first on vision for validation. On the other hand, touch is frequently used to verify the reliability of vision, as sometimes occurs in the purchase of fabrics in which tactile contact to evaluate the texture may serve as a significant factor in deciding whether that material really is as appealing as it visually appears.

Touch is a more dominant modality than vision for younger children, ages 3 or 4. As children mature, vision seems to become of equal importance or more dominant than touch (Itakura & Imamizu, 1994). This distinguishing factor becomes significant in working with adult survivors of childhood trauma or people who suffered abuses that involved violations of touch, because the age(s) at which that trauma occurred may determine the degree to which memories have been stored predominantly through a visual or tactile modality. Interpreting presenting symptomatology and implementing intervention strategies may more appropriately focus on visual or tactile modalities, depending on the age that a touch-related trauma occurred.

■ The Relationship of Touch to Memory

We focus next on the ways in which touch relates to the process by which humans experience memory. For many people, touch has potent emotional meaning—positive or negative—because of its linkage to memories. Furthermore, not all memory that is linked to touch is accessed consciously. Relevant to our discussion here are two concepts: a working definition of memory and clarification of the process of state-dependent learning.

For most people, touch triggers a multitude of emotional and physical associations. The mind and the body seem to release a rush of memories whenever physical contact is made with another person or object: Touch may be accompanied by a feeling of familiarity that guides us through a routine task; touch may alert us to a stance of alarm, as we are signaled to remember that a particular physical sensation is a precursor to danger or harm; touch may be a new experience and may increase our feelings of anxiety because we have no memory associations with which to link particular physical sensations; touch may provide an immediate calming response, as when we experience a physical contact that has strong associations with previous encounters of being nurtured or protected.

Memory is not simply a result of or a specific phase of consciousness. Rather, as Prince (1995) noted, memory is more accurately conceptualized as a process. Prince further clarified that *"conscious memory is only a particular type of memory.* The same process may terminate in purely unconscious or physiological effects, or what may be called physiological memory to distinguish it from conscious memory" (p. 29; italics in the original). In addition, recall of memory—whether at the conscious or physiological level—is influenced by whatever events have transpired between the actual time an event occurs and the time it is recalled as well as by whatever previous knowledge about that event is available at the time of recall (Ornstein, 1991).

The physical body frequently becomes the "storage container" for physiological memory, wherein prior associations with touch are deposited. We can often speculate about persons' histories with touch simply by observing their body demeanors. Many people who have been severely traumatized by physical and/or sexual abuse learn to carry their bodies in a rigid or constricted manner, whereas people who have been appropriately nurtured may be visibly more open and fluid in their manner of physical presentation. People who have received judgmental or shaming messages about their physical appearance tend to focus considerable energy on hiding their bodies or attempting to make themselves invisible, whereas people who have been positively encouraged in self-esteem more often convey a stance of being physically visible and available.

Many of the clients who present for psychotherapy may have experienced trauma from physical and/or sexual abuse or emotional and/or physical neglect. A considerable literature exists concerning the impact of traumatic experiences and deprivation on both physical and emotional dimensions of the human organism. For example, the human organism has the capacity to implement tremendous adaptive strategies when chronically exposed to stressors such as deprivation or trauma, including the ability to make psychological or physiological alterations in how the organism deals with its environment on a day-to-day basis (Yehuda, Giller, Southwick, Lowy, & Masson, 1991). Unfortunately, if such profound coping responses must be used repetitively, they can result in structural changes that can then interfere with how that organism copes with subsequent acute stressors.

Kolb's (1987) research indicates that excessive stimulation of the central nervous system during traumatic encounters may result in immutable neuronal changes that negatively affect a person's ability to discriminate various stimuli, as well as that person's style of learning and habituation. The hyperarousal startle response that is so characteristic of posttraumatic stress disorder (PTSD) is a dramatic illustration of the way such neuronal changes affect the human organism. Van der Kolk (1994) noted that current research confirms that

> there are persistent and profound alterations in stress hormone secretion and memory processing in subjects with PTSD. . . . [Furthermore, literature] has shown that trauma response is bimodal: hyperamnesia, hyperreactivity to stimuli, and traumatic re-experiencing coexist with psychic numbing, avoidance, amnesia, and anhedonia. (p. 254)

Children are affected by a similar process simply because of the developmental dynamics of childhood. In other words, living in an altered state of consciousness is a distinctive developmental feature of childhood, and it is actually normal for children to experience much of their daily living in a state of hyperarousal. Most infants spend the majority—if not all—of their time in a trancelike state of mind, moving in and out of conscious awareness with considerable fluidity, spending much of their awakened time fixating on particular stimuli in their environment that capture their nearly undivided attention and experiencing most stimuli—internal as well as external—as having global proportions within their infant universe. As children mature and widen the expanse of their world, the lure of real-world and fantasy-world experiences serves the role of inducting them into trancelike states of hyperarousal: Children's attention becomes singularly focused on the excitement and intensity of a particular experience. As children are confronted with new experiences that create extremes of fear or anxiety—such as might occur during an illness, injury, trauma, or nightmare—they again appropriately respond by entering an altered state of consciousness that allows them to cope with surviving an unknown outcome.

Information and experiences that are acquired in these altered states of consciousness are recorded as memory through a process that has come to be known as state-dependent learning (Van der Kolk & Van der Hart, 1989). It is now understood that when a child experiences stimuli while in a highly emotionally charged state—whether the stimuli are positive or negative—certain hormones, called *neuropeptides* or "messenger molecules," are released into the body as the memory of those stimuli are being stored (Cousins, 1989; Van der Kolk & Van der Hart, 1991). Two aspects of this process are significant for considerations of psychotherapy. First, subsequent experiences that replicate the highly emotionally charged state in which such stimuli were originally stored can trigger the rerelease of messenger molecules that allow for the intense recall of the original experience. Second, efforts to substantially alter the way a person deals with and manages such internalized stimuli can be accomplished only while that person is safely within the range of similar highly emotionally charged states of mind.

Because children's early development is so strongly affected by the subjective quality of touch that they receive—or fail to receive— and because so much of childhood is experienced in an altered state of consciousness, most of what people come to know and feel about touch is acquired through this process of state-dependent learning. This relationship between touch and memory creates a critical framework within which any efforts to use touch in psychotherapy will occur.

▦ Touch and Psychological Development

The presence or absence of touch influences both physical and psychological development in profound ways. After birth, the new infant experiences the environment predominantly through touch as he is handled by caregivers; by contact with clothing, surfaces, and objects that populate his environment; and by physical contact with his own body. Through these tactile experiences, the infant accumulates most of the important information about his body and about his relationship with his external environment.

By touching things in the environment, humans become acquainted with the world. Touch functions as a foundation for interacting with the world around us and provides a way of grounding ourselves. This is especially important for the newborn infant, whose initial orientation to the spatial dimensions of his world is gained primarily through tactile explorations achieved by using hands, fingers, mouth, and lips to feel objects that inhabit his environment. The young child spends countless hours exploring the qualitative dimensions of objects within reach, manipulating and testing objects in an endless effort to comprehend the complexities of their size, shape, texture, flexibility, and density. Through these simple and repetitive tactile activities, most children form the fundamental perceptions on which their world is built.

Considerable documentation exists that physical contact is essential for basic physiological development in humans and animals (Bowlby, 1952; Harlow, 1971). This appears to be true for the adult caregiver as well as the infant. Not only is touch a vital component in establishing emotional bonds between adult and offspring, self-touch is sometimes a critical ingredient both in the mother's preparation for the physical act of giving birth and for her subsequent duties of parenthood.

Just as the young human infant needs food, water, and sleep to sustain physical survival and growth, so, too, he has a constant emotional need for comfort, reassurance, and security. As the infant encounters life stressors that are a normal part of existence outside the womb, these needs are heightened. Physical contact is especially important because such interchanges between the infant and caregiver signify comfort, acceptance, protection, and a sense of being loved. These physical contacts between caregiver and infant, in effect, make up the transitional experience that provides replacements for the interaction between amniotic fluids and the fetus that was such a normal and predictable part of life in utero.

All too quickly, the infant discovers that his inherent need for positive physical contact is frequently not met. The infant soon learns that unlike life in the womb, the adult caregiver cannot or will not provide unconditional comfort and contact. Increasingly, the child must learn to mediate between himself and events in his environment.

The adult caregiver's style of parenting immediately becomes a relevant factor that begins to shape how the infant deals with basic physiological and psychological needs. Humans have not evolved any universal or comprehensive style in the delivery of nurturance and support for newborn infants. Instead, cultural context generally determines the framework within which caregiving is provided for young children. Within the social constructs of most contemporary cultures, norms impose varying degrees of disapproval about the use of physical touch. Unfortunately, these influential prohibitions function to restrict adult caregivers from providing unconditional physical contact to their offspring.

Mead and MacGregor (1951) documented wide-ranging variations among cultures in the type, amount, and duration of tactile experiences that are sanctioned for children. Although many cultures promulgate traditions that encourage tactile communication and physical contact between adult caregivers and children, other traditions impose varying degrees of restriction on the uses of touch. In most Western cultures, such as the United States, physical contact between caregivers and children beyond a certain age (usually postlatency) is viewed as unnecessary, inappropriate, and childish.

Within U.S. culture, as children mature, physical contact is increasingly defined as sexual in nature. By the time American children reach adolescence, few, if any, socially sanctioned opportunities for physical contact remain that do not carry the burden of double meaning, whereby any touch becomes subject to interpretation or misinterpretation as a sexual overture. Most channels for physical contact become plagued with sexual connotations once children enter puberty.

Some writers have noted that the decreased availability of non-sexualized touch within American culture has contributed to a collective perception that Americans, as a nation of people, are starved for nurturing physical contact (Jourard, 1968). It is not surprising that many patrons who frequent prostitutes or massage parlors verbalize that what they value most is simply the physical contact such encounters provide. This is often what they are really seeking, rather than the more erotic sexual aspects of such experiences.

Cultural norms that discourage touch are neither new nor unique to American culture. The depth of our understanding about the devastating impact of touch deficits is relatively recent, however. The reality that children may actually die from a lack of physical touch is demonstrated by historical events surrounding foundling homes and orphanages. These institutions were developed during the 19th century in response to growing public awareness of providing for the needs of neglected children. Changing social sensibilities within European and American cultures created an increased public demand that abandoned and abused children should be placed in professional care facilities, with the expectation of providing them with a better future. Throughout the 19th century and the first quarter of the 20th century, however, as many children died as survived this form of institutionalized care. Older (1982) noted some startling statistics: A German foundling home at the end of the 19th century had a mortality rate exceeding 70% for infants in their first year of life, and a 1915 study of American orphanages revealed death rates for children ranging from 32% to 75% before the end of their second year of life. That same 1915 study reported that child care institutions in Baltimore were estimated to have a mortality rate approaching 90% and that Randall's Island Hospital in New York had a mortality rate close to 100% during that year.

Foundling homes and orphanages were solidly grounded in the prevailing medical and social norms that dominated European and American cultures during that period, constructs that forbade physical contact of any type between staff and children. Although well-meaning caregivers were baffled by the astronomical mortality rates among those children who were institutionalized in orphanages, the prohibitions against physical interactions were so intense that few professionals risked even considering the possibility that these orphans might be suffering from touch deprivation.

Not until the late 1920s and early 1930s did any child care facility have the courage to challenge these prevailing norms. Bellevue Hospital in New York was one of the first institutions to defy tradition by authorizing staff to incorporate physical contact into their routine child care protocols. Staff were encouraged to pick up, hold, and physically nurture every hospitalized baby several times each day. Miraculously, the mortality rate of children on the pediatric wards at Bellevue plummeted dramatically, dropping from well over 30% to under 10%. The staff quickly realized that institutionalized children were suffering from touch starvation. Realizing that touch was an essential nutrient in the human diet, these caregivers began to view this phenomenon as an illness and proposed a name for this disease of institutionalized touch deprivation: *marasmus*, which is derived from the Greek concept meaning "wasting away" (Cohen, 1987). As professionals increasingly risked advocating for the use of touch in other orphanages and child care facilities, the mortality rates among institutionalized children decreased markedly. Having regular intimate contact with the children also made it easier for the caregivers to become aware of the signs of health problems earlier than when the children were kept at arm's length, which also increased their chances of survival.

The important lesson from this history of orphanages is the profound impact that physical contact has on the developmental process for infants and children. Subsequent research has documented the impact of physical deprivation on both animal and human organisms. The devastating consequences of touch deprivation are poignantly demonstrated by the "failure to thrive" symptomatology that develops in young children who are the recipients of severe physical and emotional neglect.

Research suggests that the absence of touch may be most critical in accounting for an infant's failure to thrive (Field et al., 1986). The dramatic realities of how profoundly these failure-to-thrive dynamics may affect human life are illustrated by one extreme case reported by a Johns Hopkins research team, which documented a touch-deprived 4½-year-old child who had achieved the size of only a normal 12-month-old baby (Money, Anneaille, & Werlwas, 1976).

Touch deprivation affects psychological as well as physical development. Reite and Field (1985) cited studies with infant primates that demonstrated that these babies exhibited intense grief, huddled in corners, and displayed classically depressed symptoms when they were restricted from receiving touch. Although the overt symptomatology disappeared if infants were allowed renewed contact with their mothers after a relatively short separation, distinct physical effects persisted. Specifically, the baby primates were found to be more vulnerable to disease, and they exhibited a more pervasive spectrum of bodily weaknesses. Some researchers suggest that disturbances in the body's immune systems, as well as psychological difficulties such as social isolation, difficulties in cooperation, and propensities toward violence, may be directly related to touch deficiencies during early childhood (Cohen, 1987; Prescott, 1975).

▓ Summary

In this chapter, we have shown that the experience of touch is a physiologically and psychologically complex phenomenon and that the meaning of a particular touch is idiosyncratic. In other words, how touch is experienced is influenced by the individual's mind as well as the skin.

The Influence
of Touch on Socialization

▓ The Language of Touch

Language is rich with references to touch. Both literally and metaphorically, people reference much about daily life experiences through the language of touch. A telephone company urges us to "reach out and touch someone." We may be casually advised by a friend to "handle her with care" because we had earlier "rubbed her the wrong way." The prevalence of these expressions highlights the extent to which physical contact is a significant dimension in our experiences of connecting with other people.

Many adjectives that address the more qualitative dimensions of language actually exist only in the context of tactile contact. Adjectives such as *rough, smooth, soft, hard, tender,* and *painful* are devoid of meaning without direct points of reference that are based in previous tactile life experiences.

Sometimes, direct physical contact can be an effective and clear modality for communication, even in the absence of any verbal expressions. For example, clubs within many cultures have historically used secret handshakes to gain entry into exclusive inner sanctums. Placing a gentle hand on the arm or leg of someone who has just been informed of a tragedy can communicate such a level of comfort and safety that the recipient may burst into tears at the moment of physical contact.

Physical contact not only is a primary means of communication but also has the capacity to function as a secondary communication, serving to influence or modify verbal interactions. For example, using tactile contact at a particular point in a conversation, such as placing a hand on a listener's shoulder and gently squeezing, can underscore or highlight that point. Exchanging a physical hug immediately after disclosing an incident about which a person felt an immense sense of joy may enhance the feeling of pleasure and may contribute a shared quality to the experience.

Often, the tactile contact that accompanies a verbal interchange will improve the listener's capacity to remember the particular comment that was emphasized or the situation in which a particular event occurred. Most people can probably recall a vivid memory that is linked to a significant physical contact, such as hugging a friend following an extended absence or a receiving a comforting arm around the shoulder after suffering a significant loss.

Physical contact frequently serves to enhance or intensify communication. The use of tactile contact adds a rich and colorful dimension to interpersonal exchanges. Touch may also provide a stimulus to open channels of communication when sensory skills have become diminished or atrophied. For example, touch, when used in conjunction with affective expression, has the potential to improve communication with older persons, regardless of whether they are oriented or confused (McCorkle, 1974). Even when verbal responses of older persons who are confused do not increase, active nonverbal responsiveness to touch frequently may be observed (Langland & Panicucci, 1982).

Touch sometimes conveys a quality of authenticity that reveals discrepancies in communication, even when the intention is to sublimate hidden or insincere messages. Careful observation of tactile cues during verbal interchanges may divulge mixed messages, revealing discrepancies between overt and covert levels of communication. For example, during a staff meeting, a supervisor may verbalize a sincere commitment to promoting gender equality and then unobtrusively pat a colleague on the hip as they leave that meeting.

Touch usually cannot be completely extricated from the context or setting in which that physical contact occurs, nor can tactile contact be totally separated from whatever verbal or nonverbal communication accompanies such behavior. Ambiguity of meaning is an inherent dimension of touch communications. Often, it is possible to decipher the true meaning of a physical contact only by examining the context in which that behavior occurred or by attending to whatever use of words accompanied that physical communication. For example, it is all too familiar to experience confusion about whether a touch has sexual overtones. Being physically held or cuddling may or may not be enmeshed with sex; context and any accompanying verbal comments are generally significant factors in helping to distinguish sexual from non-sexual intentions.

Weiss (1986) postulated that six qualitative dimensions influence how individuals respond to this inherent ambiguity of touch. Examining the interplay of these dimensions of touch assists in the attempt to interpret and define the meaning of tactile contact.

1. *Duration:* Physiological literature indicates that for a touch to be significant, it has to last long enough for the receiver to distinguish her body from the rest of her surroundings.

2. *Location:* Location measures three factors. The first factor is *threshold.* In other words, some parts of the body—for example, the face and hands—are more sensitive to touch than are other parts. The second factor is *extent*, or the number of parts of the body that are touched. The final factor is *centripetality*, or the degree to which the trunk of the body is touched compared with the degree to which the limbs are touched. Jourard (1966) and Rubin (1963) reported that touch to the torso has different meaning for most people as compared with touch to a limb, such as an arm.

3. *Action:* As discussed in Chapter 1, many of the physical sensations that are experienced about a touch are influenced by the degree and types of movement that accompany that physical contact.

4. *Intensity:* Intensity is measured by the indentation of the skin. Moderate touch has been determined to be the most therapeutic (Geldard, 1972).

5. *Frequency:* Physical sensations are experienced in qualitatively different ways in relation to whether a touch is familiar or novel.

6. *Sensation:* This dimension is focused on whether a touch is pleasurable or painful. Not surprisingly, pleasurable touch enhances the perception of one's body more than does painful touch (Thayer, 1982).

Each of these variables exist on continua. As we identify and define their location and boundaries along their respective continua, we establish a framework that allows a heightened level of clarity about tactile experiences.

Because touch experiences are subjective and highly charged, they elicit a wide range of arousal responses. Arousal has the potential to either accentuate or confuse both perception and awareness. Therefore, variations in the level of arousal that a touch generates may cause dramatic and/or erratic deviations in the perception and awareness of touch experiences.

※ Touch as a Tool for Interaction and Exchange

Touch is more than just the earliest and most elemental form of communication. It is also a source of comfort and a necessary building block to sustain life for both humans and animals. Chapter 1 discussed the critical role of touch in physiological and psychological development. Within the context of communication and socialization, touch also emerges as a significant factor. A rich variety of information can be gained by exploring social interactions among both animals and humans.

Animals frequently employ touch during the initial phases of greeting. Ritualized greetings between animals commonly include a generous portion of tactile contact, using behaviors such as embracing, grooming, kissing, touching hands, and genital or stomach nuzzling (Argyle, 1988). Through his observation of primates, Hall (1962) discovered that 11 of the 12 greeting behaviors used by the animals in his research sample involved touch. When employed in the process of greeting, touch seems to facilitate greater accessibility.

Primates are also well known for their common use of bodily contact in social interactions. Most of us probably have familiar images of observing primates at a zoo while they are engaged in grooming behavior, sometimes for hours at a time. This grooming behavior usually involves the use of hands, with periodic interventions using the mouth. Although the apparent purpose of grooming behavior is to provide mutual support for cleaning a companion's neck, back, or head—areas of the body that are generally difficult to access—there also seems to be an underlying social meaning to such focused tactile interchanges. The message inherent to this physical contact is probably appeasement, reassurance, and/or bonding. The primary effects of grooming are essentially relaxation and a reduction of tension.

Physical contact is equally significant for human primates. Leboyer (1975) offered the following description of the impact of touch on the newborn child:

> A word about the hands holding the newborn child. It is through our hands that we speak to the child, that we communicate. Touching is the primary language, "understanding" comes long after "feeling." . . . The newborn baby's skin has an intelligence, a sensitivity that we can only begin to imagine. It is through its skin that the newborn child once knew its entire world. (p. 75)

Wilson (1982) also described touch as each human's "first language" and then elaborated,

> Tactility in the newborn infant provides the basic orientation to the mother and to life. At birth, all the baby's other senses are so undeveloped that they convey very little information of value to it. It is the sense of touch on which the infant depends. While nourishment comes from the breast, contact with and manipulation of the breast are as important psychologically.

The experience the infant undergoes in contact with the mother's body constitutes a primary means of learning whether the world is a hostile, rejecting place or a warm, caring one that promotes physical and psychological growth. (p. 66)

Bodily contacts and physical interactions between infants and adult caregivers provide the most primitive experiences of interpersonal communication, from which the infants establish their earliest and most basic patterns of intimacy and affection. In essence, these patterns actually create a template by which subsequent interpersonal relationships will be formed. How infants are handled during routine encounters with caregivers—activities such as bathing, clothing, feeding, and tucking into bed—establishes the context from which they define tactile experiences in the larger world. This becomes the guideline to frame all subsequent learning about relationships that involve any component of tactile contact.

Many of the gender norms that govern social relationships are learned by young children through touch experiences with their caregivers. Dixon et al. (1981) reported clear gender distinctions in the ways touch is used to parent children from a young age: Mothers are frequently observed responding to upset infants by trying to physically contain or hold them or by actively using touch in their efforts to decrease the children's distressing motor activity, whereas fathers are more often observed responding to children's discomfort by jiggling or rocking them in a roguish and rhythmic fashion.

Lamb (1981) noted that fathers frequently use physical contact in their play interactions with young children, whereas mothers hold their infants less for play and more for caregiving, safety, and protection. Lamb further noted that fathers tend to exhibit a more physically stimulating style of play with their infant children, as contrasted with mothers, who were inclined to use more conventional approaches to play and who more often used toys and games (e.g., peek-a-boo).

How the infant feels about her own skin will be learned largely through her early tactile experiences with the external world, including contacts with the physical world and reciprocal interactions with caregivers. And how an infant expresses physical contact with her caregivers' bodies is a central influence for how her internal beliefs develop about whether the world is safe and accepting or unsafe and inhospitable.

Prescott (1975) further clarified the impact of touch on the development of a child's basic emotional capacity to feel loved:

> It is plain that the infant can only experience and express love or its absence through its body. . . . A lack of intimate bodily contact between mother and child has to be interpreted as abandonment, since, in a very real sense, the infant can only "think" with its skin. (p. 72)

How the young child comes to feel about her own skin is extremely influential in determining the image she will formulate about her own body. If the infant receives warmth, unconditional nurturance, and healthy physical comfort, it is generally assumed that she will acquire positive self-esteem about her physical body and will be better prepared to form solid interpersonal relationships. Argyle (1988) suggested that warmth is one of two primary dimensions of touch (dominance being the other) and that this dimension of warmth communicates the most basic meaning of touch: that an interpersonal bond is being offered or established.

If a child has a reference point for being physically held as a demonstration of love or an expression of affection, then she probably will have gained the emotional capacity for using tactile contact as a component of interpersonal exchanges with other people. This availability of touch as a part of relationships may be a central feature in helping her to overcome loneliness. We have all heard people describe how they sometimes feel loneliness even in the midst of their relationships with other people. Most likely, these feelings of alienation may reflect the absence of any physical contact in those relationships.

Hollender (1970) conducted research in which participants consistently identified several features they associated with being held or cuddled: security, protection, comfort, contentment, and love. These are sometimes the prerequisite features that are necessary before children feel safe enough to venture into the larger world and attempt to form relationships. These are the same features that allow us, as adults, to feel safe enough to maintain our relationships with other people in the world.

Unfortunately, many young children experience considerable abuse or neglect in their physical contacts with the caregivers who inhabit their world. Dysfunctions or disturbances in infants' experiences of physical contact may therefore contribute to dysfunctional or disturbed patterns in interpersonal relationships as the children mature. Disruptions in the availability or quality of physical contact frequently occur in interactions that are affected by the illness, anger, anxiety, or depression of caregivers. A strong sense of "skin hunger," a profound need for human contact with others, may result from a lack of physical contact (Hall, 1966).

▓ The Impact of Touch on Communication and Physical Development

Considerable research demonstrates the impact of physical contact on communication and development. Montagu (1971) cited research that confirmed that the gentle handling and touching of animals during their early days of life contributed to more activity, a reduction in fear, and an increased capacity to cope with stress. Mason (1967) found that when two chimpanzees were in an unfamiliar situation, they clung to each other, but once the situation became familiar, the mutual clinging decreased.

Collard (1967) demonstrated that kittens as young as 5 weeks old showed a feline form of stranger anxiety when handled by unfamiliar humans. In this research, one group of kittens was touched by a different person 5 days a week for 1 month. A second group was touched for the same length of time as frequently but by only one person. A third group of kittens was not touched at all during the month. At the end of each week, a stranger handled the kittens in the touch groups, with a different person being used each week. All the strangers were blind to which group the kittens came from. The kittens who had been touched by only one person during the week and the no-touch group kittens showed the most fear as measured by retreating, freezing, or attempting to escape.

Perhaps the most striking research on the importance of touch is the often-referenced work of Harlow and his colleagues at the University of Wisconsin during the 1950s and 1960s. Harlow conducted laboratory studies with primates to examine the significance of tactile contact to developmental issues. In these studies, cloth mother and wire mother surrogates were placed in a cubicle attached to the living cage for newborn monkeys. Surrogate mothers had appropriate surrogate breasts to provide the infant with access to milk, although these experiments varied whether the wire or cloth surrogate provided such nutriment. Harlow (1971) reported that as the infants developed,

> those who had been provided with a lactating wire mother showed decreasing responsiveness to her and increasing responsiveness to the nonlactating cloth mother—a finding completely contrary to the interpretation that infant love is a derived drive in which the mother's face or form becomes a condition for hunger or thirst reduction. It is clearly the incentive of contact comfort that bonds the infant affectionately to the mother. (p. 19)

The results of this research surprised those who would have predicted that the wire mother who supplied the reinforcing stimulus of milk should have been more highly prized than the terry cloth figure, which lacked access to nourishment. Further evidence of the importance of the huggable figure to the monkeys was seen when they were threatened by a large wooden model of a spider. The monkeys who had access to the cloth figure ran to it but eventually ventured away from it to explore the spider. The monkeys with only the wire-mesh mother continued to behave in a frightened manner and were less likely to move into open spaces.

Harlow's research ultimately demonstrated two crucial observations about the foundations for relationships: Comfort contact is a more significant maternal quality for an infant rhesus monkey than is feeding, and as adults, even those monkeys who were reared on a cuddly mother surrogate exhibited dysfunctions as they engaged in primary relationships or attempted to parent their own offspring. Although these studies were laboratory experiments conducted on monkeys, simple observation of life experiences in the world of humans provides a basis to at least consider that these results have direct relevance to human relationships. The second observation cited from this research is especially important because Harlow and his associates noticed that longer-term patterns for socialization began to emerge from early tactile experiences.

Subsequent research has elaborated the degree to which touch is a critical variable that has the capacity to alter fundamentally the manner in which relationships are formed—or are not formed. Suomi and Harlow (1972) reared three groups of infant monkeys under different conditions. One group was reared for 3 weeks by a human and was isolated from other monkeys for 1 year. Infant monkeys in the second group were reared normally by their biological mothers for the first year of life. The third group was provided with shelter, warmth, and food but was isolated from sight or touch from both humans and monkeys for the first year of life. During the second year, all the monkeys from all three groups were given the opportunity to interact with monkeys each day. When, between the ages of 2 and 3 years, the monkeys were placed one at a time in a chamber with a human on one side and another monkey on the other side, the monkeys who had been touched by their mother approached the other monkey rather than the human. The monkeys from the group that had been touched in the first 3 weeks of life by a human preferred to be with a human. The monkeys raised in isolation approached neither the other monkey nor the human but spent their time in the center of the chamber, devoid of any tactile contact.

Harlow (1971) reported that monkeys raised in isolation for less than 6 months tended to recover and eventually exhibited normal behavior if given the opportunity to interact with other monkeys. Monkeys who were cut off from others for more than 6 months showed social and sexual behavior that remained abnormal. Those who had been isolated for a year or more continued to show extreme fear, including avoidance of all social contact, unusual postures, and self-clutching.

The effects of touch deficiencies and/or a general lack of other stimulation can have lifelong ramifications. Mitchell (1979) reviewed social isolation studies on animals. He noted that animals that were raised in laboratory environments that permitted them to hear, smell, and see each other while restricting them from direct physical contact such as touching, sucking, or cuddling demonstrated severe problems in maintaining basic life skills. He cited common symptoms such as excessive fear and violence, failure to integrate into the prevailing dominance order, self-mutilating behaviors, and difficulties in mating or mothering.

As hopeless as this sounds, there is evidence that recovery is possible. Suomi and Harlow (1972) took monkeys raised in isolation for the first 6 months of life who showed the usual symptoms of sensory depression, including fear, strange social behavior, bizarre habits, and a tendency to attack novel stimuli, and placed them with young female monkeys who had been raised normally and were not aggressive. After 26 weeks of interaction, the formerly isolated monkeys were able to learn appropriate social behavior.

■ Touch as a Facilitator of Attachment and Affect Development

Frank's (1957) research identified touch as the first sensory response to develop for humans and most animals. As we noted previously, tactile contact is actually the first language an infant learns, the most primal mode for communication. In this primitive initial stage of development, touch cues function primarily to facilitate orientation either toward or away from the source of a stimulus. Some animals have developed antennae, or "feelers," that provide them with an actual physiological mechanism to ascertain their way through their world, an evolutionary response that is particularly essential for animals that live underground, in light-restricted environments, or at depths where vision simply is not possible.

Although humans do not have antennae or feelers, we do use our skin in a similar manner to find our way through the world. Chapter 1 elaborated the process by which humans receive and process contacts with an external stimulus through the skin. As children begin to notice the world around them for purposes other than basic survival, touch emerges as a basic, fundamental, and possibly necessary ingredient for the healthy development of their earliest social attachment bonds. It is generally agreed that attachment bonds are primary for the normal development and integrative functioning of all high primates, especially human beings. The bond between infant and mother is perhaps the earliest and most fundamental attachment relationship for humans and other high primates.

For humans, the early stages of life are dominated by oral and skin contact between infant and caregiver. Because the infant initially can communicate only by tactile reference, touch serves as the primary message system between caregiver and infant. Context is fundamentally important, however, in determining the meaning of that touch message. For example, Brazelton and Cramer (1990) noted that touch could be used with infants either for quieting or for the opposite purpose of alerting and arousing. Reporting the results of some of their studies of infants, they stated

> that a slow patting motion is soothing whereas more rapid patting becomes an alerting stimulus, and that the threshold is very specific. With patting any faster the baby becomes upset. . . . When babies are quiet, a tactile stimulus serves to alert them and bring them up to an alert state. When babies are upset, a slow, modulated tactile stimulus seems to serve to reduce their activity. (pp. 61-62)

The child's demands will be responded to in a sufficient manner only if her adult caregivers have the capacity to elicit and interpret her signals adequately. The task for the caregivers is to name the multitude of sensations and emotions the child seems to experience: "You must be tired." "Are you hungry?" "Are you frightened?" "You look very happy." By providing positive bodily contact in conjunction with these verbal responses, the adult caregiver not only satisfies the physical and emotional needs of the child but also begins to demonstrate the constructs of a language for emotions. In essence, the child is conditioned to sublimate certain tactile behaviors and to use instead specific linguistic symbols that have been defined by others to represent the verbal equivalent of those physical behaviors. The child thereby progresses beyond searching in a trial-and-error manner and learns instead to formulate strategies to release the tensions that accompany physical and emotional sensations.

When distressed, however, young children frequently require more than just a verbal response to help them calm. Through time, children who learn to trust the availability of physical contact to help them calm will begin to incorporate self-calming and self-soothing responses merely on the basis of the awareness that they have access to touch if needed. On the other hand, children's level of agitation may actually increase when they perceive that accessibility to comforting touch is unavailable in any given situation.

It appears that a child's sense of security that touch is available and accessible if needed is equally important to the formation of a capacity for attachment as is whether direct physical contact actually occurs (Montagu, 1971; Parkes, Stevenson-Hinde, & Marris, 1991). In other words, a child's perception that touch is available if needed may be just as significant for promoting healthy development as is any actual physical contact that occurs between child and caretakers. The evolution of smiling and crying may reflect an effort to communicate a symbolic bridging between child and caregiver in the absence of direct physical contact. In this regard, smiling or crying may be a symbolic expression for a type of nonverbal holding or soothing when such is not available in the form of direct physical interaction.

If the child successfully shifts into the world of verbal language, she is increasingly able to employ concepts and symbols as a methodology for organizing sensory experiences, allowing the child the capacity to interpret experiences and thereby establishing patterns for stabilizing the environment. Because linguistic symbols are culturally defined, cultural traditions prescribe what is an appropriate meaning for each symbol. Therefore, as the child moves from a world dominated by tactile experiences to one governed by the symbolic rules of language, responses to sensory experiences are increasingly culturally patterned and prescribed.

Although the infant initially assimilates everything about her world through the medium of tactile contact, the maturing child begins to learn restrictions about touch through the prohibitions and limits that are verbally imposed by caregivers and the social order of her expanding physical world. As the child increases her level and range of activities, she begins to "reach out" and into her surrounding environment, trying to touch and handle whatever object she can bring into her direct contact. While the child is using such exploration to gain a mastery of space-time orientation, she quickly encounters verbal warnings commanding her, "Don't touch," "Keep your hands off that," and "Stay away from there." Sometimes, these warnings are reinforced by direct physical responses from the caregivers that seek to stop, divert, or perhaps even punish the child for her determined efforts to make physical contact with a particular object.

Children gradually transform these repetitive verbal and physical admonitions from caregivers into self-administered inhibitions. Most children learn, at a young age, to distinguish the signs and symbols in their environment that serve as cues that touch is not allowed. Ultimately, children must establish an internalized sense of which forms of tactile contact are permissible and which are prohibited and to differentiate cues that imply, "It's OK to touch" from signals that are intended to communicate, "Don't touch me."

As children progress toward adulthood, symbolic communication increasingly becomes predominant. Tactile communication is never fully superseded, however, and the meaning of many symbols depends on previous tactile experiences. This is especially illustrated within English-speaking Western culture by the frequency of tactile figures of speech. For example, the early pages of this chapter referenced many words and phrases that imply a tactile and/or emotional response. Likewise, many adjectives (e.g., *smooth, rough, warm,* and *painful*) imply or reference a tactile sensation; these adjectives have little or no meaning without prior tactile experiences.

Cultures rely on symbolic communication to differing degrees. Less complex cultures are more tactually oriented and reflect less emphasis on symbolic communication. For example, interactions of members within Aboriginal tribes in Australia have been observed to function largely at the level of tactile and nonverbal communication (Morgan, 1991). In contrast, cultures that are highly technological in their structure—the case for most contemporary Western societies—are more reliant on the use of symbols for communication. Verbally based milieus assume that a person has had early tactile experiences that provide an appropriate context to understand the symbols that are exchanged for purposes of communication.

The emergence of an internal state of homeostasis provides humans with the capacity to distinguish between their internal experiences and their awareness of an external world. Early tactile experiences, which originate in the external world, are critical to assist in the development of internal homeostasis. As infants develop and the other sensory modalities (e.g., kinesthetic, auditory, and visual) mature, infants are increasingly socialized to rely on symbolism rather than tactile contact as a primary method for communication. Dysfunctions in early tactile experiences can be disruptive to the formation of internal homeostasis, which may thereby contribute to an inability for some infants to shift from tactual dependency to linguistic-symbolic communication. Consequently, this type of early childhood deprivation may subsequently be manifested in gross physiological disturbances such as speech retardation and learning disabilities as well as by emotional or affective problems.

The positive sociological effects of touch are those that increase the ability of individuals to live in harmony with the world around them. A number of studies have noted the relationship between parental physical contact with their children and the ability of the children to explore the surrounding world (Ainsworth, 1978; Harlow & Harlow, 1962). Children who were denied close physical contact were deemed *anxiously attached* and were more frightened to be out of the sight of their parents. Those who did receive physical touch were labeled *securely attached* and were able to initiate more exploratory activity and to tolerate a parent's absence for short periods.

By the second year of life, infants who are healthy and who have developed a secure attachment to their caregivers display an anger response following most situations involving stressful separation from their caregivers. Rejection of physical contact by an attachment figure has specific consequences, generally first prompting children to initiate increased approach efforts and, if the rejection persists, eventually triggering anger and conflict. Harlow and Harlow (1962) reported that maturing infants sought physical contact with their mothers when they became frightened. They further noted that mothers who refused their infants' efforts for physical contact in a fearful situation aggravated the children's anxiety while withholding their primary means for alleviating the anxiety.

Infants who have primarily experienced anxious attachments with their caregivers will exhibit the phenomenon of *avoidant attachment,* characterized by an absence of anger on stressful separation from caregivers (Ainsworth, 1982). Unfortunately, infants who feel avoidant attachments tend to vent considerable anger toward their caregivers in stress-free situations, with the anger frequently seeming out of context and without reason. Avoidantly attached infants also demonstrate a much higher incidence of disobedience, hitting, and banging of objects during play and characteristically exhibit idiosyncratic behaviors such as rocking and trancelike states, unexplained fears, and hand-flapping. Ainsworth further noted that babies who developed avoidant attachments all had mothers who manifested behaviors that he labeled the *rejection syndrome,* characterized by a deep aversion to physical contact that leads the mother to rebuff her infant's attempts to initiate physical contact.

Other research studies have demonstrated that tactile contact can be used to influence human behavior in positive ways. One of the pioneering studies in this area was a field experiment that measured how the attitudes of library patrons could be positively influenced merely by a casual touch from a librarian (Fisher, Rytting, & Heslin, 1976). In this experiment, a librarian administered a cursory tactile contact to some borrowers during their process of checking out a book, while abstaining from any physical contact with other borrowers. Interviews with the borrowers revealed that those patrons who had received touch reported much more positive attitudes toward the library and its staff. The dramatic results of this study provided the first experimental data that even a brief physical touch could influence attitudes and feelings between total strangers.

Subsequent research has generally found that touching has a positive correlation to self-disclosure. Jourard and Rubin (1968) reported a low but significant association between touching and self-disclosure. Several studies (Goldman & Fordyce, 1983; Pisano, Wall, & Foster, 1986; Willis & Hamm, 1980) have revealed that participants who were touched on the upper arm by a stranger who approached them and then asked to complete a time-consuming task were more likely to comply with the request than were participants who were not touched during the process of making the same request. These results were true regardless of the gender of either the requestor or the requestee. Similarly, Heslin and Alper (1983) have reported that touch frequently influences recipients to talk more about themselves.

Sometimes, however, caregivers are unable or unwilling to facilitate this important process of helping children make the transition from the primitive level of tactile communication into the development of a verbal language for emotions. This level of caregiving is frequently absent in situations of severe abuse or neglect or when some significant trauma causes physical separation between children and adult caregivers. In such cases, there is an increased risk that preverbal, bodily expression may become fixated and persistent, a condition known as *alexithymic communication* (Sivik, 1992; Taylor, Bagby, & Parker, 1991).

Alexithymia is commonly employed as a coping and survival strategy by trauma victims, although it is seldom named or labeled as such by clinicians as they seek to provide treatment for those survivor clients. *Alexithymia* is derived from the ancient Greek terms *lexis* (meaning "speech") and *thymia* (meaning "mind" or "spirit"). Alexithymia is, essentially, a cognitive and emotional deficiency. According to Sivik (1993), alexithymia "is generally defined as a psychic dysfunction in which expression of symbolic thinking and fantasy is reduced, somatization is common, feelings are poorly communicated, empathy is impaired and intimate interpersonal relations are difficult to maintain" (p. 130).

Alexithymia is characterized primarily by impaired ability to use emotions as inner signals; basically somatic reactions, consisting of physiological aspects of affects, with minimal verbalization; diminution in the verbalization of affects; difficulty recognizing or naming specific emotions even for basic states such as hunger, pain, and pleasure; an accompanying impairment in the capacity for self-care; and tendency to focus on external processes and activities (Krystal, 1988).

Because alexithymia as a coping and survival tool is grounded primarily in a decreased capacity to verbalize feelings, people who exhibit alexithymic communication patterns are at greater risk for developing severe psychosomatic symptoms and disorders. This may thereby create the prerequisite conditions for the development of longer-lasting dysfunctional personality traits (such as alexithymia, hypochondriasis, hysteria, and depression), for a greater hypersensitivity to touch, and for an increased propensity for pain to be experienced subjectively (Sivik, 1993).

During the 1970s, Prescott (1975, 1976), a neuropsychologist at the National Institutes of Health, began to explore the relationship between physical contacts that human infants receive and their likelihood of exhibiting violent behaviors as adults. Although some researchers have questioned the validity of Prescott's research, his studies warrant serious consideration. Prescott postulated that sensory stimulation is a necessary component for the normal development of the cerebellum. Furthermore, he suggested that sensory stimulation is like a nutrient and that sensory deprivation adversely affects the developing brain in a similar way as malnourishment negatively affects growth of the physical body. In brain physiology, however, different sources of sensory stimulation have disparate impact. For example, movement and touch have considerably greater significance to the healthy development of the cerebellum than do sight, hearing, and smell.

Prescott (1975) studied 49 cultures to examine child-rearing practices and levels of adult violence. He reported a strong significant statistical relationship between the degree of deprivation of infant physical affection and adult physical violence. According to Prescott, adults who experience extreme sensory undernourishment during childhood are at much greater risk to develop a neurophysiological addiction to sensory stimulation as adults. Although some adults who are touch deprived as children develop an actual physical aversion to physical contact, other touch-deprived adults may undertake to fill the void of unmet sensory needs from childhood. This second category of adults may, therefore, be more vulnerable to the increased stimulation that is available through involvement with drugs, violence, and crime.

Other research studies have demonstrated conclusions that support the work of Prescott. For example, Biggar (1984) observed mothers during play sessions with their infant children and noted that

> the greater the mother's observed aversion to physical contact with the infant during the first three months, the more anger seemed to direct the infant's mood and activities nine months later. In addition, the more the mother had shown an early aversion to physical contact with the infant, the more frequently the infant struck or angrily threatened to strike the mother in relatively stress-free situations. (p. 69)

▦ Touch as a Facilitator of Separation and Individuation

Separation and individuation are equally significant to the social development of children as is attachment. Just as with issues related to attachment, these developmental dynamics are fundamentally affected by touch. In ideal situations, young children receive positive and frequent tactile contact in the form of cuddling and affectionate touching from caretakers. For most children, the amount of touching they receive from their adult caregivers is maximal during infancy. During the preschool stage, children become increasingly ambulatory and are able physically to move away from their primary caregivers. Most infants use their experiences with tactile contact to establish and maintain a secure base as they begin this process of exploring their environment.

Those children who feel secure from their base of tactile contact begin to venture away from the immediate reach of their primary caregivers on "investigative forays" that become increasingly frequent, longer in duration, and more distant from their caregivers. Usually such explorations end with children dashing back to their caregivers to gain reassurance through brief tactile contact. As children incorporate increasing levels of security and trust into their experiences with separation from caregivers, the need for reassuring tactile contact becomes less important, and the amount of touching between children and caregivers decreases.

The continued development of individuation behaviors, however, requires that the caregivers remain available and receptive to such touch, although the tactile contact does not necessarily need to be reciprocal between children and caregivers. Harlow and Harlow (1962) reported that when an infant is denied tactile contact with her mother, all exploratory activity is halted immediately, even if the mother remains in contact with the infant via visual, auditory, or olfactory senses.

The process of healthy detachment is also of critical importance for a child's positive development. In other words, although the child develops a level of security from the availability of physical contact, she must increasingly be allowed free choice concerning the degree to which such touch interactions are desired. An adult caregiver who lacks the security and ego strength to tolerate a decrease in the level of tactile contact with her child threatens the positive maturation of that child just as significantly as when physical contact is deprived. Therefore, it is important that the adult distinguishes between healthy detachment and unhealthy denial regarding the availability of touch. Harlow (1971) interpreted this detachment process as primarily a function of the young child's emerging powers of curiosity and wanderlust. The adult who resists this developmental process and clings to her child risks undermining the child's future capacity for forming healthy and successful relationships.

Considerable research elaborates on the frequency with which gender differences are observed in the ways males and females use touch in the process of parenting (Brazelton & Cramer, 1990; Lamb, 1981). Most often, females tend to use touch as a component of routine caregiving tasks and to facilitate provisions of safety, whereas most males use touch for purposes of play or social interaction. Chapter 1 identified much of the literature regarding the significance of maternal physical contact with infants and children. Less frequently discussed in the literature, and in society in general, is the value of paternal physical contact with infants and children.

Ross (1994) discussed the developmental impact on children of physical contact with adult male caregivers. He described the typical style of fathers' play with their children as consisting of "romping, roughhousing, and tossing them up in the air, especially during the end of the first year or beginning of the second year" (p. 28). He noted that these behaviors had a significant importance to the young child's developmental needs, as such physical interactions "resonate with the toddler's inherent thrust toward muscular activity . . . [thereby enhancing] the child's 'sense of body self,' and encouraging the exploration of space" (p. 28).

By school age, children generally receive less tactile contact from their adult caregivers—female and male alike—than was the case during the preschool stage. At this age, they are more likely to begin seeking touch from peers or to engage in self-touching behaviors. Harlow (1971) discussed the phenomenon of *physical free play*—playful interactions that involve a considerable intensity of physical contact, such as roughhousing and wrestling—that frequently characterizes children during this developmental stage. Although this stage sometimes tests the limits of tolerance and coping skills for adult caregivers, Harlow observed that no other single configuration of play was more critical to basic socialization than this process of physical free play.

The amount of touching between children and caregivers generally continues to decrease as children mature. Some of this decrease in physical contact can be attributed to the healthy process of detachment and individuation. Much of the loss of physical contact between children and adults in our society, however, results from the unfortunate and unhealthy cultural norms that govern the "acceptable" ways Americans as a whole have chosen to socialize children. Studies by Goldberg and Lewis (1969) revealed that touch differences exhibited by male and female children as they mature were more indicative of differential modeling and the circumstances of reinforcement than of any physiologically based gender factors.

For many Americans, particularly northern European Americans, touching between children and primary caregivers tends to be quite minimal by the time children have reached adolescence. As children progress through their developmental stages, verbal contact increasingly replaces tactile contact as a major channel of social interchange, between peers as well as with adults. Similarly, as children grow older, touch is less likely to be responded to than talking. Most instances of contact among elementary-age children reflect intentional touching, primarily involving the hands. In contrast, by junior high school, interactions are dominated by the verbal mode, with most instances of physical contact being accidental, primarily involving shoulders and elbows. By adolescence, the meaning of touch has largely been transformed from nurturance to sexual/erotic. The question must be raised, however, whether the need for nonsexual physical contact has actually decreased as dramatically by adolescence as the shift in the norms governing touch seems to indicate.

Hollender (1970) postulated that much sexual behavior is actually motivated by a need or wish to be held. Our culture seems to have accepted as fact the common image of adorable and cuddly children growing into sulky, rebellious, noncommunicative adolescents. How much of this change in teenagers' personalities is biologically based, and how much of this transformation might rather reflect the dramatic decrease in physical contact that is available between adults and children following the onset of puberty?

Most adults become more fearful about issues of sexuality as their children enter adolescence. For example, much more attention is paid to concerns that touch between an adult caregiver and a same-gender teenager might be perceived by observers as homosexual behavior or that engaging in such contact might promote homosexuality for that child. Equally problematic, physical contact between an adult caregiver and an opposite-gender adolescent risks being perceived by observers as sexually suggestive or provocative. It is not surprising that most adults respond to this minefield of cultural double binds by simply refraining from touch as soon as the adolescent children in their lives begin to exhibit any signs of their emerging sexuality.

Such approaches to caregiving, however, seem ill conceived and counterproductive to the needs of adolescents. In the absence of nurturing and nonsexual physical contact, teenagers understandably begin to equate touch with sex (or with violence—physical contact through athletics or gangs is the primary other avenue that remains available for most adolescents).

Dunne, Bruggen, and O'Brien (1982) reported on the positive results of an adolescent treatment program in which staff were trained to incorporate touch into a variety of clinical activities. As nonsexual physical contact became an acceptable part of the cultural milieu on the treatment unit, the adolescents exhibited a noticeable decrease in violent and sexual behaviors. It seems feasible that similar results could occur if society as a whole adopted a commitment to continue offering nonsexual contact to adolescents, if adults helped teenagers learn that becoming sexually aroused does not require that they have to act on such arousal, and if adults taught adolescents that feelings of emotional or sexual attraction to another person of the same gender are normal and that such feelings do not necessarily imply a homosexual orientation.

Helping children form healthy adult sexual relationships must start much earlier than adolescence. Healthy sexual transactions directly involve the use of touch. Therefore, values, beliefs, and feelings about touch that are acquired during childhood will become an important factor as children enter adulthood and face the inevitable developmental issues surrounding sexuality. Offit (1977) clarifies the fundamental significance of touch to the formation of a healthy adult relationship:

> What I shall call "touch bonding," then, seems to be the first requirement for the establishment of sexual feelings. It is also necessary to the creation of one's first dependent attachment. The road map to old-fashioned marital joy requires a firm relationship between dependence, touching, and sexuality. Warmly nurturant parenting is thought to groom us into becoming delightful lovers and dedicated parents ourselves. (p. 31)

■ The Impact of Touch Dysfunctions on Child Development

Some children are also affected by unusual types of touch dysfunctions. For example, Smith (1989) cited a rarely discussed disorder known as *sensory integrative dysfunction*, in which children have difficulty interpreting information they receive through touch. It is developmentally normal for young children to exhibit a proclivity to breaking and spilling things while they are acquiring basic mechanical skills. Such behavior is generally dismissed as indicative of children's "clumsy" phase. Children who are affected by a sensory integrative dysfunction, however, generally extend beyond this phenomenon of clumsiness into the additional realm of a general awkwardness or outright dislike of being touched by others. Furthermore, they may display a more global tendency to shun physical contact with objects and people because they actually find the sensations of light touch unpleasant and disturbing.

Other research studies have identified infant children who do not seek comfort and soothing from physical contact. In one study, Schaffer and Emerson (1964) reported on individual differences regarding physical contact during the first year and a half of life. They observed children who fit into two categories of response to physical contact: cuddlers and noncuddlers. Schaffer and Emerson noted that both contact-seeking and non-contact-seeking infants sought out their mothers equally in situations of fear or stress, but the cuddlers desired direct physical contact, whereas the noncuddlers preferred visual or minimal physical contact (e.g., holding the mother's dress or hiding the face against the mother's knee). Noncuddlers were observed to be more resistant to all forms of direct physical contact than were cuddlers, even in circumstances when they were tired, physically ill, or emotionally upset.

Children who are born physically addicted to drugs face an additional risk for abuse because it is common for such infants to exhibit a decreased desire for, or an actual aversion to, touch. Malfunctions in an addicted infant's nervous system frequently cause her either to sleep or to cry excessively. She may also shun physical contact, be nonresponsive to being held, and experience difficulties in bonding with her caregiver. Such children can be extremely frustrating for even the most competent and well intentioned adults, and it is common for caregivers to feel rejected, irritated, and/or incompetent when such children fail to respond to efforts to soothe or nurture them. If adult caregivers for these children are also addicts, chances are that they have diminished self-esteem, a low tolerance for stress, and difficulty forming intimate relationships, all of which increase the risk that children in their care may be abused.

Some researchers have observed that hyperactive children frequently have negative reactions to being touched (Bauer, 1977a, 1977b). Following physical contact, hyperactive children regularly demonstrated reactive behaviors such as negative verbal responses, physical withdrawal, and rubbing or scratching of those areas of the skin that had been the points of physical contact. Many professionals who work with hyperactive children may be aware that the common expression that someone is "very touchy" has a directly physical as well as emotional dimension when applied to this population of clients. Thayer (1982) alerted clinicians to be aware of the profound social implications of this extreme negative sensitivity of hyperactive children.

Although mental health professionals have become much more aware of the negative impact of abuse, far less attention has been given to the equally destructive implications of neglect and deprivation on child development. Therapists who work with clients who have issues involving aggression and antisocial behaviors should consider how issues of touch may be a factor in understanding the underlying causes of these behaviors, as well as the potential value of using touch as an intervention to facilitate healing. A growing body of literature has linked aggressive, violent, and antisocial behaviors to sensory deprivation during early childhood (Mitchell, 1979; Older, 1982; Prescott, 1975). Evidence suggests that children who experience sensory deprivation as a routine style of caregiving grow up with a diminished capacity to feel, including a reduced ability to initiate touch with, or receive touch from, other human beings. In its more extreme presentation, clients exhibit a distinct lack of affection or feelings for anyone or anything and are frequently assigned a diagnostic label of *antisocial personality disorder.* Older, however, cautioned us to be aware that this diagnostic label may sometimes serve as a dumping ground for troublesome people who do not seem to fit other labels. As previously noted in Chapter 1, Prescott has been an early pioneer in advocating that touch deprivation may play a significant part in a client's violent or sociopathic disturbance. His research has identified a strong relationship between the amount of physical contact that children receive during infancy and the propensity for those children to become violent adults. Prescott offered evidence that the less children receive touch, the more likely they are to grow up to become violent.

Neglectful parents are not the only source of touch deprivation for young children. Equally significant is the lack of touch that may accompany institutionalized treatment. For example, young infants who require extended medical treatment on an intensive care unit are vulnerable to the longer-term implications of touch deprivation. Although some hospitals do incorporate physical contact into the treatment regimens for such children, some of the worst culprits for creating the circumstances for institutionalized touch deprivation are those facilities that rely on the most highly sophisticated technical equipment and/or are the most conscientious about hygienic concerns.

Similarly, children who require extended stays in foster homes or residential treatment programs are frequently denied even nonsexual touch because of fears of legal suits that could result from physical contact between staff and children. Even teachers and day care staff, who sometimes spend more time with children than children's own parents, are restricted from using touch because of the increasingly litigious social climate. The frequency with which children in U.S. society spend time in agency and institutional settings outside the home raises serious concerns about the longer-term implications of a general social climate in which adult caregivers are afraid of touch interactions or are restricted from such forms of interpersonal engagement with the children they serve.

▦ The Relevance of Touch With Older Persons

At the other end of the developmental continuum is the relevance of touch for persons who are old. Americans live in a society that is obsessed with youth. Consequently, we tend to diminish or overlook the needs of older persons. Much of the emphasis on touch for older persons is focused on the maintenance of youth. For example, we tend to substitute face lifts and skin creams for nurturing touch. In our love affair with youth and materialism, we overlook the value of touch in keeping the human spirit young as we move gracefully through the process of aging.

Within the constructs of most Western cultures, people unfortunately encounter an increased loss in opportunities for touch as they age. Older persons are at greater risk for social isolation, with heightened feelings of alienation and disengagement from the world around them. Some of these feelings are a response to the natural losses in their support system due to illness and death, some of these feelings are the consequences of failing vision and hearing, and some result from a decreased capacity for physical mobility. Although some loss in physical faculties and general perceptual skill is an expected part of the aging process, the sense of touch seems to remain intact for most older people, and, for some, touch actually becomes a more significant source of sensory communication by which they maintain contact with the world around them (Hollinger, 1986).

Too often, however, we deprive older persons of touch, thereby increasing their already growing sense of isolation and alienation. We often assume that decreases in physical agility imply lesser needs for physical contact. We fail to consider how difficult it must be for older persons to deal with failings in their own physical capacities or to grieve the losses of loved ones if they are spending extended time alone, if they encounter periods of hospital confinement, or if they are relegated to the care of an impersonal nursing home. Barnett (1972), reporting on the results of a survey on the use of touch by health care professionals with an intergenerational sample of hospitalized patients, found that older patients received the least amount of touch. In another survey, Huss (1977) noted that 60% of the professional caregivers reported uncomfortable feelings and some degree of anxiety when touching older patients.

Evidence suggests that tactile discrimination thresholds do increase as a result of aging. In other words, older persons may experience a greater degree of impaired sensitivity to light touch. Woodard (1993) explained that this phenomenon is not accounted for by any particular changes in the compliance abilities of the skin but rather seems to be attributed to some factor or factors associated with age itself. This means that older people may be less sensitive to tactile stimuli and may require a greater degree or intensity of contact in response to a tactile need; this in no way, however, implies a lesser degree of need or desire for touch.

Unfortunately, many of the ways in which older people within our culture are treated are based on the assumption that older persons have a greatly decreased interest in sexual dimensions of life and a corresponding assumption that older persons are less needy of physical contact. As older people become increasingly vocal and assertive in expressing what the aging process really feels like, many of the prevailing assumptions are being challenged. We believe that older members of our society need touch to thrive just as much as do infants. We believe that generous, appropriate, and nurturing touch across the life stages could greatly facilitate the process by which people are able to age and die with dignity.

▓ Summary

In this chapter, we have briefly surveyed the variety of ways that touch influences the socialization processes for human beings throughout the developmental stages of life. We have reviewed much of the research on nonhuman primates and humans concerning the impact of touch. Although not all researchers agree on the exact ways or the degree to which touch is significant to socialization experiences, few disagree that touch is a primary and essential variable that affects how people form and sustain interpersonal relationships.

Traditions of Touch
Within Various Cultures

The use of touch in the art of healing has a long and rich tradition, transcending time and boundaries among the diverse cultures throughout recorded history. Although the norms governing the acceptability of touch have varied tremendously in different times and places, touch has been an important feature during every period of human history. People have employed touch in their quests to increase personal well-being; in their search to access the spiritual realm of a higher power, a god, or a positive life force; and in their efforts to find and/or demonstrate goodness in the world.

Cave paintings in the Pyrenees, estimated to be more than 15,000 years old, offer visual evidence that touch was used for purposes of healing. Greek mythology is populated with lessons that are influenced by the use of touch.

Touch as a significant tool for healing is well understood within many of the Native American cultures, although modern-day evidence for the existence of many of these practices is largely anecdotal (Kaplan & Johnson, 1964; Murphy, 1964).

▪ Christian and Other Religious Traditions

Religious traditions in nearly all parts of the world have incorporated touch into spiritual rituals. Literature from early religions and the Eastern world that date from 5,000 years ago include generous references to the existence of therapeutic touch as healing art (Miller, 1979). Those who have emerged as spiritual leaders within various religious traditions have characteristically been imbued with special powers of touch. For example, faith healers—religious leaders such as Jesus of Nazareth, Ali, and present-day evangelists—are believed to have magical powers that allow them to use touch to exorcise diseases and evil from the bodies of their true believers.

Within the settings of the Islamic mosque, the Taoist temple, and the Buddhist shrine, religious followers regularly engage in practices that involve both real and symbolic touching of consecrated garments and religious icons. Kissing the Pope's ring is a symbol of prestige and honor within the Catholic tradition. The Jewish faith invests considerable importance to ceremonial rituals surrounding the touching of the Torah. The vast outpouring of Renaissance art that accompanied the proliferation of Christianity in Western Europe frequently portrayed spiritual scenes that emphasized physical contact.

Most of the norms and beliefs that define social constructs within Western culture have been filtered through the traditions of Christianity and have been influenced by Christian beliefs. In actuality, however, Christianity is quite ambivalent about the value of touch. Narratives in the New Testament of the Bible illustrate the basic contradictions about touch that exist within Christianity.

Much of the grandeur that surrounded Jesus of Nazareth emanated from his reported awesome abilities to perform miracles. The laying on of hands was generally an essential part of these celestial miracles, as is clearly illustrated in the following passage describing Jesus' healing touch: "And when Jesus entered Peter's house, he saw his mother-in-law lying sick with a fever, he touched her, and the fever left her, and she rose and served him" (Matthew 8:14-15, Revised Standard Version).

Jesus used his hands to anoint people with oil as well as to perform acts of healing. He was frequently portrayed as using touch to mend the crippled, to heal the sick, and to offer strength to the downtrodden. Jesus' willingness to touch the sick and the outcast so freely, however, soon became controversial with more established Jewish authorities.

The New Testament of the Bible freely documents both sides of this traditional Christian conflict involving the issue of physical touch. On the one hand, numerous examples of how Jesus demonstrated his healing powers directly through such physical contact are included. Henley (1977) noted that the New Testament documents 25 miracles of healing that are attributed to Jesus, 19 of which take place within a range that would allow for touching, and 14 of which are accomplished through direct physical contact. In all but one of these cases, Jesus touched the person who was afflicted, rather than the recipient touching him. On the other hand, Christianity has historically devoted considerable attention to dissuading people from indulging in pleasures of the flesh and has consistently chastised believers when they have ventured too close to "sins of the body." Traditional religious doctrines and official church policies within most denominational wings of Christianity ultimately have supported a negative view of earthly pleasures associated with the physical body and, thereby, have incorporated into notions about touch the concept of sin or of being less than spiritual.

Well into the Middle Ages, however, Christian literature and art abound with accounts of miracle healing through the use of the laying on of hands. For example, Michelangelo's magnificent portrayal of the Creation on the ceiling of the Sistine Chapel is a clear illustration of the degree to which touch was imbued with heavenly powers. Henley (1977) noted,

> When Michelangelo painted the scene of creation in the Sistine Chapel, he chose to portray the giving of life as a *touch* from God to Adam, rather than what is described in Genesis, that God "breathed into his nostrils the breath of life." And few observers have noted this difference: the magic of touch is seen as so natural one almost senses the spark of life jumping the gap between the outstretched hands. . . . Michelangelo's use of touch reminds us of the special place this gesture has had in human history, particularly as an act of divine and magical connotation. (p. 94)

Particularly significant about this Michelangelo painting is the motion toward physical contact that is represented in the portrayal. It is significant that the actual moment of physical contact is not shown but is left to the emotional interpretation of the viewer. Perhaps this symbolizes the spiritual longing to touch or to be touched that is an inherent part of the human experience.

The Christian Church was focused on gaining influence and consolidating power during the Middle Ages. In this regard, Christian leaders discouraged people from engaging in physical contact outside the sanction of official Church policies. Nonsanctioned touch was viewed with intense suspicion and was portrayed to represent witchcraft or curses of the devil or was simply judged as nonsensical. Through time, Church policies became increasingly restrictive and punitive against those who violated the established Christian norms about physical contact.

Thomas (1994) offered the following summary that clarified the transition of attitudes about touch within the context of changing Christian norms:

> During the first eight centuries after Christ, church members experienced *healing touch* in the sacraments and in their homes. . . . Then, gradually, through the Middle Ages both church and culture grew preoccupied with levels of authority [hierarchies]. . . . In this period healing touch disappeared among laity and became *power touch*, exercised by religious and political authorities. Later, with the birth of science in the Sixteenth and Seventeenth centuries, both healing touch and power touch were considered superstitions of the past, and *no touch* became proper scientific philosophy. Finally, the unhealthy behavior modeled by no touch in helping professions, religious communities, and families produced *touch gone wrong*. (p. 27)

■ The Practices of Medicine

The use of touch is also prevalent in the early roots of medical practice. The basic concept of disease is actually based in the conceptual framework of touch. Ford (1989) noted that the word *disease* was derived from the Latin roots *dis* meaning "not," and *ease*, from *adiacens*, meaning "adjacent" or" touching." Thus, *dis-ease* means separate or not touching. *Disease* usually designates a condition of the body that implies the opposite of healthy.

Within ancient Eastern cultures, documentation dating from 25 centuries includes references to medical procedures involving touch that were employed by yogis (Miller, 1979). The Hindu traditions of yoga are grounded in the idea that the human body is composed of energies that travel through nonphysical pathways (Cohen, 1987). Within this framework, acupuncture and Chinese massage emerged as healing techniques by which these energies could be supported or regulated.

The art of healing began to evolve into the science of medicine during the Middle Ages, increasing the tensions between Christian Church and secular leaders within European societies. The growing ability of medical doctors to assist in the process of healing was intensely threatening to religious teachings that were grounded in concepts of miracle healing. The miracles of science provided earthly explanations that challenged traditional beliefs about religious miracles previously attributed to heavenly forces. The stature of scientists grew exponentially during the Renaissance, undermining public respect for royalty and religious leaders and thereby eroding their positions of power and privilege.

Medically trained physicians increasingly turned to scientific data to demystify and invalidate religious miracles, whereas religious leaders vehemently discredited scientific advances as heretical. In the middle of this battle, the "chirthetists"—touch healers who had long been honored and respected by the common people in the countryside—gradually lost clout as they were negatively stigmatized by both medical and religious proponents (Cohen, 1987).

By the 17th century, the scientific and religious communities reached an unofficial compromise that defused the intensity of this church–secular conflict (Cohen, 1987). When medical doctors were officially sanctioned by Church leaders to conduct autopsies of human corpses, the Christian Church essentially relinquished its domain of control over healing touch. In essence, the Christian Church conceded control over the physical body to medical science in exchange for retaining control over the realm of mind and spirit. This important historical compromise established the fundamental framework for the Western construct of a split between body and mind/spirit, a construct that has prevailed since the Middle Ages.

Such historical processes provide a context within which to understand the radically different ways in which contemporary Eastern and Western cultures have approached issues related to healing. Within the traditions of many Eastern cultures, shamans have been the archetypical healers. Shamans are usually granted special status because of their wisdom at attending to the physical, emotional, and spiritual needs of members of the community. Although the shamans characteristically approach healing as a process involving the mind, body, and spirit as integrated aspects of the human life force, Western culture responds to each of these dimensions of the human experience as separate entities. In the technological view of the world, medicine is viewed as an industry and healing as a process to be adapted to the mechanical constructs of assembly-line production. Therefore, these three aspects of the human organism are separated and subdivided to allow them to be allocated to different professional healers: Physicians are granted access to the physical body, psychotherapists focus on the mind and emotions, and clergies attend to the needs of the spirit. This separation of the mind and spirit from the physical body has, perhaps more than any other factor, drastically influenced Western approaches to touch and physical contact.

Many of the ancient traditions of healing that had used touch were abandoned or restricted during the Middle Ages because of the growing love affair with emerging science and technology. Therefore, for several centuries, the relevance of touch within the healing professions was largely ignored.

Although physical touch has undeniably been a fundamental aspect of routine physician–patient interactions, most contemporary medical doctors seek to minimize, rather than to enhance, their contact with patients. In this modern age, traditional diagnostic procedures involving touch and physical probing have increasingly been replaced by sophisticated technological machines that produce complicated statistical data. The deft hand and eye of the master surgeon are quickly being superseded by robotic tools and monitor screens that foster an ever-increasing reliance on technological approaches to surgery. The physician's reassuring touch and nurturing attention that used to accompany treatment for a routine illness have been supplanted by impersonal drug therapies that require little more physician–patient contact than is required to exchange a pharmaceutical prescription. In today's technological medicine, physical contact has become nearly irrelevant, frequently viewed more as an interference with the larger goals of efficiency in the delivery of services than as a cornerstone to humane medical treatment.

▓ Child Rearing

Schreber (1955) was a physician and preeminent authority on child rearing in Germany during the mid-1800s. Dr. Schreber believed that his nation and his age had become contaminated by several evils: softness, moral decay, and weakness. His writings were dedicated to teaching his fellow citizens about the "proper" ways to raise children. He was adamant against "unnecessary" touching of children by parents and caregivers. Discipline and absolute obedience were the essential goals to be achieved in his approaches to child rearing, and he cautioned that physical contact that was kind and soft was generally toxic, undermining any parental efforts to achieve these goals.

Attitudes and practices toward child rearing were strongly transformed during the early part of the 20th century as a result of the influence of behaviorism, which emerged as a prominent school of thought within the professional community of psychology. The philosophical basis of behavioralism closely paralleled the views of Schreber. Watson (1928), the founder and leading advocate for this approach, authored a landmark book titled *Psychological Care of Infant and Child.* In this book, frequently referred to as the "standard book of child psychology" and so widely read that it went through at least five large printings, he warned mothers not to touch their children. The focus for this command is illustrated in the following passage from his book:

> A certain amount of affectionate response is socially necessary but few parents realize how easily they can overtrain the child in this direction. . . . Mothers just don't know, when they kiss their children and pick them up and rock them, caress them and jiggle them upon their knee, that they are slowly building up a

human being totally unable to cope with the world it must later live in. (pp. 43-44)

Further expounding his philosophy about the proper way for raising children, Watson included the following advice:

There is a sensible way of treating children. Treat them as though they were young adults. Dress them, bathe them with care and circumspection. . . . Never hug and kiss them, never let them sit on your lap. If you must, kiss them once on the forehead when they say goodnight. Shake hands with them in the morning. Give them a pat on the head if they have made an extraordinary job of a difficult task. (pp. 81-82)

By the 1930s, social attitudes in general and child-rearing practices in particular solidly reflected the institutionalization of the taboo against touch. The pervasiveness of this "no-touch" norm was apparent within American culture. American society as a whole increasingly evinced a hands-off attitude that supported the growing trend toward the superiority of individual (vs. shared or collective) endeavors. During the early and middle period of the 20th century, orphanages and foundling homes rigidly adhered to policies that strictly forbade any physical contact with the children who were entrusted in their care, reflecting a strong social mandate to uphold the taboo against touch. (Chapter 1 addressed the failure-to-thrive phenomenon that so pervasively plagued orphanages for much of the 20th century.)

▦ Summary

In this chapter, we have surveyed a variety of traditions within various cultures. Perhaps most significant in these traditions is the extent to which social and political interests, compared with clinical concerns, have determined the degree to which touch has been interpreted as acceptable or contraindicated.

Chapter 4

Traditions of Touch in Psychotherapy

For most of the 20th century, the American psychotherapy community has remained almost silent regarding the issue of whether there might be any positive value in using touch as a tool for healing. Not until the late 1960s and 1970s did literature begin to appear within the mainstream psychotherapy professional journals that approached the topic of the potentially positive value of touch in healing. Winnicott (1965) took a professional risk by publishing anecdotal case materials that disclosed his clinical practices of using touch with his patients.

Forer (1969) is one of the earliest contemporary pioneers who suggested that there could be positive value in the touching of patients by therapists. He pointed out that continued adherence to a rigid "don't touch" stance was fostered more as a result of social beliefs than of clinical theory: "The puritan ethic and the engineering, technologic, antihumanistic stance of our middle class society has fostered ritualistic interpersonal relationships. It has preferred rationality and discipline to emotional expressiveness and tenderness, and emphasized verbal rather than body contact" (p. 229).

Older (1977) was courageous enough to continue the process of questioning and challenging the taboos against touch. In his article titled "Four Taboos That May Limit the Success of Psychotherapy," he boldly stated that clients can definitely benefit from touch and examined the prevailing clinical practices and attitudes that imposed limits on therapeutic effectiveness.

The roots of the abandonment of touch within the field of mental health can probably be seen most clearly in the framework of psychoanalysis, which emerged as a significant influence during the late 1800s. Psychoanalysis has had a pervasive influence on the development of nearly every aspect of medical and mental health throughout the 20th century. Therefore, we begin our examination of psychotherapeutic history with the work of Sigmund Freud.

Space does not permit an in-depth examination of the many men and women who wrote on the use of touch within the various traditions of psychotherapy, but we will now provide a brief overview of some of the thinking of the early pioneers. Readers who wish more detailed information are directed to the materials contained in the reference list.

▨ Psychoanalysis

Freud

Freud's work has had a particularly profound impact on the use of touch within the field of psychotherapy. In his early professional career, Freud was a physiologist who routinely examined the body as part of his standard protocol. This led him to study neuropathology, focusing on diseases of the nervous system. Freud (1960) advocated that an individual's experience of the body at least partially influenced the development of the experience of ego:

> The ego is first and foremost a bodily ego; it is not merely a surface entity, but is itself the projection of a surface. . . . The ego is ultimately derived from bodily sensations, chiefly those

springing from the surface of the body. It may thus be regarded as a mental projection of the surface of the body. (p. 16)

Freud initially employed touch during his therapeutic interactions with patients, using physical contact in ways that were adjunctive to the process of verbal therapy (Breuer & Freud, 1955). When he began his work on hysteria, Freud observed that a dynamic therapeutic intervention for patients who were distraught or suffering from somatic symptoms was to touch or massage them. During this early period of his practice as a psychotherapist, he not only routinely stroked the head or neck of his patients for stimulative effect but also permitted his patients to touch him.

Freud reported positive results when he used the technique of holding a patient's head between his hands as the patient struggled to answer a question to which the patient did not know the answer (Breuer & Freud, 1957). Freud offered the following account of his approach to treatment during his early work as a psychotherapist:

I proceeded as follows. I placed my hand on the patient's forehead or took her head between my hands and said: "You will think of it under the pressure of my hands. At the moment at which I relax my pressure, you will see something in front of you or something will come into your head. Catch hold of it." (p. 110)

As Freud focused more precisely on the dynamics of transference, however, he increasingly advocated that the correct therapeutic relationship required a therapeutic stance of nonintervention. During the early 1900s, Freud was instrumental in outlining the governing concepts for the classical model of psychoanalytic treatment. A primary focus of psychoanalysis was to make unconscious material conscious through the use of free association and by analyzing the transference process from patient to therapist. It was critical to this process that the analyst assume the role of a blank screen, remaining impersonal, objective, and nonjudgmental, avoiding any interaction that could contaminate the transference process.

Within the context of orthodox Freudian psychoanalysis, touch was increasingly viewed as a response that gratified the patient's desires, thereby interfering with the development of the transference neurosis, lessening the patient's energy, and ultimately leading to stagnation in the analysis. Freud's attention to the concept of transferential reliving of early attachments highlighted the importance of the analyst's understanding and attention to the unconscious meanings of body contact. As the field of psychoanalysis gained stature, theoretical rationales that supported strict prohibitions against touching became commonly accepted, thereby evolving into an institutionalized taboo forbidding the use of touch in this form of psychotherapy.

Eventually, the traditional psychoanalytic model came to see touch as serving the detrimental purpose of seductive wish fulfillment. Within this context, any physical contact between analyst and patient was viewed as colluding with the patient to sidestep, rather than work through, whatever painful experience was at hand. From this set of constructs, Freud established a consistent technique of having the patient lie on a couch, without seeing or being touched by the analyst.

This hands-off approach included refraining from any physical contact, even during the greeting and departure phase of an analytic session. According to this model, the analyst was to be impenetrable to the client, with the analyst acting solely as a mirror to reflect back to the patient nothing more than what the patient revealed.

Menninger (1958), a psychoanalyst, wrote that the psychoanalyst must remain "neutral and aseptic." This meant that the analyst must not "chat" with patients or "touch them unnecessarily" (p. 36). Unfortunately, Menninger globally branded *all* touch as ruthlessly criminal in nature, failing to consider any distinction between therapeutic, sexual, and aggressive touch. Menninger's prohibitions against touch were quite wide reaching; he even regarded any physical contact by the analyst—including handshakes—as "incompetent and criminal" (p. 36). Mintz (1969a, 1969b), however, reported that many analysts who responded to confidential interviews admitted that they did sometimes permit physical engagements with their patients, such as a shoulder touch, a handshake, or an embrace.

Contemporary European psychoanalysts have not seemed as rigid about the use of touch as those in America. For example, van der Waals was quoted by Menninger and Holzman (1973) as stating,

> I think every analyst in Europe, at least every analyst I know, shakes hands with his patients at the beginning and end of the

hour. It gives valuable information about the mood of the patient, his reaction to the hour, etc. In Europe it would be a technical error not to do this. (p. 36)

Ultimately, it is important to understand that the evolution of this strong taboo against touch within the tradition of psychoanalysis has a political, as well as a clinical, basis. As we previously outlined, the clinical context for this taboo emerged from the theoretical principle that transference, the cornerstone of psychoanalysis, should occur with a minimal influence by the real personality of the analyst. Therefore, this basic rule of abstinence justifiably contradicts the use of any form of physical touching by the analyst.

The political reasons to explain the emergence of this taboo from psychoanalysts are more complex. Mintz (1969b) offered some historical insight regarding external, nonclinical circumstances that probably influenced the psychoanalytic community. These circumstances cast a political hue on the touch taboo. According to Mintz's analysis, Freud developed his theories during the Victorian era, a period that was characterized by unyielding sexual prudishness and a strong emphasis on the products of the mind. Considerable tensions existed between religion and science. Members of the newly emerging scientific community desperately sought to gain legitimacy to support their pursuits of knowledge while religious leaders continued to compete for people's souls.

For those members of society who sought to maintain their stance as defenders of the status quo, the original psychoanalytic practices of using techniques such as stroking, hypnosis, and therapeutic massage were viewed as proof that Freud and his associates were nothing more than sexual perverts. Within the context of such intense social struggles, the decision by psychoanalysts to avoid any form of physical contact with their patients, no matter how neutral its intent, can be seen as reflecting political expediency as much as clinical efficacy. In the end, Freud and his associates probably had enough wisdom to understand the political dimensions of their quest to establish themselves as legitimate scientists. Political savvy may well have persuaded them to embrace the tactical strategy of dissociating themselves completely from any clinical practice having the appearance of magical or religious overtones.

Ferenczi

Ferenczi (1952) was originally trained in the psychoanalytic model but later became a proponent of using touch in analysis. He experimented with providing touch for some of his patients who were victims of early parental abuse and neglect. At one time, Ferenczi suggested that the analyst could facilitate trust with the patient by hugging, holding, kissing, and nonerotic fondling. He believed that the use of such therapeutic touch would be experienced as nurturing, providing reparative parenting to correct and heal early damage in the patient's experience.

Although Freud was initially supportive of Ferenczi's experiments, he later withdrew that support when he learned that Ferenczi was romantically and sexually involved with at least two patients (Masson, 1988). Ferenczi was expelled from the ranks of orthodox psychoanalysis because of his refusal to discontinue his use of touch. Ironically, Ferenczi later took the opposite position—not only discouraging analysts from touching patients but also discouraging patients from touching themselves by masturbating. It has been suggested that Ferenczi's conflict with Freud had a chilling effect on the growth and development of psychoanalysis, because others feared it was a sign that if they dared to experiment with analytic technique or challenge the accepted theory they would be punished by Freud and his closest followers.

Reich

Reich, also an early psychoanalyst, initially gained significant stature through his membership in Freud's inner circle. By the middle of his professional career, however, he began to suggest that neuroses could be observed in the muscles as well as in the mind. He postulated that stiff body posture, shallow breathing, and/or an awkward gait often disclosed as much therapeutic information about a person as did fears and fantasies. Eventually, Reich (1972) devised the concept of *character analysis*, which emerged as a radical departure from the rigid tenets of Freudian psychoanalysis and which, in essence, replaced psychology with somatology.

Reich advocated that seven rings of muscular armoring cut across the body transversely from front to back: eye area, mouth and jaw, neck, chest, diaphragm, central abdomen, and pelvis. His method was to observe breathing patterns by having his clients undress and lie on a couch. Reich suggested that body tensions are frequently encapsulated as "character armor," which he proposed are actually habitual physiological rigidities that correspond to barriers against the stimulation of emotions.

Reich departed from the traditional stance of Freudian psychoanalysis by initiating direct physical contact with his clients, for which he was censured and eventually excommunicated from the psychoanalytic community (Older, 1982). Although there is only sparse direct information to clarify the type of touching Reich employed, it is generally agreed that he would touch the client's body to help identify areas of physical tension. His writings make passing references to the use of physical interventions such as pressing muscles and palpitation as he sought to attack directly the appropriate areas of character armor, dissolving the muscular tension and thereby releasing the "bound up" emotion.

Reich's courageous departure from traditional Freudian psychoanalysis set the context for a proliferation of alternative body-oriented approaches to healing that have been developed during the 20th century. Reich is frequently credited as the father of body-oriented psychotherapy. Body-oriented approaches to healing, however, as distinguished from mainstream psychotherapy itself, have a long and rich history, considerably predating the work of Reich. Reich's most significant contribution is more appropriately focused on his efforts to deconstruct the barriers and restrictions to touch that had been imposed by the domineering influences of psychoanalysis. Riechian therapy continues to be actively practiced, particularly in Europe. Contemporary Riechians regularly make use of touch during therapy with both children and adults (Schoener, 1997).

▨ Body-Oriented Psychotherapies

Body-oriented psychotherapy is actually an umbrella term that refers to a wide spectrum of approaches. Because most contemporary body-oriented psychotherapies challenge the basic assumptions of psychoanalysis, it is not surprising that most of these alternative approaches that have emerged have been greeted with considerable doubt and skepticism by those healing professionals who are the defenders of the Medical Model Establishment. Most of the body-oriented approaches to psychotherapy share an inherent ideology of responding to psychological events by focusing more on the physical than on the cognitive aspects of those experiences. Most body-oriented psychotherapies emphasize experiential learning rather than transferential relationships.

Bioenergetics

Bioenergetics was developed by Lowen (1958, 1976), a psychiatrist who studied with Reich. He believed that a person's physiology was significantly affected when emotions and desires were repressed or inhibited during infancy, childhood, or adult years. Lowen advocated that chronic muscle tension resulted from the conscious or unconscious repression of emotions, eventually interfering with the body's potential to be vibrant and robust. Although orthodox Reichian therapy emphasizes concerns with orgasmic performance, bioenergetics focuses instead on the larger realm of pure feelings. Lowen wrote,

> We work with the hypothesis that there is one fundamental energy in the human body whether it manifests itself in psychic phenomena or in somatic motion. This energy we call simply "bioenergy." Psychic processes as well as somatic processes are determined by the operation of this bioenergy. All living processes can be reduced to manifestations of this bioenergy. (1958, p. 18)

Bioenergetics training institutes exist throughout the world, and practitioners continue to contribute to the psychotherapy literature.

Adler

Adler interpreted disease psychologically and concentrated on the specifics of body language (Ansbacher & Ansbacher, 1964). Adler was especially interested in the body's capacity to compensate for organic damage, a phenomenon that he believed occurred in both the psychological and physiological spheres. He made important contributions to the evolution of body therapy through his attention to physical defects and bodily expressions of character traits.

▒ Human Potential Movement

The human potential movement, sometimes referred to as touchy-feely therapy, attained considerable notoriety during the 1960s because of its permissive approaches to physical contact. This movement emerged from the sociopolitical milieu of the 1960s, and many of the techniques employed by human potential practitioners—usually within the context of group therapy—were defiant and nonconformist in their nature. Such techniques were designed to assist participants in their quest to become liberated from prevailing social norms.

A primary feature that distinguished human potential therapy from other existing mainstream group therapies was the willingness to sanction the inclusion of therapeutic maneuvers that involved some form of physical contact. Therefore, common activities included massage; hands-on relaxation exercises; back rubs; "love baths" in which everyone in a group would hug one another; trust exercises, such as one person's falling back into the arms of other group members; and exercises, sometimes including various degrees of nudity, to enhance self-esteem and self-acceptance of one's physical body (Rogers, 1970, p. 62).

Spontaneity was valued by human potential therapists. Rogers (1970) described the therapists ability to be spontaneous as "the most precious and elusive element" he knew (p. 57). He advised therapists to avoid "gimmicks and exercises," and have faith in the ability to authentically respond to the group members. This attitude made it possible to experiment with the use of touch as part of the group experience. Rogers (1970) wrote,

> Slowly I have learned to respond with physical contact when this seems real and spontaneous and appropriate. When a young woman was weeping because she had had a dream that one in the group loved her, I embraced her and kissed and comforted her. When a person is suffering and I feel like going over and putting my arm around him, I do just that. Again, I do

not try consciously to *promote* this kind of behavior. (pp. 58- 59, italics in the original)

A main tenet of Gestalt therapy is making contact between client and client, as well as therapist and client. Although such contact can take place through any of the senses, touch is viewed as particularly useful. Polster and Polster (1973) wrote,

> The immediacy of touch breaks through the intellectual layers into palpable personal recognitions. For example, in one group a lively but sexually naive woman told about her tomboy background and observed that she had never had the sense of really being close to a man. I asked her to touch several of the men in the room. At first she was reluctant, although she was obviously not thrown by the suggestion. Gingerly, she touched one man's hair, and she began to lose her self-consciousness, slapping the next man on the shoulder and stroking another's cheek. She began to be tuned in, at first incredulously, to the fact that she was actually making contact with the men, and that each was receptive to her touch and respectful of her exploration. (p. 143)

Eventually this woman climbed into the lap of the male psychotherapist and began to cry about the death of her father. What is not discussed in this example is whether the male clients were asked prior to the physical contact if they were open to being touched by the female client.

Gestalt therapists such as Fritz Perls (1969) believed that most psychotherapies, especially psychoanalysis, ignored the dimension of physical sensations, thereby making them overly intellectual. Perls believed that unresolved traumas are stored in the physical body as repressed emotions, so he advocated the expression of these emotions, which he terms *unfinished business*. During such expression, touch was frequently involved. Unfortunately, in the permissive times that fostered the development of Gestalt therapy the touch was sometimes allowed to become erotic. For example, Perls appeared to have some difficulty distinguishing between love and lust when he stated,

My hands are strong and warm. A dirty old man's hands are cold and clammy. I have affection and love—too much of it. And if I comfort a girl in grief or distress and the sobbing subsides and she presses closer and the stroking gets out of rhythm and slides over the hips and breasts. . . . (Shepard, 1975, p. 159)

It was just this type of inappropriate use of touch that reinforced the idea that any form of touch between client and therapist led to sexual contact. Eventually, in some cases, all boundaries were eliminated and group sessions ended in orgies. One such experience was described by Shepard (1972), which led to the loss of his license to practice.

▓ Behaviorism

Behaviorists (e.g., Lazarus, 1976; Skinner, 1938, 1969, 1971, 1974; Wolpe, 1990) did not believe that transference was the primary issue in the treatment of psychological problems. Thus they did not focus on the possible negative effects of the use of touch in the treatment relationship. Behavior therapists have not extensively discussed the possible positive effects of touch between the behaviorist and the person receiving treatment. Neither did later cognitive-behaviorists (e.g., Beck, 1976; Dobson & Craig, 1996; Ellis, 1962; Ellis & Bernard, 1985; Yankura & Dryden, 1994) write specifically on whether touch was to be avoided or used in the treatment of emotional/behavioral problems.

However, when watching films or witnessing demonstrations of the therapists, one sees that they did engage in physical contact with those they were treating. For example, Wolpe used touch during the process of systematic desensitization.

▓ Marriage and Family Therapy

When watching training films in which the pioneers of this form of psychotherapy appear (e.g., Satir, 1967, 1972), one is able to see the ways in which touch was used. However, discussions about the efficacy of using touch, are largely absent from the professional literature that is identified with marriage and family therapy. A survey of the indexes for 20 basic textbooks that serve as cornerstones for marriage and family therapy does not identify a single reference to the terms *touch* or *physical contact*. These textbooks include some of the milestones in marriage and family therapy. In the nearly 50 years of marriage and family literature that is covered in *Family Therapy: A Bibliography* (Lubin, 1988), the term *touch* appears only once. In the one text that did include a listing on *touch* (Ferber, Mendelsohn, & Napier, 1972), the actual discussion of the topic consisted of 28 words in the description of the technique of body sculpture: "This technique has a number of interesting virtues. One is that it entails touching, a fact of great importance in families which have minimized this modality of communication" (p. 299).

Those marriage and family therapists who did specifically mention the use of touch suggested caution but did not forbid it. For example, L'Abate, Ganahl, and Hansen (1986) wrote,

The therapist should also be attuned to the potential power of touch. . . . Touch can be encouraged by the therapist and evaluated as family members respond to each others' touch and proximity. The therapist can also encourage this by touching the sculptor in offering guidance or gentle support. (p. 179)

Although written materials focusing on the use of touch within marriage and family therapy are sparse, training films in which the pioneers of the field appear (e.g., Satir, 1967, 1972) are numerous. Watching these films makes it apparent that touch was frequently used.

▦   Sex Therapy

Masters and Johnson (1966, 1970a, 1976) and Kaplan (1974) are perhaps the most well known of the early sex therapists. Their treatment approach focused on directly modifying the sexual responses and behaviors of their client. Masters and Johnson proposed the use of "sensate focus" (1970b, p. 71), a form of structured exercise done by the client. Although not engaging in touch with the clients, the treatment providers described the exercises as a method allowing each member of the couple to "comfort or solace, convey reassurance, show devotion, (and) describe love or physical need" (1970, p. 71) to their partner.

Masters and Johnson's (1970) controversial technique made use of paid surrogate sexual partners for the treatment of sexual dysfunction. Within the framework of this approach, a professional sex therapist functioned in the role of a sexual surrogate, literally engaging in sexual activities with clients to help them learn or relearn sexual behaviors or to address areas of sexual dysfunction. Employing sexual surrogates within this framework generated such ethical controversy that Masters and Johnson eventually discontinued using this technique in their treatment program.

Other professionals have continued to use these methods under the auspices of a Professional Surrogates Association that was established to define and regulate ethical standards for such practitioners. In some states, however, a mental health professional who refers a client to a sex surrogate can be liable for criminal prosecution, under prostitution and antifornication statutes (Berkowitz, 1980).

▓ Hypnotherapy

The use of touch in hypnotherapy is common. It is used to induce trance, deepen trance, focus attention, check for the existence of amnesia, and assess level of trance. Spiegel and Spiegel (1978) give the following instructions to hypnotherapists who are administering the Hypnotic Induction Profile to determine the hypnotizability of a subject:

> This is an excellent opportunity to touch the subject's left arm by actually placing it on the arm of the chair gently, but firmly. Touching as you begin immediately establishes touching as a standard part of the procedure so that it will not startle the subject later. Touch is used by the examiner to focus the subject's attention on the physical sensations which may occur in response to verbal instructions. Touching also gives the tester the opportunity to actually measure the subject's physical response to some items on the test. For example, how light, heavy, stiff, or flexible the subject's left arm feels to the examiner is essential to measuring Item E, the instructional arm levitation.

Touching encourages a trend toward regression and atavism. Remember that too soft and indefinite a touch may be seductive and distract the subject's attention rather than help focus it. Be firm and definite. (p. 45)

Perhaps because both Speigel and Spiegel are physicians, and they assume the subject will expect some form of touch between doctor and patient, they do not suggest discussing the issue of touch prior to utilizing it.

▉ Contemporary Factors That Influence Individual Views on the Use of Touch in Psychotherapy

Psychotherapists Are Members of the Wider Culture

Contemporary Western societies remain generally confused and conflicted about the place of touch within their cultures. Americans, particularly those of Germanic and northern European descent, have historically been restrained and reserved when it comes to actually touching one another, engaging in minimal physical contact during routine daily living. Many Americans maintain a hands-off stance even during contacts with their closest friends, fearful that the intentions of their touch could be misconstrued. Americans generally reserve expressions of physical affection, even with lovers, to private times to avoid the risk of offending people in more public settings. This general stance of touch abstinence seems to be one of the traits that characterize the Anglo-Saxon and Puritan heritage.

On the other hand, touch remains a powerful and magical force within the everyday practices of modern society. People swoon at the opportunity to touch famous athletes or legendary movie stars who serve as the icons for our culture. It is common to pay our last respects at funerals by touching the casket that contains the body of our beloved deceased. The common human compulsion to reach out and "feel" great works of art requires that guards routinely patrol the galleries of museums. Politicians prize any opportunity to be photographed holding a baby.

Touch and Taboo

Taboos traditionally serve the dual function of imposing prohibitions that put roadblocks in front of pleasure as well as creating protective devices that define collective boundaries. The value system to which persons subscribe establishes the framework that frequently determines whether a taboo is experienced as a prohibition or as a protection.

Whether we agree or disagree with the prevailing cultural taboos against touch, it is important at least to identify and label those taboos that continue to influence psychotherapists. We can articulate the following list of taboos, which have similarities to a framework first postulated by Cohen (1987).

Don't Touch Opposite-Gender Friends Too Much. Most Western cultures are severely lacking in providing positive and healthy images, training, and experiences concerning nonsexualized touch. Therefore, there is the suspicion that any form of touch is a sexual advance.

Don't Touch Same-Gender Friends. This taboo is strong and pervasive in Western cultures. Even if they are not gay, most people are conditioned to label any same-gender physical contact as "homosexual." Unfortunately, this taboo is so deeply entrenched that it even encourages many parents to disengage from touch with their same-gender children once they reach puberty, from fear that their physical contacts might be misconstrued by outsiders or that such behaviors might contribute to the development of "homosexual tendencies" by their children.

Don't Touch Yourself. Perhaps even stronger than the taboo against touching others is the taboo against self-touch. Children first learn it as, "Don't touch down there."

Don't Touch Strangers. Touching strangers is avoided because it can provoke violence or lead to a sexual response. It is often viewed as an intrusion into another's personal space.

Don't Touch If the Recipient Is Elderly or Ill. This is the American version of the "untouchables." This taboo is subtle because Americans tend to deny the reality of our cultural favoritism toward the young and the healthy. Close observation of our social behaviors reveals that we are a society that is obsessed with youth and beauty. Therefore, we learn the cultural protocols that sanction us to be warm and receptive toward those whom we view as attractive and sexually desirable while grooming us to be more physically "cool" and aloof toward the sick and the infirm.

Not surprisingly, these subtle norms are even absorbed by our dominant institutions. For example, Ainsworth (1984) noted that nurses in intensive care units used supportive touch more than nurses in other types of medical units. This is what we expect. The surprising and more interesting result of Ainsworth's study, however, was his discovery that these intensive care nurses still adhered to an unspoken hierarchy of who was less desirable to touch: They exhibited an underlying bias toward touching those patients who were listed as in "good" or "fair" condition more frequently than they did those patients who were designated as in "poor" or "critical" condition.

The advent of the spread of AIDS has begun to have an impact on the use of touch with the sick. Some people believe that the mainstream medical community was slow to respond to the needs of AIDS patients, and this led to the use of alternative treatment techniques. In several major cities, massage therapists and others with touch-related training go to the homes of AIDS patients to provide massage and therapeutic touch.

Don't Touch Those of Higher Status. Those who are savvy about the implications of touch regarding status place heavy taboos on certain power gestures, which may or may not be intentionally or innocently given. In other words, a person's status frequently determines whether it is permissible to touch another person. Unfortunately, this taboo is violated frequently in almost every aspect of daily existence within the context of Western culture. The inherent contradiction between this implied norm and the realities of its application creates dilemmas in our understanding as we seek to establish a coherent framework to define the ethical uses of touch.

For example, it is commonly accepted that the status of physicians allows them to touch patients, whereas reciprocal touch from patient to doctor is often judged as disrespectful of established status protocols. Henley (1977) pointed out that touch can often cancel itself out in power plays but that touch taboos also have created a nontactile society. (A discussion of the power dynamics of touch is included in Chapter 5.)

The Taboo of Touch
Within Psychotherapy

Given the pervasiveness of the above attitudes toward touch in Western culture, it is easy to see some of the reasons why psychotherapists have developed a taboo against touch with clients. The attitudes and practices of healing professionals both grow from, and are reflective of, the larger social milieu. Most of the prevailing trends within the field of psychotherapy are toward the public denouncement of using touch, with a sizable number of clinicians tending to rate the professional environment regarding the use of touch as "unfavorable" or "very unfavorable." Within the prevailing climate, most clinicians have resolved the cultural and professional tensions surrounding the issue of touch by adopting a one-word guideline: *Don't.*

Wolberg (1954) stated, "It goes without saying that physical contact with the patient is absolutely taboo" (p. 352). Langs (1987) saw any form of touching as pathological. Gabbard was quoted (Slovut, 1992) as saying that it is the ethical duty of all psychotherapists, whether clergy, psychologists, psychiatrists, male, female, heterosexual, or homosexual, to keep their hands off their patients: "No hugging, nothing" (p. 1).

Although empirical evidence exists, and continues to grow, that some forms of touch in psychotherapy not only are not harmful when used properly but are indeed helpful, the attitudes of psychotherapists change as slowly as the attitudes of other people. This is not a new observation; Cowen, Weissberg, and Lotyczeuski were aware of the same dynamic in 1982:

The point to be stressed, however, is that changing times, cultural norms, and views about the causes of psychological problems have led to the reality of changing practices in regard to physical contact with clients. Such contacts doubtless occur far more often today than they did a generation ago. Although the fact is recognized more and more often (and perhaps implicitly legitimized in popular magazines and in speculative commentary in professional journals), there is still a noteworthy lag between de facto change in practice and scientific study of the nature and consequences of such change. (pp. 219-220)

Despite a Hostile Environment, Touch Is Used in Psychotherapy

Given Watson's (1975) definition of touch—the "intentional physical contact between two or more individuals" (p. 104)—it seems likely that psychotherapists are touching clients. Numerous confidential studies have confirmed that within the privacy of therapeutic interactions, a large number of clinicians actually do use touch.

For example, a survey of clinical social workers (Schultz, 1975) found that 65% of those who responded approved of the use of touch as an adjunct to psychotherapy. Holroyd and Brodsky (1977) found that approximately one third of the psychologists who responded to their survey reported using some form of touch with their clients. It appears that more recent attitudes among psychotherapists reflect an increased receptivity toward considering the use of touch with clients, although anecdotal reports continue to indicate that many clinicians may have difficulty in articulating how they made the decision to use touch with a particular client and may not realize the importance of explaining the use of touch to clients.

Those clinicians who do use touch tend to employ such techniques in ways that reflect the inherent biases of the larger culture. Cowen, Weissberg, and Lotyczeuski (1983) found that clinicians tend to touch child clients more than they touch adult clients. They also found that female therapists touched child clients more often than did male clinicians; doctoral-level practitioners reported using touch less than did those without this level of training; private practice clinicians reported less contact than did those working within agencies; social workers and psychologists reported more frequent use of touch than did psychiatrists.

▓ Our Position on the Use of Touch in Psychotherapy

As a result of pervasive and entrenched taboos, much confusion, contradiction, and change exist regarding the relevance of touch within the mental health professions. That many professional helpers do use touch in the treatment of clients suggests that considerably more attention needs to be devoted to education, training, supervision, and consultation by professional certification and licensing programs.

In their book on ethics within psychotherapy, Keith-Spiegel and Koocher (1985) cautioned that "no program of psychotherapy or psychotherapeutic technique should be undertaken without a firm theoretical foundation and scientific basis for anticipating client benefits" (p. 146). Throughout our book, we will attempt to provide such a basis for the use of ethical touch. Touch, like any therapeutic activity, should not be used by any therapists who view it to be practicing outside their competency without first obtaining training or supervision. At this time, however, there are no widely known and accepted standards for therapist–client physical contact within any of the professional disciplines. The only guidelines that exist focus on what *not* to do—that is, no sexual intimacies.

There has been insufficient research, as well as an absence of leadership from master psychotherapists and professional psychotherapy organizations, to provide guidance for mental health clinicians concerning the effective and ethical application of psychological healing techniques that incorporate the use of touch. Open and frank discussions are needed within all mental health disciplines to determine how best to use touch, to set standards for its use to avoid harming clients, to reduce therapists' fear of litigation, and to promote research. Bringing the issue of touch "out of the closet" is a more responsible way to promote quality and ethics within the healing professions than to continue promoting an environment of silence and censorship about this important issue.

Because touch can be helpful in the process of healing, is it not unprofessional, irresponsible, and perhaps unethical to forbid the appropriate use of touch within the process of psychotherapy? Yet few, if any, clinical training programs openly address the issue of how to use touch in an ethical and responsible way. This collective failure to incorporate discussions of touch into course curriculum is an underlying factor that contributes to professionals' entering the field of psychotherapy ill equipped to deal with touch in an appropriate and ethical way.

It is important that the mental health community deal with the unfortunate reality that our collective negligence in dealing with this issue openly within our respective professions actually lays the groundwork for attorneys to decide—through litigation—how touch will be used within the context of psychotherapy. As we have seen in other areas—for example, debates regarding the validity of memory versus false memory—legal interventions to define the parameters of psychotherapy create a cumbersome layer of bureaucratic controls and sometimes move us in directions that are dissonant from our desired clinical goals.

Henley (1973b) estimated that nonverbal behavior has four times the effect of verbal behavior on a recipient. Therefore, to be effective, touch must be used carefully and must be applied skillfully. Of course, this is true with any potentially potent technique. Certainly, psychotherapists routinely treat clients whose psychological wounds are the result of shaming, abusive language. Yet we just as routinely continue to use language in the healing process. Clinicians realize that it is not the use of language but rather the type of words and how those words were used that caused a client's injury.

So, too, it is with touch. The question is not, "Does touch hurt or heal?" We know empirically that it can do both (see Chapter 6). Rather, the question ought to be, "What forms of touch are most effective and efficient when treating what type of problems with which type of clients at what phases of the therapeutic relationship by which therapists?" Therapists must know when to avoid touch as well as how and when to make use of it. Without a doubt, some clients should never receive touch as part of their treatment, just as some therapists ought not to use touch as a treatment option.

Recommendations for the Field of Psychotherapy

Wilison and Masson (1986) pointed out several aspects of touch that ought to be studied. They identified the development of baselines based on nonclinical populations; response to touch as affected by socioeconomic level, cultural background, education level, personality, and age; the effects of touch in the therapeutic relationship through time; the identification of critical junctures that can be affected positively or negatively by the use of touch; the effects of touch on various diagnostic groups; and the origins and usefulness of therapist beliefs about touch.

To this list, we add the effect of therapist and client affectional preference on the impact of touch; the effects of verbally processing each experience of touch compared with not discussing it; the effects of various specific types of touch, such as hugging, rocking, and hand-holding; and the effects of movement during touch versus static touch (i.e., stroking or patting the client's hand versus merely resting the hand on hand of the client). Finally, because the literature on the use of touch focuses almost entirely on the dyadic therapeutic relationship, we recommend that the use of touch with couples and families and in group therapy settings be more adequately explored.

Recommendations to the Reader

To this point, you have examined the historical and current factors, both cultural and within the field of psychotherapy, that have probably also influenced your view of touch in general and within psychotherapy in particular. As you begin the next section on the clinical applications of touch in psychotherapy, we ask that you bear in mind those influences on your thinking.

We end this part of the book with the thoughts of two authors whose work preceded us by many years but was toward the same end, the acceptance of respectful touch as a method for healing suffering.

> Perhaps what is missing from the current emphasis on touching in psychotherapy is an awareness of its differential significance for individual patients at different junctures in the treatment relationship, and using this awareness to enlarge the therapist's understanding of his patient. (Fuchs, 1975, p. 175)

> We know that touching another person is a significant act. Touches can convey love, goodwill, hate, and myriad other meanings. Lovers arouse their paramours, mothers soothe their infants, and healers relieve their patients, all with a touch. . . .

As investigators, we have encroached upon many realms deemed sacrosanct. We have enquired into people's sex lives, probed their religious sentiments, peeped into their unconscious fantasies, we have even eavesdropped on the psychotherapeutic interview. But for all this, we know little about the conditions under which a person will permit another to touch him, the meanings people attach to touching and being touched, the loci of acceptable touch, and little of the consequences of body-contact. It is as if the touch-taboo most of us learned in childhood has produced a scotoma of our professional vision, making us describe man in our text-books as if he did not get closer to his fellow than a foot or so. (Jourard, 1966, p. 221)

▩ Summary

This chapter has identified historical trends that continue to influence contemporary thinking. Although literature supports the usefulness of touch in psychotherapy, the attitudes of most psychotherapists remain unchanged about their willingness to consider ethical ways to use touch in psychotherapy.

Part **II**

Clinical Application of Touch in Psychotherapy

Part II begins our exploration of the direct clinical application of touch within the context of psychotherapy. The beginning chapters in this part offer some additional theoretical material to provide a more solid and comprehensive framework to support the ethical use of touch in psychotherapy. We believe that it is helpful for clinicians to understand such theoretical material in a sound and thorough way before they venture into specific efforts to employ touch techniques.

After establishing a solid framework and specific guidelines to support the use of touch in psychotherapy, Part II moves on to elaborate the variety of ways that touch can be used by skilled and ethical clinicians. Numerous examples to illustrate the use of touch are interspersed throughout this section. The final portion of this part expands on these basic examples to provide actual clinical vignettes and case material to further elaborate the clinical application of touch within the psychotherapy setting.

Chapter 5

Power Dynamics That Effect the Use of Touch in Therapy

It may seem odd for us to begin a section designated as "Clinical Application" with a chapter that does not immediately offer a plethora of examples to demonstrate how touch is used within actual settings of psychotherapy. Some readers may react with questions about the relevance of material on power dynamics in a book that is intended to address the ethical uses of touch in psychotherapy.

We wrote this chapter, however, with much intention and thought. Its position is placed strategically within a planned conceptual theme of how to organize the material for this book. The content was written with deliberate attention regarding what information is relevant to practitioners who seek to employ touch ethically and responsibly.

Too often, clinicians embrace the newest techniques without a clear understanding of the intricacies and implications of those methods. Many professionals employ therapeutic interventions that are increasingly sophisticated. Many clinicians, however—sometimes even those who have many years of experience in the field—bypass the fundamental process of establishing for themselves an adequate frame-work for how to conduct basic, solid psychotherapy. We firmly contend that the most innovative therapeutic technique will be grossly lacking, or even perhaps counterproductive, if delivered by clinicians who do not possess a working command of the rudimentary tenets that create a context for that method. In other words, progressive therapeutic techniques will be effective only if they are used to enhance an already solid foundation of good clinical psychotherapy skills.

Therefore, we have chosen to begin our journey through this dis-cussion of the clinical application of touch in psychotherapy by first addressing the dynamics of power. Without a basic awareness of the dynamics of power, we believe that any use of touch in a therapeutic relationship is irresponsible at best and potentially dangerous at worst. Ultimately, the dynamics of power—whether understood consciously or unconsciously—constitute the underlying foundation from which any use of touch will emanate.

Considerable opposition against using touch in psychotherapy has traditionally focused on the real or perceived linkage between touch and the abuse of power. Much of this criticism is valid. Many clients have been victimized by the misuse of touch, and many psychothera-pists have abused their power through the misuse of touch. We believe that it is our professional responsibility to find ways to use touch in an ethical manner, not to avoid the use of touch. Because touch and power are so closely linked, it makes sense that the first step toward the ethical application of clinical techniques that involve touch should be to pro-mote a more careful examination of the dynamics of power. By so doing, ethical therapists will have a more solid context within which to under-stand the power that accompanies the methods we will be discussing throughout the rest of this book. From this base of knowledge, ethical therapists have the capacity to be more respectful and responsible concerning the power dynamics that will be operating—overtly or covertly—in the therapeutic relationship whenever touch is a factor.

Many psychotherapy clients have been mistreated by those with more power. For example, clients who were physically abused, sexually assaulted, or battered—whether as children or adults—are victims of the misuse of touch; clients who experience posttraumatic stress from combat service were usually exposed to overwhelming physical assault; clients who struggle with attachment difficulties and other repercussions from neglect or deprivation are dealing with the consequences of a lack of adequate physical contact; clients who seek recovery for sexual addictions or eating disorders are frequently grappling with an inability to manage their experiences surrounding physical contact, or they attempt to regulate their feelings resulting from a void of significant touch; clients who are dealing with issues of intimacy sometimes experience excruciating emotional distress in their efforts to achieve a healthy balance between the degree of contact versus noncontact in their relationships. This list of client issues, although not all-inclusive, illustrates the ways in which many clients will already be dealing with issues related to the linkage between touch and the use of power even before they begin their therapeutic relationship.

The goal for many of these clients is first and foremost to establish an environment of safety and trust. No therapy of a corrective nature can occur until clear and safe boundaries within which to hold the therapeutic relationship have been established.

Within this context, finding a process to address the dynamics of power with openness and with intentionality becomes an issue of therapeutic technique, not mere theoretical concern. Therefore, we encourage psychotherapists to consider the material in this chapter from the perspective that attending to the dynamics of power is the first step in the clinical application of using touch in psychotherapy.

▓ An Introduction to the Dynamics of Power

Western cultures are grounded in hierarchies of power, with most Westerners conceptualizing social organization as vertical models in which relationships are defined from top to bottom and in which energy flows from the more powerful to the less powerful. In contrast, members of Native American and Eastern cultures conceptualize social organization as horizontal or circular models in which relationships are defined in more consensual terms and in which energy flow has a quality of mutuality.

Within the constructs of most Western cultures, touch is closely linked with images and feelings ascribed to power. Therefore, touch both illuminates and enforces the existing power hierarchies that characterize relationships within Western cultures. For example, Henley

(1973b) conducted research on intentional touch and found that men were more likely to touch women than vice versa, that older persons were more likely to touch younger persons than vice versa, and that people of higher socioeconomic status were more likely to touch those of lower socioeconomic status.

Discussions of touch sometimes ignore this dimension of power. In its essence, however, touch is actually a supremely political interchange between and among people. The basic fabric of interpersonal transactions is prescribed and regulated by sociopolitical constructs, regulatory norms that may be communicated by the culture overtly or covertly. These constructs are fundamental to support the maintenance of prevailing power relationships as defined within the dominant cultural environment.

In and of itself, power is neither positive nor negative. In its most generic sense, power is actually a neutral force that serves to promote balance and equilibrium in the world. The subjective and qualitative dimensions of power really emerge from context and application. Power is not inherently monolithic but rather a dynamic force that exists on a continuum. Power can be autocratic or compassionate; it can be used to dominate or to empower; it can be exclusive or shared; it can assist in activating or suppressing human desires.

Equally important, touch is not inherently a tool of power or domination. Touch can be an effective tool to promote and enhance an atmosphere of mutuality and teamwork. For example, Forer (1969) noted that touching has the capacity to support mutuality and is a significant factor in the process of testing whether one can risk to become or will be allowed to become an equal. Henley (1973a) noted that touch may be likened to the nonverbal equivalent of summoning another person by his first name.

Touch increases intimacy in any relationship, and with increased intimacy, there is also increased vulnerability. Within the context of forming a therapeutic relationship, it is crucial to remember that clients are already vulnerable when they seek assistance from a therapist. Any action that increases their vulnerability must, therefore, be carefully considered.

It is our position that a power differential is inherent to the nature of a therapeutic relationship, with the therapist always holding the superior power position. Not all authors agree with this viewpoint. For example, Wright (1985) wrote, "The therapist is every bit as much in the power of the consumer, as the consumer is in the power of the therapist. In that sense, the relationship is no different from any other human interaction" (p. 117). We believe, however, that numerous dynamics cause the client–therapist relationship to be, by definition, unequal.

Most basic is the power that all therapists have because of the benefits of extensive formal education and the high social status and mystique that the larger culture has traditionally assigned to the role of healer. Healers have historically been imbued with the powers to relieve pain and suffering through the use of skills that are unfamiliar to recipients. In addition to the role itself and its accompanying physical trappings, such as style of dress and diplomas and professional licenses to adorn an office wall, those therapists who also have personal characteristics highly valued by the dominant society—Anglo, male, and heterosexual—are awarded even more power.

Although a power differential is both an inevitable and a necessary element in the therapeutic relationship, discussions of power are usually ignored by training programs that prepare psychotherapists for clinical practice and by psychotherapists who are active in the field. This collective failure to discuss the dynamics of power within the therapeutic setting seems a glaring deficit and reflects a lack of maturity by the professions of psychotherapy. Psychotherapists are simply expected to exercise ethical and appropriate use of power without ever receiving guidelines for how to do that.

This power differential between client and therapist is evident from the beginning, as illustrated by an interaction reported by a colleague who received a phone call from a client who found his name in the business section of the telephone directory. The client spent a great deal of time and energy during the initial phone inquiry both exulting the therapist's status and simultaneously mocking his credentials. For example, the client expressed, "I suppose you have a million years of education and some big title," and "You charge twice as much as I do per hour, and I bet you don't have grease under your fingernails." These statements revealed the degree to which this client was already feeling vulnerable, merely by asking for help, let alone actually meeting the therapist one on one.

Another illustration of this power difference between therapists and clients is illuminated when clients are addressed by their first names, whereas the therapists are referred to as "Doctor" or "Mr./ Mrs./Ms." Brown and Gilman (1960) pointed out that the reciprocal use of first names indicates solidarity but that nonreciprocal transactions in this same realm of interpersonal exchanges indicate a difference in status. A nontherapeutic example is the father who calls his son by his first name but who would be offended if his son addressed him by any term other than "dad" or "father" or "sir."

Henley (1973a) addressed the degree to which touch is nonreciprocal and is perceived as a sign of power in Western culture and the ways in which physical contact is used to reinforce existing norms of hierarchical power relationships. In her discussion of this topic, she invited the reader to consider interactions of specific pairs of people—for example, doctor and patient, teacher and student, police officer and accused, and executive and secretary—and to consider which member of the dyad would be more inclined to touch the other by placing a hand on the back, by putting an arm around the shoulder, by holding the wrist, and so on.

Most people are acculturated to believe that the normal and acceptable mode for interaction between these types of social pairings allows permission for the superior-status person to touch the inferior-status person but casts a tone of defiance or insubordination on the inferior-status person who is the initiator of touch within those same pairs. This norm is deeply ingrained within our culture and affects even the most intimate of relationships. Henley (1973a) offered a poignant illustration: "Did you ever see a family portrait made with the wife standing resting her hand on the husband's shoulder rather than the other way around?" (p. 425).

Alyn (1988) wrote that touch "carries great risks, especially in interactions involving male therapists and female clients" (p. 432). Her concern focused on the political nature of touch because of the "culturally prescribed power differences between men and women" (p. 433).

Certainly, gender is an issue when it comes to exploitive touch. Holroyd and Brodsky (1985) found that the prevalence for male therapists who were sexual with their clients was six times higher than for female therapists. In addition, only 35% of nonoffending male therapists surveyed identified having anger toward offending therapists or recommended that such colleagues be punished. This compares with

65% of the female respondents who indicated they felt anger and/or recommended that colleagues who are sexual with clients should be punished.

We strongly advocate that power should not be ignored or avoided. It is essential that therapists facilitate the process of making power dynamics conscious and intentional. Paying attention to the power dynamics in the formation of the therapeutic relationship and throughout any interactions that involve the use of touch can help promote a positive outcome for clients.

Within the context of any therapeutic relationship, the therapist ultimately assumes the burden of responsibility to consider and monitor whether power is used positively or negatively and whether touch is used for domination or to promote mutuality. Thomas (1994) poignantly reminds us that "reclaiming healing touch means basically that we come to grips, so to speak, with addictions to power. It means we loosen our grip and reach out from compassion, not compulsion" (p. 42).

▤ Relevant Dimensions of Power

If a decision is made to use touch as a part of therapy, three dimensions of power dynamics are particularly relevant to the paradigm of the therapist–client relationship: status/role norms, cultural/ethnic norms, and gender norms. Let's now turn our discussion to a more specific consideration of how each of these dimensions influences therapists' efforts to use touch as a tool for helping and healing clients.

Status/Role Norms

Status is closely associated with power: The person who is in a position of higher status generally has more power to prescribe the status quo, or what is normative for a particular situation. Touch is frequently employed as an instrument to demonstrate power. Physical contact is so commonly associated with closeness and intimacy that the very act of offering, imposing, or withholding touch can become a vehicle to express the degree of equality or inequality that exists within a relationship. In most instances, reciprocal touch promotes intimacy and equality, whereas nonreciprocal touch reinforces distance and dominance/submission.

Major and Heslin (1982) advocated that touch has two primary dimensions of meaning: warmth and dominance. Addressing the issue of perception of the touch and the person being touched, they noted that the person who is doing the touching generally is viewed as having enhanced status, assertiveness, and warmth, whereas the recipient of touch is considered to have less.

When used in exchanges with peers, touch reflects a quality of reciprocity or unity; when used in exchanges with those who are identified as either superior or subordinate, however, touch is employed with a quality of nonreciprocity or rank. In other words, the general norm is that a person of superior status has inherent permission to touch another person of equal or lower status, whereas permission to touch someone of higher status is usually denied or discouraged to the inferior-status person. Within most relationships, the higher-status person generally has more power and, therefore, has a greater ability to define the parameters of the relationship as nonreciprocal: "I can do this to you, but you cannot reciprocate."

Research supports the conclusion that the initiation of touch is more often evaluated by people as denoting higher status or dominance than is the receipt of touch (Major & Heslin, 1982; Summerhayes & Suchner, 1978). Goffman (1956), when studying the social ranks in hospitals, noted that "doctors touched other ranks as a means of conveying friendly support and comfort, but other ranks tended to feel that it would be presumptuous for them to reciprocate a doctor's touch let alone initiate such contact with a doctor" (p. 474).

All psychotherapists, via their role, have power greater than their clients simply because of the reality that the therapists are being sought after for assistance. Although a client may be an astute consumer of mental health services, his inability to solve his problems by himself inherently places him in a vulnerable position when he seeks assistance from a professional.

This difference in role allows the therapist more latitude than the client in defining the formation of the relationship and its fundamental rules. The client looks to the therapist for what is acceptable. Because the client is dependent on the therapist to lead the way, there is always the potential for abuse of whatever degree of power is attributed to the role of therapist.

Another way status is imposed is through age differences. Most adults consider themselves free to touch children without obtaining permission beforehand. Cowen et al. studied the touch that took place between children and those in roles to care for them. In their first study (1982), they observed the interaction between female nonprofessional child aides and "maladaptive children" who had been referred to school-based programs. The children ranged in age from kindergarten through sixth grade. The training that the aides received did not specifically address the issue of physical contact, so the touch that occurred was spontaneous. The researchers found that four types of touch took place with differing frequencies: child sitting on an adult's lap (4%), hugging (25%), hand-holding (57%), and other touching (81%). Both gender and age were variables that affected the level of touch. All types of contact occurred significantly more often with girls than with boys, and more contact, except for hugging, occurred with younger children than with older children.

In their second study, Cowen et al. (1983) examined how children were touched by female and male psychologists, social workers, and psychiatrists in various settings. They found that in comparison with the nonprofessional aides, the professionals had lower frequencies of touch. The tendencies to touch girls more than boys and younger children more than older children, however, were similar.

A higher status is inherent to the professional member of a dyad within the context of any professional–client relationship. Within the field of mental health, there also exists a hierarchy of status. Status follows wealth and education in the mental health field, in that psychiatrists are viewed as having the highest status, followed by doctoral-level clinicians. Master's-level therapists, with some distinction between the various disciplines, come in third, followed by those not allied with a particular discipline and holding undergraduate degrees. Practicing clinicians must exercise professional and personal integrity not to abuse the power that accompanies their status within the profession.

Openly acknowledging and addressing the power differential between psychotherapist and client minimizes the risk for abuses of power. Furthermore, it is important for the professional to always be cognizant of how this difference in status affects the therapeutic relationship. Because the appropriate use of touch is generally intended to promote closeness, it is important to assess the degree to which each particular client is capable of managing feelings of intimacy before engaging in any degree of physical contact with that client. Closeness must often be regulated within the context of therapy.

For example, offering touch to a client prematurely may elicit fear if that client has a history of physical abuse. The client who has been sexually exploited may be confused about the meaning of a particular gesture of physical contact if that offer of touch is perceived by the client to have been initiated in a manner that is overly friendly. The client who is struggling with feelings of homosexual panic may become extremely threatened by a well-intended overture of touch from a therapist of the same gender.

When considering the use of touch, it is critical to consider the influence of power dynamics that distinguish therapist from client. Older (1982) noted two ways to facilitate reciprocity within the context of a helping relationship: "allowing the patient to touch the healer, and responding to the patient's wishes not to be touched" (p. 240). Many clients, particularly in the early development of the therapy relationship, find it difficult to decline a suggestion that touch be used as part of the therapy.

Facilitating reciprocity includes attention to dimensions of the therapeutic relationship that may seem trivial on the surface but that are actually subtle reinforcers of power. For example, because a therapist should not assume that a client wants to make physical contact at the first meeting, it is advisable to allow the client an opportunity to initiate any handshake if it is to occur. A therapist's stance during this initial meeting may seem innocuous, but in reality it communicates a fundamental expression of power regarding client empowerment or therapist control.

Cultural/Ethnic Norms

Although virtually all cultures use touch as a medium of communication for support and nurturing, there are vast cultural differences in the way touch is interpreted, and the boundaries within which touch occurs vary considerably from culture to culture. Culture creates the basic framework that prescribes the fundamental boundaries for the appropriate and inappropriate use of touch. Cultural norms about touch are sometimes identified most easily by observing the traditions governing how members of a society present their physical bodies to the world. Much can be ascertained about the norms of touch simply by noting the traditions of how and the degree to which people cover their bodies with clothing versus exposing their skin to the world—or the ways in which people encourage or discourage others to approach them by decorating their bodies with jewelry, using paints or makeup, donning masks, and/or piercing their bodies. In many parts of the world, people stoically accept physical contact through participating in rituals that involve body mutilation. Cultural norms, sometimes enforced through laws, both define and restrict the context in which people are permitted and/or excluded from the privilege of engaging in physical contact. For example, many societies, such as the United States, subscribe to strong social taboos that severely restrict same-gender physical contact.

Although there is considerable variation in how greetings, farewells, and expressions of congratulations occur within different cultures, some form of bodily contact is most often included during the process of such engagements. For example, Americans commonly shake hands when meeting and departing. Japanese offer bows to one another as a symbolic touch of respect. Rubbing noses is a routine part of the greeting ritual between Eskimos, clearly intended as a way to express loving friendship. Greeks and Italians characteristically exchange hearty embraces.

Considerable research documents that members of certain cultural groups, such as Mediterraneans (including both Jewish and Arabic societies), Latin Americans, southern Europeans (Greeks and Turks), eastern Europeans, and some African societies, frequently and freely engage in physical contact, whereas other groups, such as Americans, Germans, and English, tend to be much more restrictive in their use of touch (Argyle, 1988; Mehrabian, 1971; Scheflen, 1973). Unfortunately, Western cultures seem to be more inclined to imbue touch with sexual intent.

Jourard (1966) documented cultural differences in the rates of interpersonal touch between pairs of people. This landmark study involved the observation of dyads in four countries as they engaged in routine conversations within the setting of a coffee shop. During an hour, the average number of touch exchanges between the members of these dyads ranged from 180 in San Juan (Puerto Rico) to 110 in Paris (France) to 2 in Gainesville, Florida (United States) to 0 in London (England).

Latin American and Mediterranean cultures tend to exhibit the highest frequency of physical contact (Argyle, 1988). Much of the touch within these cultural groups occurs between people of the same gender. It is commonplace for males to embrace or kiss at formal occasions (such as weddings, celebrations, and holidays), to hold hands in public, and to place an arm freely around the shoulder of another male. In contrast, females within these same cultural groups are rarely touched in public.

The norms for physical contact within Japanese society vary widely, depending on whether a person is in a public or a private setting (Barnlund, 1975). Japanese routinely exchange considerable physical contact within public settings such as subways, trains, and shops simply because the conditions of their society are so crowded. Cultural traditions, however, impose strong restrictions that discourage physical contact within the more private confines of Japanese homes.

The United States is generally considered to be a noncontact culture. As noted above, Jourard (1966) documented a low rate of physical contact between pairs of Americans in a coffee shop setting, compared with pairs from three other countries. Similarly, Henley (1973a, 1973b) reported low rates of touch from her observations of people in public settings in Baltimore.

Much of American culture reflects a high degree of dissonance concerning the settings in which touch is permissible. Physical displays of affection in public settings are generally discouraged. On the other hand, tactile contact (even same-gender contact) is usually quite acceptable within the context of physical encounters such as athletic events or military activities. Therefore, the physical embrace between two football players after a touchdown may often be perceived more positively by most Americans than two people on a date cuddling while waiting to eat at a restaurant. Without question, most people are probably conditioned to evaluate the latter situation more negatively if the couple on the date are of the same gender.

Within large portions of American culture, there is a propensity to either infantilize or sexualize physical contact. Gestures of touch are frequently judged to be childish, inappropriate, or motivated by sexual desires. Therefore, Americans commonly simply avoid touch to mini-mize the risk of their intentions being misinterpreted. It is difficult for these Americans to conceptualize physical contact as simply a desire to be held or to imagine touching another human body for nothing more than emotional nurturance. Patrons of prostitutes or massage parlors frequently report that being touched and held is a more significant aspect of their encounters than is whatever degree of sexual contact that occurs.

Huss (1977) noted the popularity of pets within American culture and the degree to which pets demand physical contact from their owners. It is not far-fetched to consider the hypothesis that the high prevalence of pets in the United States may reflect the degree to which many Americans feel touch deprived. Huss speculated that "touching and being touched by a pet [may be] acceptable when human touch interaction is denied" (p. 13).

Because the United States is actually a melting pot of ethnic heri-tages, considerable variations in the use of touch can be observed across the spectrum of American culture. For example, Californians seem to touch each other more casually and more often than do New Englanders (McNeely, 1987). California is an ethnically diverse state, however, and Californians whose heritage is linked to Far Eastern cultures generally engage in less touching behaviors than do citizens with other ethnic origins (Samovar, Porter, & Jain, 1981). Midwesterners, many of whom are strongly rooted in German and Scandinavian heritages, are some-what restrained in their physical contacts. In contrast, Americans who share a Latino heritage, a segment of the population more commonly found in southern regions of the United States, can more often be observed sharing bear hugs or *abrazo* greetings (Heslin & Alper, 1983).

Some social scientists have suggested that it is a misnomer to categorize American culture as nontactile. For example, Goffman (1971) observed that middle-class Americans actually exhibit considerable physical contact. Halberstadt (1985) further noted that many African Americans employ a lot of touch in the complex handshakes that characterize greetings and farewells (e.g., "high fives," "giving skin," the "dap," and the "Black Power" handshake).

Extensive research has explored the contrasts in physical contact between American and Mediterranean cultures. Because the differences in the norms governing touch within these respective cultural milieus are so dramatic, they provide an easy point of comparison to understand the degree to which the meaning of touch is culturally prescribed. Overall, people who live in America can be observed to touch each other less often than do people within most Mediterranean societies. McNeely (1987) noted that kissing is more freely indulged in within Mediterranean societies than in Western cultures. In a study that compared interactional patterns of American and Arabic male students, Watson and Graves (1966) observed that the Americans sat farther apart from one another and maintained less direct body orientation than did their Arabic counterparts. The Americans in this study never touched their compatriots, whereas Arabic participants did occasionally touch one another.

The example of India's "untouchable" class is a clear example of the degree to which a no-touch norm can become institutionalized within a particular culture. Within the context of Indian traditions, the untouchables are not completely denied touch. Rather, the untouchables are allowed to have physical contact with other members of their same class and are permitted to be touched by someone of a higher class. Anyone of untouchable status is strictly prohibited, however, from *initiating* any physical contact with persons of a higher social status.

Within the U.S. cultural heritage, master–slave relationships that were prevalent during the emerging years of the American Republic reflected many of the same dynamics that are observed in the social norms of India's untouchable class. Despite alleged advances in civil rights for African Americans since the mid-1960s, many of the unspoken protocols and fundamental biases that continue to inhibit touch between Caucasians and African Americans in modern U.S. culture reflect the same sensibility as the norms that support the Indian culture of the untouchables. The continued presence of these restrictive norms is illustrated by the reality that many people remain quick to judge as inappropriate interracial physical contact when it is observed even within the norms of present-day American society.

Social norms that regulate the use of touch are institutionalized in many other ways as well. Touch that crosses these socially prescribed boundaries is often judged to be inflammatory or provocative. For example, a same-gender couple who hold hands while walking down a street will generally elicit a radically different response from observers than will a different-gender couple exhibiting the same behavior in the same location. Adorno, Frenkel-Brunswick, Levinson, and Sanford (1950) found that individuals who are rigid and intolerant and have a narrow conception of gender roles are less likely to be comfortable with touching, particularly same-gender touching.

Within most Western cultures, racism and homophobia impose severe restrictions on both interracial and same-gender physical contact. Many young people who secretly yearn for physical contact with their peers, regardless of gender or race, find such interactions in their communities only through contact sports or gangs. Unfortunately, many athletic encounters require that participants endure bruises as a price for gaining access to touch, and the bonding that can be gained through participation in a gang frequently requires that participants be willing to jeopardize personal safety and perhaps even their lives.

The enforcement of social norms regulating the use of touch ensures a level of collective security that members of society will understand their roles and will remain compliant by living within the boundaries of their defined status. Because people tend to internalize cultural norms, the comfort level with touch that is experienced by different segments of people within a society may reflect the degree to which touch barriers have been institutionalized. Compliance with these prescribed norms seems to be a particular preoccupation for those members of society who occupy or who seek access to positions of power.

When the ethnic backgrounds of a therapist and a client are different, it is critical to explore how any form of touch might be interpreted by the client. The therapist must also strive to open channels of communication by which cultural differences and blind spots can be acknowledged and processed by both therapist and client.

Gender Norms

Considerable controversy exists within the research literature concerning the influence of gender on touch. Although a number of researchers have reported that men tend to initiate touch to women more frequently than women initiate touch to men (Henley, 1973a, 1973b; Major, 1981; Major, Schmidlin, & Williams, 1990), other researchers have reported the opposite conclusion—that women are somewhat more likely to initiate more opposite-gender touch than are men (Hall, 1984; Stier & Hall, 1984; Willis, Rinck, & Dean, 1978).

Much uncertainty and disagreement exist concerning how the dynamics of gender influence touch. We live in a culture and a time in history in which many of the prevailing norms, beliefs, and roles that define masculinity and femininity are in tremendous flux. Perhaps this accounts for some of the variation that emerges from research about gender and touch. The conclusions about any particular study may be highly influenced by time, place, and the gender beliefs of both the researcher and the participants.

Research is not a neutral endeavor. Some researchers and some research studies validate and reinforce the traditional norms about gender relationships, whereas other studies challenge and promote changes about gender within the dominant culture. Despite the variations and sometimes outright contradictions that are reflected in the research studies that are included in this section, it does seem important to survey some of the observations about gender and touch that are available within the existing literature. It may be particularly relevant to note the dates of research studies that are cited to guide the interpretation of some of the discrepancies in the conclusions.

Some of the literature suggests that males tend to react to touch more negatively than females and that males are more inclined than are females to try to avoid touch (Larsen & LeRoux, 1984; Whitehurst & Derlega, 1985). On the other hand, Silverman, Pressman, and Bartel (1973) offered observations that revealed males to be more generous in their use of touch. This study found that participants who scored higher on an inventory of self-esteem reported having an easier time with the task of communicating with another participant through the use of touch than did participants who scored lower. Their research indicated that males found it easier to employ touch than did females. This study also added to the idea that touch is a means of self-disclosure and that those who fear such disclosure will have more difficulty than those who do not.

It is dangerous, however, to globalize these conclusions about gender response across generational categories, because age appears to be a variable that influences how males and females respond to touch. For example, Hall and Veccia (1990) reported that the tendency for males to touch females decreases with age, whereas the tendency for females to touch males increases with age.

Numerous authors have written about the variety of ways in which touch is affected by cultural prescriptions for gender (Jourard, 1966; Jourard & Rubin, 1968; Montagu, 1971). Contrasts in gender differences across cultural borders suggest that variations in how gender is viewed may be more reflective of cultural norms than any distinctions that are biologically inherent to males and females. In essence, people are groomed to obey the gender norms of their cultural milieu, and by extension, these same gender biases influence how the respective genders use touch during daily life.

Issues of gender become easily fused with the dynamics of status. Physical contact may often reflect the social hierarchy of gender, in which touch is employed by males to demonstrate and reinforce their elevated status over females. Females often respond to touch by female helpers more positively than males respond to touch that is provided by females. Henley (1977) suggested that who initiates touch within opposite-gender dyads may often be more indicative of power dynamics than gender; therefore, males' tendency to be socialized for establishing or reinforcing dominance may explain why an increased tendency of males to initiate touch toward females is often observed.

Many of the different ways that males and females view touch may be a result of the divergent ways males and females are socialized. The process of gender socialization starts at a young age. Lamb (1977) studied gender differences concerning the ways that mothers and fathers interacted with their infants during the first year of life and noted that fathers and mothers tended to have physical contact for divergent reasons: Fathers usually maintained physical contact with their young children for play, whereas mothers usually held their children for caretaking (e.g., feeding, bathing, comforting, and diaper changing).

Jourard's (1966) research studies of infants documented the greater frequency with which touch was offered to female children. Jourard noted that not only did both fathers and mothers touch their daughters more often than they touched their sons but also daughters touched both parents more often than did sons. Jourard and Rubin (1968) elaborated on these findings and reported that mothers demonstrated more frequent touch with their sons than did fathers and that fathers more frequently touched their daughters than they did their sons. This same study reported that female children are touched in more areas of their body by both parents than are male children and that, reciprocally, female children touch both parents in more areas of their bodies than is the case between male children and either parent.

Noller (1978) suggested that boys are socialized to be less physically expressive than girls and that fathers are less expressive with sons than with daughters. Noller observed 3- to 5-year-old children during the process of being separated from their caretakers, such as when young children are dropped off at day care centers. This research reported fewer instances of physical affection (e.g., hugging, cuddling, holding, and kissing) between adult caregivers and male children than between girls and their caretakers.

Similar patterns of behavior have been observed outside the family environment. Jourard (1966) noted that touching most frequently occurred between opposite-gender friends, followed by same-gender friends and parents. Especially relevant to gender dynamics was the observation that males touched close female friends in more areas of their body than was reported for females who touched close male friends.

Contemporary interpretations of masculinity are so highly restrictive that most males within Western cultures tend to be emotionally expressive and intimate only with females. On the other hand, females are socialized to be less competitive with one another, to be more emotionally expressive, and to serve in more nurturing roles, thereby granting them more permission to engage in same-gender physical contact without risking such immediate negative judgments. Touch between females seems to occur at a much higher frequency, perhaps as much as twice as often, than does touch between males.

Within Western culture, the impact of socialization is especially restrictive in regard to same-gender physical contact. In general, same-gender physical contact is both confusing and controversial within American culture. Male-to-male touching is observed less frequently than is the occurrence of touching between females and males and between females and females. This seems to be the case within most family constellations and within the context of close friendships, as well as in most public social settings. Men are conditioned from a young age to suppress any desires for tactile intimacy with other men. It is rare within Western societies to observe a man holding hands with another man, exchanging a mutual hug, clasping his hand around the waist of another man, engaging in nongenital caressing, and so on. In contrast, a Mediterranean man is more likely to touch another man than is an American man.

Within the context of the contemporary Western social milieu, competition is a strongly valued attribute of masculinity, and men's relationships with one another are traditionally achievement oriented (Thompson & Pleck, 1987). We have become acculturated to negative sanctions prohibiting expressions of affection between men, especially if they involve any degree of physical contact.

Derlega, Lewis, Harrison, Winstead, and Constanza (1989) found that in greeting rituals, males displayed less tactile communication with male friends than they did with female friends. The majority of males used a handshake to greet friends, even females, whereas the females were more likely to engage in more physical contact, including hugging.

Henley (1977) used the example of the common handshake to illustrate gender differences regarding touch. She noted that the shaking of hands is a much more predominant behavior within the confines of the male subculture. Women were observed to exchange handshakes much less frequently, with handshaking between women or between women and men more likely to occur within the context of an interaction that involved men. Henley commented that "[as] a masculine ritual of recognition and affirmation, [handshaking] serves to perpetuate male clubbiness and to exclude women from the club" (p. 110).

In their surveys of male and female college students, Larsen and LeRoux (1984) found that females had a more positive attitude toward same-gender touching than did males. Using a sample of schoolteachers, Andersen and Leibowitz (1978) found that males had a higher level of same-gender touch avoidance than did females, whereas females had a higher level of opposite-gender touch avoidance than did males. Heslin and Boss (1980) observed travelers at airports to document naturally occurring reciprocal touch within male and female dyads during greetings and farewells. They reported that pairs of females were more likely than pairs of males to touch one another on the arm, back, or head or to give and receive solid hugs.

Hollender and Mercer (1976) reported no significant differences based on gender in either the wish to hold or to be held; they suggested, however, that men may have more difficulty pursuing this wish because men are socialized to become more easily aroused sexually by physical contact, and, therefore, they have a lesser capacity than do women to remain focused on the wish to be held as a goal in itself. The lack of permission for physical contact of any sort, including touch, between men is strongly related to the entrenchment of homophobic norms within Western culture. An unfortunate result of the cultural phobia against same-gender physical contact for men is that men seem to have a higher likelihood of responding negatively to being touched in general, whereas women more often tend to respond positively to touch.

An exception seems to be the willingness within some segments of gay culture to defy prescribed prohibitions against same-gender touch. Another exception can be observed within the subcultures of sporting encounters, military, fraternal orders, and gang-related activities, in which same-gender touch is routinely accepted as long as the participants stay within the prescribed boundaries of the activities that have brought them together.

At a societal level, gender-based avoidance of physical contact permeates our collective consciousness. Self-conscious attention to behave according to the rigid norms of gender prescriptions undermines our ability simply to be spontaneous in our manner of using touch. Eventually, we learn to approach physical contact with an undercurrent of fear, and as a society, we exhibit a collective anxiety even while we engage in healthy touch. Perhaps our fear of violating the norms of gender is one of the factors that has contributed to our evolution toward an age of "disembodiment." In many respects, we are increasingly becoming a touch-phobic and touch-deprived culture, at least as regards nurturing, nonsexualized touch.

Crawford (1994) reported that participants who were highly ranked on a scale of androgynous values and traits were more comfortable with same-gender touch than were participants who subscribed to more traditional norms of masculinity or femininity. Nguyen, Heslin, and Nguyen (1975) focused on the meanings associated with touch and reported that males were more dependent on the type of touch (e.g., pat, stroke, squeeze, or brush) for meaning, whereas females were more inclined to interpret the meaning of touch according to the place on the body that was touched.

In many respects, it sometimes seems that the prevailing "touch vocabulary" is limited to only sexual meanings. Most Westerners face a cultural double bind that results from living in a society that bombards them with images of provocatively sexualized touch and then imposes normative restrictions against discussing sexuality or touch openly. From fear and ignorance, they are left with images that confuse physical touch with sexual contact or with a void of understanding of and models for nonsexualized touch. As noted by Morris (1971), this confusion of physical contact with sexual contact results in a more globalized response of avoiding nonsexual contact as well.

Especially in regard to cross-gender interactions, touch has sexualized overtones within American culture. Men are commonly socialized to sexualize intimacy, especially when any physical contact is involved. Derlega et al. (1989) found that when witnessing other persons touching, men, more than women, tended to view those hugging or having an arm around the waist as sexually involved whether the two people observed were two men, two women, or a man and a woman.

A number of studies have examined differences in the degree to which male and female clinicians employ physical contact as a part of therapeutic interactions. Cowen et al. (1983) reported a greater frequency of physical contact between female clinicians and child clients than was the case for males. Pope, Tabachnick, and Keith-Spiegel (1987) reported that female therapists were more likely than their male counterparts to hug clients during therapy. Holroyd and Brodsky (1977) reported that female therapists generally employed touch more often in their transactions with clients than did male therapists.

▦ Summary

Numerous factors related to the dynamics of power must be considered prior to using touch in psychotherapy. A therapeutic relationship does not exist in a vacuum, so it is important to acknowledge the ways that touch will be processed through the context of prevailing power dynamics. Issues related to status, cultural/ethnic background, and gender will affect the outcome of efforts to employ touch ethically as a part of the therapy process. Therefore, the responsible psychotherapist will take these factors into account prior to engaging in any form of ethical touch with a client. Readers who are interested in additional information on the issues of power, boundaries, and ethical conduct are referred to Flores, 1988; Gabbard & Lester, 1995; Goldman, 1980; Gonsiorek, 1995; McDowell, 1991; Peterson, 1992; and Reeck, 1982.

Chapter 6

Functions of Touch
in Psychotherapy

■ Factors Influencing the Interpretation of Touch

Before beginning any movement toward the actual use of touch within the context of psychotherapy, it is important to attend to the subjective quality of most people's experience with touch. How the recipient of touch interprets her experience is the result of a complex set of interactions. It involves the individual's ability to gather sensory information and use it to determine the intention of the individual offering the touch, the context in which the touch is experienced, the expectation of what the touch will mean, and her prior history and experience of being touched.

Sensory Experience

Reality is validated through an individual's ability to discriminate among various and sometimes conflicting stimuli to arrive at a satisfactory interpretation. To accomplish this, a person needs to use her sensory organs and accompanying discrimination skills. When one or more senses are impaired in some manner, the individual adjusts as best she is able and may rely more heavily on other functioning senses. An obvious example is a blind person who relies on touch and hearing to compensate for the lack of sight.

The interpretation of touch will be influenced by both the ability to gather accurate information and the ability to apply accurate meaning to the information gathered. It may be that the sensing organs are working perfectly, but the information gathered is interpreted differently from what may have been intended by the sender. An example might be someone who senses a soft patting touch on the shoulder and interprets it as condescending, when it was actually intended as an expression of genuine caring. In this case, the touch sensory information was experienced correctly, but the meaning of the touch was interpreted incorrectly.

In some cases, the actual sensory experience can be different from what actually occurred. Another individual might experience the soft patting touch to the shoulder as painful. In this case, the sensory-gathering organs may have adapted by turning up the "sensitivity barometer" to alert the individual to the harmful impact of any type of touch.

For the therapist who is considering the ethical use of touch, it is important to gather information ahead of time about the client's physiological and psychological responses to touch. This can provide a framework for understanding what can happen and what may need to happen for this individual to begin to reinterpret and, in some cases, reexperience touch.

Intention of Touch

Weiss (1966, 1984) proposed that the qualitative dimensions of touch—frequency, duration, and location—convey different meanings. She suggested that the more frequent the touch, the more likely it is to convey affection and approval. In addition, the longer the duration, the greater the affection and approval intended. Weiss (1984) believed that varying the location of a touch can send the nonverbal signal "I like all of your body, not just some of it" (p. 136).

Although the best intentions of the therapist may be misinterpreted, intention is one of the variables that can be controlled and that needs to

be made clear ahead of time. Boguslawski (1979) offered nine characteristics that can assist the therapist in providing a clear intention:

1. A desire for the client to be well
2. An ability to maintain a focus on therapeutic touch as a conscious process not to be employed in a perfunctory manner
   with one's thoughts elsewhere
3. An ability to harmonize one's energy levels in relation to the
   client
4. A state of wellness without any undercurrent of fatigue
5. A feeling of compassion or love
6. An ability to keep the ego uninvolved in the process, which
   includes giving up any predetermined agenda to be fully available for the needs of the client
7. An ability to allow the equalization of energy that is allowed to
   flow between caregiver and recipient
8. A capacity to mentally visualize aspects regarding the process
   of therapeutic touch; for example, the client's being well or the
   flow of energy between caregiver and recipient
9. A sense of confidence in the potential positive outcome of
   therapeutic touch as an effective intervention and that, as caregiver, one is competent to use it

Context of Touch

The potential for eliciting emotion is present whenever there is
physical contact between people. Much of this potential for response
emerges from social conditioning and the resulting norms that define
or restrict the range of permissible touch. For example, we feel warm
and fuzzy when the telephone company invites us to "reach out and
touch somebody"; in contrast, protocol leaves us with a feeling of guilt
if we fail to apologize to a person whom we may have accidentally
touched. People who are riding on a crowded bus as they return from
a sporting event may feel a positive sense of community that is enhanced as bodies bump and collide with each other; people may un-
comfortably constrict their bodies and rigidly guard against any physi-

cal contact, however, when confronted with a crowded elevator at their workplace.

As a matter of course, most of us carefully guard our bodily contact, monitoring directly and indirectly our potential for physical interactions with others. People have vastly contrasting levels of comfort regarding the degree of intentional and accidental contact they can tolerate. For some people, the experience of physical contact is so intensely aversive that they are motivated to avoid even contact with traces of another person's body. For example, the sensation of sitting down on a public toilet seat that is still warm may instinctively prompt some people to move immediately to a different toilet that has not been so recently used.

Expectation of Touch

Unexpected touch can be startling and disturbing. In a relationship in which touch is not an expected aspect of the usual interaction, any touch may be upsetting. For example, if the mail carrier hands an individual her letters and bills and then gives her a hug, she would likely be shocked. Even if touch is a familiar aspect of an established relationship, most people experience some level of disturbance if a particular touch does not fit the expected type of physical contact for the context of a situation. For example, persons may expect to be touched by a barber or hairstylist, but if the touch takes place below the shoulder, they are likely to be surprised, if not disquieted.

Not receiving touch when in a relationship or situation in which it is socially acceptable to expect touch can be equally bothersome. For example, at a wedding, if the guests were to file past the bridal party and not hug them or shake their hands, the bride and groom would probably be quite confused.

Previous Experience

Clearly, prior experience with touch will affect how current touch is perceived. If touch has frequently been associated with violence, a person is likely to view an attempt to touch as a potential assault. If her history contains sexual abuse, then touch in the present is likely to be seen as a prelude to sexual contact. If she is familiar with touch as a source of nurturance, then she may well be an eager recipient or assertive initiator of physical contact.

▓ Possible Negative Effects of Touch

It takes little imagination to consider the many negative applications of touch. We read, listen, watch, participate in, or are the recipients of negative touch daily in our lives. Unfortunately, the abuse and exploitation of others through touch have occurred—and will continue to occur.

A number of studies have focused on the adverse effects of touch in the therapeutic setting. Sussman and Rosenfeld (1978) compared the effects of touch with or without permission and found that unanticipated touch is perceived negatively. Seagull (1968) illustrated the strong negative effect that inappropriate touch can have on a client when he described his experience with a psychotic patient who believed that she could make anyone who touched her sick. During the initial interview, she disclosed this delusion to him, and he touched her without permission as she left his office. She became catatonic for 5 days.

Fuchs (1975) wrote the following passage concerning his education on the use of touch with clients:

> I myself was educated in the traditional atmosphere of circumspection. I recall one of my earliest patients in an analytic child guidance agency, a young teenage boy. As he left my office I touched him on the shoulder. My supervisor (for whom I had great respect) pulled me aside afterwards and warned me that body contacts were dangerous, especially in a boy whose psychosexual development was tenuous and who could easily be led into homosexual channels. (p. 169)

O'Hearne (1972) also cautioned against touching at specific times.

> When the patient is likely to misinterpret the touch, e.g., when the patient is paranoid or acutely hostile; when the therapist feels strong sexual or hostile feelings toward the patient. If

touching is incongruous with his theoretical orientation and he would be uncomfortable with it, he should not touch. If the touch is impersonal and mechanical, like injecting penicillin, rather than being spontaneous, I believe it should be withheld. (p. 453)

Geib (1982) reported about female participants in a research study who experienced nonerotic touch as a part of their psychotherapy and found it detrimental. Four themes were discerned from the feedback given by these female participants: They felt "trapped in the gratification of being close" (p. 248B); they felt guilty toward the therapist, whom they perceived as nurturing; there was a reversal of roles, in that they felt responsible for the therapist's well-being; and the relationship with the therapist was a recapitulation of the client's childhood family dynamics.

Most of the negative effects of touch within the psychotherapeutic field involve sexual exploitation of clients by therapists. At least 40 authors (including Freud, 1915/1983; Masters & Johnson, 1976) have commented that sexual contact between therapist and client parallels incest dynamics. The predominance of research to date shows that the perpetrators in such boundary violations between therapist and client are predominantly male, whereas the victims are predominantly female. Unfortunately, there exists a no-talk rule about both incest and therapist–client sexual contact. Furthermore, when therapists are confronted about boundary violations of physical contact, the mental health and/or character of the person bringing the complaint usually comes under scrutiny in an effort to silence the complainant or to divert attention away from the charges. Pope (1990b) suggested that these dynamics have led the field of psychotherapy to be resistant to addressing the issues of incest and therapist–client sexual contact. In his words,

The male professional's sense of identification with the male perpetrator (intensified because both roles—health care professional and sex abuse perpetrator—involve being the more powerful member of a private dyad) may, according to this view, elicit the professional's collusion in exonerating the perpetrator's accountability for his acts and/or enabling the perpetrator to continue the abuse (e.g., through unsubstantiated claims of "rehabilitation"). (p. 229)

The potential that physical contact might lead to sexual exploitation is one of the most pervasive reasons why touch as a therapeutic technique has not been employed by many therapists. Within the professional credentialing and licensing boards, there are clear prohibitions against the sexual exploitation of clients through touch but few sources of training or information on how to use touch ethically and therapeutically—or even how to safeguard against the potential for its misuse. One of the primary motivations for writing this book has been our desire to provide psychotherapists with information that will assist them in providing safe, ethical, and effective therapeutic touch.

▪ Possible Effects of the Lack of Touch

As sparse as the literature is about the positive and negative effects of touch in the therapeutic relationship, it is not surprising that almost nothing has been written on the effects of the *lack* of touch during psychotherapy. Yet it is clear that the absence or withholding of touch can have intense meaning. The refusal to exchange touch with a close friend, family member, or partner may communicate anger or hostility more intensely than any exchange of words. The failure to offer touch within a context of freely engaging in touch with other people who are present may be a strong statement of dislike or indifference. Once a relationship has developed a level of intimacy that includes touch, to then have touch suddenly withdrawn may be experienced as an expression of rejection or abandonment.

As we previously noted in Chapter 3, the word often used to imply the opposite of health—*disease*—is derived from the Latin *dis*, meaning "not," and *ease*, from *adiacens*, meaning "adjacent" or "touching" (Ford, 1989). Therefore, *dis-ease*—or lack of health—means "separate" or "not touching."

Wilison and Masson (1986) observed that vigorous transference and countertransference issues are frequently raised when touch is used. They also pointed out that equally important transference issues may be triggered by the lack of touch from a therapist. They wrote, "Absence of any physical contact is likely to cause transference distortions (i.e. the client may view the therapist as a cold, withholding parent figure)" (p. 498).

While working in a physical health setting, Wilson (1982) noticed that an integral part of promoting a patient's physical and mental health involved providing her with an acceptance of her body and that touch was an important tool for this task. When she began to work in a mental health setting, however, she was told that all touch between staff members and clients was forbidden. She argued, "To disregard all physical contact between therapist and client may deter psychological growth" (p. 65).

One of us (Hunter) had a similar experience. Throughout his career, as his level of training and responsibility advanced, his ability to use touch was increasingly discouraged. As an orderly on a medical unit with no formal training other than a high school diploma, he was required to massage the bare backs of both female and male patients nightly with no supervision. While obtaining an undergraduate degree and functioning as an aide in an outpatient therapy unit, he was openly encouraged by his supervisors to massage the shoulders and necks of phobic clients undergoing in vivo behavioral therapy to help them relax. As a chemical dependency counselor with a bachelor's degree, he was expected to hug his clients. Once he obtained a graduate degree and became licensed as a psychologist, however, he began working in a mental health center in which he was informed that it was inappropriate to have any physical contact with clients for any reason.

▪ Possible Positive Effects of Touch

Research Supporting the Ethical Use of Touch

Much of the existing literature that examines the use of touch in psychotherapy has focused on the negative effects of touch—specifically, research that addresses the issue of sexual exploitation of clients—rather than on the positive effects of physical contact. The predominance of research on the positive effects of touch is laboratory based, anecdotal, or speculative in nature. Therefore, much of the literature supporting the use of touch in clinical settings has been theoretical or has emerged from the experiences of particular therapists. The existing literature is worth considering, however, as we explore ways that touch may be used ethically within actual clinical settings. For example, Freeman, McGhie, and Cameron (1957) discussed the holding and stroking of schizophrenic clients to facilitate their development of a sense of their physical and psychical separateness.

Although the literature is not universally consistent in supporting the view that touch enhances a client's perception of the therapist or the counseling experience, a number of studies attest to the increase in a client's positive perception of the therapist who uses touch as a means of conveying reassurance and caring. Boderman, Freed, and Kinnucan (1972) found that female participants who were touched by a female experimenter were more likely than nontouched controls to see the experimenter as likable and responsive and to express a preference for working with her on a subsequent experiment. Alagna, Whitcher, Fisher, and Wicas (1979) reported an increased positive evaluation of the counselor experience when touch was used. Hubble, Noble, and Robinson (1981) found that touch by a therapist to the shoulder or back of a client resulted in the perception by that client of the therapist as more attractive and trustworthy and as having greater expertise versus a no-touch therapist. Patterson (1973) found an increase in client self-disclosure as therapists increased their use of touch. On the other hand, Stockwell and Dye (1980) found no significant difference regarding perceived counselor effectiveness between clients who were touched and nontouched controls.

LaCrosse (1980), addressing this issue of whether touch affects a client's positive perception of the therapist, commented that "many writers have observed that positive therapeutic outcome requires, among other things, preexisting helpee perceptions of helper credibility, prestige, status, and possession of special, expert knowledge (e.g., Frank, 1973; Shapiro & Morris, 1978; Strong, 1978; Strupp, 1973, 1978)" (p. 325). Levitan and Johnson (1986) found that when physical touch was used to induce trance, it shortened the induction time and increased the depth of the trance state. Other research (Alagna et al., 1979; Patterson, 1973) has indicated that clients who were touched during the process of psychotherapy engaged in deeper self-exploration and evaluated their therapy experience more favorably. Several studies have highlighted an important element in the impact of touch between therapist and client, that is, a client's response to touch is based on a complex interaction of perceived intention, expectation, and prior experience (Knable, 1981; Levitan & Johnson, 1986; Lynch, 1978).

The problems with most of the research on the use of touch in clinical settings are that the participants are generally student confederates from college settings rather than general clients from actual clinical settings and that most research studies are conducted during the early stages of therapy when touch is least likely to occur or when such a therapeutic intervention is most vulnerable to being received as inappropriate. Milakovich (1993) and Horton, Clance, and Sterk-Elifson (1995) are two exceptions that offer data from clients in actual psychotherapy settings.

Horton et al. (1995) reported that 69% of the respondents in a sample of 231 clients who were actively participating in psychotherapy indicated that touch fostered a stronger bond, facilitated deeper trust, and contributed to greater openness with the therapist, and 47% indicated that the use of touch by the therapist enhanced their self-esteem. This study noted that clients identified touch as a contributing factor that helped them to feel valued and that this subsequently contributed to their feeling better about being in therapy. A number of clients in Horton's study cited touch as a concrete expression of their physical self by the therapist.

Milakovich (1993) interviewed 84 therapists to examine how they made decisions about whether to use touch as well as to evaluate the personal and professional characteristics of those therapists who used touch within the context of their therapeutic relationships. Milakovich reported that therapists who employed touch were less concerned about risk and tended to trust their own judgment about the appropriateness of when to use touch. She also reported that psychotherapists who used touch tended to operate from belief systems that supported the value of physical contact within a clinical setting.

O'Hearne (1972) provided several examples to illustrate when touch might be beneficial within a therapeutic relationship, such as

> times when the individual is most likely to profit from receiving a different feedback than he usually receives. Examples would include touching the patient who holds himself rigid while showing despair or rapidly increasing anxiety; when the pa-

tient's conviction about his unlovableness is at maximal intensity; as a congratulatory reward for changing characteristic games and scripts; when I believe that a more basic mode of communication than words will facilitate the patient's change. (p. 453)

Touch, however, can have the effect of assisting a client in fixating on gratifying her emotional needs within the therapeutic relationship because it is safer to do so. Who wouldn't like a consistently available source of physical comfort who didn't ask anything in return? The assumption that when a client has reached her fill of this type of embryonic bliss, she will get on with her development may not happen. Touch, just like any other therapeutic intervention, needs to propel a client forward along the developmental path. Spotnitz (1972) advised, "A taboo against touching for the therapist's gratification, the patient's gratification, or for their mutual gratification is wholly justified. A good experience that is primarily gratifying smothers the incentive for change and fixates the patient at his current level of development" (pp. 458-459).

Geib (1982) reported five conditions that appeared to be centrally related to a positive outcome when using nonerotic touch in psychotherapy: (1) The patient and therapist discussed the "touch event," the boundaries of the relationship, and the actual or potential sexual feelings; (2) the patient felt in control of initiating and sustaining contact; (3) contact was not experienced as a demand or need for the satisfaction of the therapist; (4) the overall expectations of the treatment were congruent with the patient's experience of the treatment; and (5) the emotional and physical intimacy were congruent.

Aguilera (1967) noted the following when nurses touched patients in an inpatient psychiatric setting:

Patient verbal interactions with the staff increased.

An improvement in rapport took place. Not only did the patients report a more positive attitude toward the staff, but the nurses also noted that they viewed the patients in a more positive manner.

The patients became less avoidant of the staff.

The comfort level index and acceptance of the touch by the patients were not related to the diagnosis or gender of the patient.

These changes were noted after touch had been used for approximately 8 days.

This last point deserves an additional comment because the positive impact of touch may not be immediately measurable. Therefore, it is possible that clinicians who undertake to employ touch may not fully realize the positive results of their efforts if effectiveness is measured only within the context of short-term outcome. For example, a member of a treatment center staff or a clinician who is operating within the restrictions of managed care might search for—or need—prompt results. In such cases, clinicians might experiment with the use of touch in a treatment group once or twice and, when no immediate results were observed, might conclude that it is not an effective technique.

The use of touch may not be effective within many forms of the contemporary clinical setting, in which an excessive pressure to demonstrate short-term results has emerged. The ethical use of touch implies that time be permitted to allow both therapist and client to develop sufficient clinical rapport for touch to occur as an appropriate therapeutic engagement, rather than be administered as a prescribed treatment intervention.

Positive Functions of Touch

The use of touch can enhance the therapeutic experience for a client in many ways: to provide real or symbolic contact; to provide nurturance; to facilitate access to, exploration of, and resolution of emotional experiences; to provide containment; and to restore touch as a significant and healthy dimension in relationships. These features represent the actual clinical functions of ethical touch when it is incorporated naturally into the process of a therapist–client relationship.

These functional aspects of touch are addressed here in this chapter from the perspective of their clinical role within the context of therapy. Some of this material is based on existing professional literature (McNeely, 1987; Schultz, 1992). Many of these functions will be revisited in the following chapter, in the discussion on appropriate situations for using touch in psychotherapy. In that section, these functional aspects will be addressed within the framework of the clinical purpose for using touch within a therapeutic setting.

To Provide Real or Symbolic Contact

Touch often helps in the establishment of communication between two or more people. In such cases, touch functions as a bridge. For example, touch provides a kinesthetic experience by which people can convey their psychic and/or physical presence. In this regard, touch sometimes facilitates the function of establishing, deepening, and/or maintaining an awareness of trust between people. Within the framework of Gestalt therapy, touch is often used as a technique to assist clients in overcoming distractions and in focusing their attention on being "in the moment" to make contact with the here and now of a particular experience.

To Provide Nurturance

Touch can be an effective expression of nurturance. This often revitalizes a client who has become unaware of her physical sensations. Touch can trigger profound transference responses that when properly managed, can facilitate the healing of past emotional wounds through a reparenting experience. In this context, the reassurance that can accompany touch often facilitates a corrective experience or promotes reparenting for a client. When touch is used in a clinical setting for the function of nurturance, a client may symbolically receive from the psychotherapist what was missing from the child–parent relationship in her early years of development. Sometimes, nurturing touch is so powerful that the increase in awareness and energy level experienced by a client may remain even after the actual physical contact is terminated.

To Facilitate Access to, Exploration of, and Resolution of Emotional Experiences

Touch is valuable during the process of helping clients deal with emotions. Tactile contact is frequently a viable tool in helping a client access previously subconscious or unconscious emotional material. Touch helps this goal in two ways. First, it increases a client's awareness of her body and the sensations associated with emotions. Second, a relationship that provides enough safety to experience nurturing touch usually also provides enough safety to express felt emotions.

Emotions often remain buried in a client's internal psychic worlds, hidden under the debris of shame. Sometimes, the simple act of a therapist's making physical contact—symbolically or in real terms— serves the function of communicating to the client that she is worthy and/or likeable. This alternative message may be sufficient to catapult a client through a psychological obstacle or a "stuck spot." Using touch for the previously described functions of contact and nurturance, as well as attending to the following function of containment, will then become useful components of the process of moving toward resolution of emotional material.

To Provide Containment

A psychotherapist's use of touch can provide a sense of safety so that what would otherwise be emotionally overwhelming becomes manageable for a client. In this context, touch may serve the function of diminishing a client's anxieties and isolation.

Touch for the function of containment frequently occurs when a psychotherapist provides direct assistance to a client, such as might occur by joining in some physical experience with a client, for example, if a client needs something to push against. The containment of touch is particularly important during spontaneous abreactions, planned abreactive sessions, and occurrences of age regressions. (See Steele & Colrain, 1990, for a detailed explanation of the clinical dynamics of abreactions.)

To Restore Touch as a Significant and Healthy Dimension in Relationships

By promoting an increase in a client's level of body awareness as well as reducing a client's overall emotional level of shame about herself and/or her body, touch serves a reparative function. For some clients, the goal is not simply to restore touch as a desirable aspect of life, because they may never have experienced nurturing touch in the first place. Rather, for clients who are victims of severe neglect or deprivation, the goal is sometimes as fundamental as introducing the *idea* that touch can be a positive experience. For touch to become fully satisfying, clients must ultimately explore touch at all levels of intimacy. Therefore, clients must eventually also experience touch with someone other than a psychotherapist, because no sexual touch is to be exchanged in the therapeutic relationship.

▦ Summary

Like all dynamic interventions, the use of touch in psychotherapy is a technique that must be used with caution. Similarly, the withholding of touch is also a technique and must be used just as thoughtfully. How any touch is experienced by those involved is influenced by many interacting factors. The ethical psychotherapist will be familiar with these factors and take them into conscious consideration prior to and during engaging in any touch with a client.

The Dynamics of Touch When Applied in Psychotherapy

Touch is an aspect of many types of relationships, personal and professional. Chapter 7 begins our journey into more specific applications of touch in psychotherapy.

▓ Initial Considerations

Once a psychotherapist accepts physical contact as a viable option, the issue of where to touch and where not to touch becomes a fundamental concern that requires more specific guidelines. Certainly, there are areas of the client's anatomy that are untouchable, such as the genital regions. Generically defining "permissible" locations for touch or prescribing how touch is to be applied according to rigid and predetermined formulas does not really give a therapist an operational framework within which to make realistic clinical decisions about using touch.

Sometimes, the application—not the location—of a touch might be problematic, such as the likelihood that a hand pat on a client's head may easily be perceived as a condescending and patronizing nonverbal statement, even if the intention of that physical contact was support or nurturance. In general, the most acceptable parts of the body to touch are the hand, lower and upper back, shoulder region, and middle back (Jourard & Rubin, 1968). Even those areas of the body, however, may be unsafe to touch for a client who was the recipient of abuse that was targeted on any of those body regions.

Ultimately, there are two general guidelines to consider in deciding where to touch on a client's body:

1. *Never* touch a client *anywhere* unless and until you have first identified a "map" of those physical locations that are connected to subjective meaning—such as abuse experiences and erogenous zones—for that client.

2. *Never*—under *any* circumstance—touch the breast, buttock, or genital areas of a client.

The essence of touch is really about communication. As with any form of verbal or nonverbal communication, touch is multidimensional and is influenced by a myriad of factors. The touch gesture itself has four components: the message, the sender, the receiver, and the context of the situation (Weiss, 1966). As a method for communication, touch is highly subjective, and each of these four components will influence the meaning of any particular touch gesture. Spotnitz (1972) highlighted three observations about touching that have been supported by research in neurophysiology: "(1) The same touch can have divergent meanings for different recipients; (2) the message one is attempting to convey through touch can be modified by the attitude of the recipient; and (3) repetition alters the meaning of a touch" (p. 456).

The same touch gesture used or received by different people in different situations may have various meanings. Within the context of a therapeutic relationship, however, three primary features of touch emerge as having consistency, regardless of message, sender, receiver, or context: When used appropriately for therapeutic reasons, (a) touch is employed by the sender with intentionality, (b) growing from a context of compassion, and (c) with the desired outcome of facilitating healing in the receiver.

Krieger (1979) has consistently emphasized that the *intention to heal* is a key factor in distinguishing therapeutic from other types of touch. Goodman and Teicher (1988) noted that the intent of any touch can generally be characterized as either holding or provoking and that therapeutic touch has the intent of holding. They elaborated that the purpose of the holding "is to communicate the presence of a net of safety within the therapeutic relationship, offering assurance or reassurance, restraint, [or] comfort" (p. 492).

Even within the context of healing, the concept of appropriate and permissible touch has remained highly charged and intensely controversial. In most Western cultures, "appropriate touch" is nearly an oxymoron when viewed within the context of a therapeutic relationship. Consequently, it is impossible to consider the use of touch as a tool for healing without first establishing clear boundaries for what constitutes permissible touch.

The most basic definition of permissible touch includes conduct that is grounded in solid professional judgment, that stays within a practitioner's area of competency, and that conforms to accepted standards of professional conduct. In other words, the therapist thinks about the effect of the touch prior to offering it and believes that professional colleagues would agree that it is appropriate. Thomas (1994) stated that therapists who use touch ethically do not seek to control clients, do not have their egos tied to the results of the intervention, and are mindful of their intentions and the possible consequences of their actions.

Other authors have attempted to define more clearly what constitutes appropriate touch within the psychotherapy relationship. Nguyen et al. (1975) suggested that the therapist use touch in one of four ways, which they described as a pat, a brush, a squeeze, or a stroke. Bacorn and Dixon (1984) assessed the differential impact of a counselor's touch in an initial interview on depressed and vocationally undecided clients. Within the framework of this study, they stated that a counselor's hands should come in contact only with a client's hands, arms, shoulders, legs, or upper back. They defined appropriate touch as lasting only "long enough to establish firm contact, but not so long as to create an uncomfortable feeling in the subject" (p. 491).

Sometimes, a person's experience with touch is related to qualitative features that are subjective in nature. Smith (1985) referred to three categories of touch that convey distinct qualitative tones: hard, expressive, and soft. According to this typology, hard touch tends to be dramatic in the style of delivery, often being received as uncomfortable and sometimes even painful. Examples of hard touch are pushing, hitting, and kicking. Within the therapy setting, an example of hard touch is a psychotherapist's use of deep and/or insistent touch to access and mobilize awareness in a client about some aspect of his physical body.

Expressive touch is geared more toward facilitating action or catalyzing the active expression of emotion. Examples of expressive touch are the types of physical contact that routinely accompany structured activities in Gestalt, psychodrama, and psychomotor therapies. The psychotherapist who uses touch to facilitate emotional expression should employ such physical contact only after patterns of denial and dissociation have been significantly addressed because such techniques can often trigger anxiety, disorganization, and/or dissociation for the client.

Soft touch is generally supportive in nature and tends to focus attention, provide containment, or facilitate movement. Examples of therapeutic soft touch include suggesting to a client that he notice how tightly he is holding his muscles, suggesting that a client pursue an activity because the therapist is present to support him, and encouraging a client to focus his attention on relaxing the tension he is exhibiting in a specified place in his body.

As is the case in most types of interpersonal communication, the meaning of touch generally emerges from the interplay between message, sender, receiver, and context. Heslin and Alper (1983) suggested that the meaning of touch is affected by the following factors:

What part of the body touched the other person?

What part of the body is touched?

How long does the touch last?

How much pressure is used?

Is there any type of movement after the contact has been made?

Is anyone else present?

If others are present, who are they?

What is the situation in which the touch occurs (such as a funeral or athletic event), and what is the mood created by that situation?

What is the relationship between the persons involved?

▦ Touch and the Variability of Meaning

The meaning of touch is variable and multidimensional. Although touch does not always fall into neat, descriptive groupings, for purposes of understanding it is helpful to organize touch into several distinct, but sometimes overlapping, functional categories. Drawing on the work of existing research (Edwards, 1984; Jones & Yarbrough, 1985), we propose that the various types of touch can be organized into the following categories: accidental touch, task-oriented touch, attentional touch, celebratory/affectional touch, emotional/expressive touch, aggressive touch, sensual touch, and sexual touch. These categories actually reflect a continuum of levels of physical contact, moving from unintentional touch, to businesslike and sometimes ritualized touch, to more personal touch, and finally to a highly intimate degree of touch. As you read the following sections, you may notice that a particular behavior may be cited within more than one category. This is due to the reality that behaviors involving touch can be used for different reasons and have different meanings, depending on the context in which they occur.

We encourage you to consider examples from your own life experience as you are reading about these categories. You may find that some of this information validates what you already know, that some of the examples give you a more precise label to understand touch that you have experienced or that you seek to use in psychotherapy, and that some of this information expands your awareness beyond your current level of understanding.

Accidental Touch

Accidental touch is physical contact that occurs without intention or purpose. Such physical contact is generally spontaneous in nature, such as a momentary brush against another person. Accidental touch may also include the sense of discomfort and anxiety that is often experienced following an intrusion into someone's psychic comfort zone. Such a feeling of trespassing may result from touching someone's personal space even without the involvement of direct physical contact.

Examples of accidental touch include the physical contact that occurs between people when they are confined to small or crowded spaces (such as elevators or subway trains), casual contact that occurs during a movement-oriented activity such as dancing, and the sense of discomfort that may result during a conversation when someone stands closer than is tolerable.

An example of such a touch in psychotherapy is when the psychotherapist uncrosses his leg, and his foot accidentally bumps the client's foot. Although this touch may seem meaningless in a nonpsychotherapeutic setting, the psychotherapist ought to be alert for the client's reaction and may wish to discuss it. In most cases, the psychotherapist will want to acknowledge the physical contact verbally (e.g., "oops," "sorry," or "pardon me") since not to do so may lead the client to wonder if perhaps the touch was actually intended. Clients who have been incested or otherwise groomed for sexual abuse may interpret the touch as a method for testing their reactions or the beginning of more and more intrusive forms of touch.

> *Pausing to apply this material:*   What actions, if any, would you take in the event that accidental touch took place between you and a client?

Task-Oriented Touch

Task-oriented touch is physical contact that accompanies the performance of activities that are work related, that seek to accomplish a goal, or that focus on completion of a particular function. The physical contact itself is sometimes one and the same with the task that is being completed. Although the physical contact is self-explanatory, verbalizations are frequently made to reference the touch that occurred.

In other situations, the touch is merely auxiliary to the task at hand, such as physical contact that occurs incidentally or unintentionally during the process of accomplishing a task. Although the touch is not necessarily intentional, such as hands that touch during the exchange of an object, a verbal explanation or acknowledgment that the touch occurred is often made by either or both parties involved in that transaction.

Examples of task touch include offering a hand to help someone stand up, bracing an arm around someone's shoulder to keep him from falling, and helping a person hold an object while completing a task. Gathering information may sometimes have a task focus, as when a nurse touches a client for purposes of taking his pulse.

Unintentional task-oriented touch takes place in psychotherapy, sometimes in ways that go unnoticed by psychotherapists who lack adequate awareness of touch. For example, unintentional touch frequently occurs when a client hands the psychotherapist payment for a session or when a box of tissues is offered to a client during a therapy session. Psychotherapists often overlook that even these brief, and seemingly innocuous, transactions involving physical contact may have a significant effect on a client.

Psychotherapy creates a framework for therapist and client to interact on the basis of the safety of nonsexual, nonviolent physical contact. Therefore, for some clients, the healing aspect of this type of therapeutic relationship can be promoted by including a specific treatment goal that focuses attention on the intentional aspects of touch. As noted, verbalizations usually accompany task-oriented touch in most nonpsychotherapy settings; therefore, when this type of touch takes place between psychotherapist and client, some verbal exchange ought to accompany or immediately follow it.

> *Pausing to apply this material:* Which of the task-oriented forms of touch have you experienced in psychotherapy? How did this touch affect the therapeutic relationship?

Attentional Touch

Attentional touch is primarily used to help focus attention or control behavior. Such physical contact is functional in nature and is frequently used to facilitate information gathering, to prompt a particular outcome, or to assist in moving an interaction toward a specific outcome. In some cases, touch may be used as a lubricant to move a communication in a desired direction, offered in such a way or with a certain timing to underscore a particular word or in a manner that allows a statement to stand out from the rest of a conversation. Frequently, this type of touch involves the use of the hand, such as an accompanying gesture to emphasize a point or to create a signal.

Attentional touch may be employed either to gain or to hold someone's attention. In some cases, such as when a person has escalated to an out-of-control emotional state, physical contact may help focus the recipient's attention on the need to reestablish a sense of groundedness. Attentional touch is often paired with a verbalization, such as when physical contact is made with an object while emphasizing a particular point during a discussion.

Examples of attentional touch include placing a hand on someone's arm or shoulder to gain nonverbal feedback about his level of anxiety, the gentle tap to someone's arm or shoulder to alert him that it is his turn, and reaching for someone's hand to assist him in reaching his intended destination. There are several forms of attentional touch, including touch for greeting and departure, referential touch, and courtesy touch.

Touch for Greeting and Departure

Greeting touch is used to acknowledge the beginning of an encounter. People use an incredible array of behaviors in their manner of extending a greeting, ranging from a glance, to a quick exchange of physical contact, to a complete physical embrace. A variety of factors influence the type of greeting that is used, including age, status, gender, culture, and context. For example, males frequently use handshakes when they greet other males, whereas females more often use hand-to-body contact in female-to-female greetings (Jones & Yarbrough, 1985). Sometimes, greetings include a significant degree of affectional touch, as when people exchange a hug and/or kiss when they meet.

Departure touch is used to acknowledge the end of an encounter. Most departures that include touch consist of pats, hugs, and brief touches, although, like greetings, the degree of affection is sometimes enhanced during a departure by the inclusion of a hug and/or kiss.

The use of touch in the process of greeting or departure is sometimes used within the context of psychotherapy. We normally do not begin sessions with a ritualized touch. We prefer to use verbal greetings. We acknowledge, however, that many clients desire a handshake when they meet a therapist at the initial session. For some clients, this ritual of exchanging a handshake may actually help relieve their anxiety or allow them to establish a feeling of rapport. Therefore, we agree that a handshake in situations of first meeting a client may be appropriate if the request for this type of physical contact is initiated *by the client.*

Once rapport and safety have been established, some clients can benefit from the physical contact of a brief handshake or hug at the beginning and/or end of a therapy session. We emphasize that if touch is used during greeting or departure within the psychotherapy setting, the physical contact should consist of a brief touch to the arm or shoulder, a handshake, or a *brief* hug.

It is also important that the therapist remain cognizant of the therapeutic appropriateness of such physical contact each time such an interaction occurs. In other words, exchanging a handshake or hug does not necessarily establish a precedent that such a level of physical contact will be appropriate for all future greetings and/or departures. Context must always remain the determining factor for whether such physical contact is clinically and ethically appropriate.

Referential Touch

Referential touch is used to announce a response or to reference something about the appearance of another. This type of touch is sometimes used to implicitly solicit the affectional response of another or to call attention to a body part or overall appearance. The point of reference is frequently noted via the use of touch. For example, the person who is the sender in this type of interchange might touch the body part in question or extend a brief touch to the arm or hand.

An example of referential touch in psychotherapy is a therapist who taps the arm or shoulder of a client following a structured activity during a group psychotherapy session, using the touch to indicate that it is time for that client to share his experience with the other group members. Another example of the use of this type of touch is described in Chapter 10 and is termed "the tattoo." When commenting on a client's overall appearance, it is usually better to avoid any physical contact. Touch at such a moment can easily be misinterpreted as flirting.

Courtesy Touch

Courtesy touch is an attentional touch that is generally employed in social etiquette. Such physical contact may communicate a particular social affiliation (e.g., secret handshakes that are used to gain entry to certain fraternal orders) or enhance the meaning of an interpersonal affiliation (e.g., the "bravado" hug that frequently characterizes social greetings in Mediterranean cultures).

Examples of courtesy touch include the handshake or hug that sometimes accompanies greetings and departures, physical contact that occurs during the exchange of the peace greeting within certain religious ceremonies, and the holding of hands during a closing circle at an experiential therapy encounter workshop.

> *Pausing to apply this material:* Write a list of your experiences with attentional touch within psychotherapy. How did these uses of touch affect the course of the clients' treatment?

Celebratory/Affectional Touch

Celebratory touch often occurs spontaneously and is usually an expression of joy, excitement, or pride. This type of touch tends to reflect a tone of inclusiveness and is generally reciprocal in nature. The inclusive quality of celebratory touch calls attention to the emotional connection between the recipients.

Affectional touch is an expression of friendly, helpful, or playful emotional energy. Such physical contact is usually nurturing, caring, encouraging, comforting, or reassuring in nature. Affectional touch is used to express positive regard. It is not uncommon for people to want physical contact, especially the desire to be held, simply as a way of feeling needed. Therefore, affectional touch is frequently accompanied by a light, brief touch or a hug.

Examples of celebratory touch include the handshake at the conclusion of a performance, the high five exchanged between participants in a contest, and the hug given to the winner of an athletic competition. Examples of affectional touch include the gentle squeeze added at the end of a handshake before an extended separation, the casual arm extended around the shoulder of the person who has just learned some disturbing news, and the warm hand briefly placed on someone's cheek before he ventures into some difficult encounter.

This form of touch can be a significant adjunct when used within the context of a solid psychotherapy relationship. For example, the client who has expressed being lonely or isolated in a group therapy session may find that he becomes more a part of the group when another client puts his arm around his shoulder or offers him a hug. The therapist, however, must remain attentive to the ways in which such an expression of affection is vulnerable to misinterpretation. Context, timing, and the nature of the therapeutic relationship have a lot to do with how affectional touch will be translated by a client. The psychotherapist's touch that may be intended to send the message "You are worthy of respect" may be received as "I want to be your friend or lover." Therefore, it is important for a psychotherapist to pair the touch with a verbal explanation of the intended meaning of the touch.

Pausing to apply this material: Have you made use of celebratory/ affectionate touch within the therapeutic relationship? If so, what was the effect?

Emotional/Expressive Touch

Touch frequently accompanies the expression of emotions or is used as the actual method for expressing emotions. There are several categories of emotionally expressive touch, including appreciative touch, reinforcing touch, supportive touch, protective touch, playful/affectionate touch, and touch for catharsis.

Appreciative Touch

Appreciative touch is used to express gratitude and includes hugs and brief touches, such as a pat, squeeze, or handshake. If this form of touch is to take place within the psychotherapy relationship, then the initiator ought to be the client. Although psychotherapists receive rewards from professional roles, we can think of no situation in which expressing gratitude to a client by hugging would be appropriate. Gratitude concerning the rewards of the psychotherapy profession are better expressed to colleagues than to clients.

Reinforcing Touch

Reinforcing touch is physical contact that is administered to strengthen a particular behavioral or emotional response. Reinforcing touch may be offered with fully conscious intent. It may also occur as a fully or partially unconscious behavioral response that may be an auxiliary and habitual reflex, such as the way some people impulsively lash out or strike whatever or whoever happens to be within their proximity when they are unexpectedly angered.

The use of touch as a reinforcer may provide either positive reinforcement (functioning as a reward) or negative reinforcement (functioning as a punishment). Sometimes, reinforcement touch has the dimension of compliance, as when a person seeks to direct the behavior of another.

Because the use of touch as a negative reinforcer is generally controversial, Older (1982) offered several guidelines for using touch for this purpose:

> (1) The pain or danger caused by the condition must be considerably greater than the pain caused by the touch, (2) painless methods must have been tried and exhausted before painful ones are considered, and (3) fully informed consent must be obtained from the patient or the patient's guardian before the procedure is employed. (p. 213)

Examples of reinforcing touch include the hug of congratulations that is sometimes extended to a person after the completion of a task; the spanking that may be administered as a punishment to a disobedient child; and the giving of a physical object, such as a trinket or a stuffed animal, to a person to keep with him during a separation to facilitate his desire to retain memory and awareness of a person or an interpersonal experience.

Supportive Touch

Supportive touch is used to nurture, reassure, or protect. This type of touch frequently involves the use of the hand or some physical gesture.

Support is perhaps the primary use of touch in psychotherapy. The important feature is the use of the hand as opposed to other parts of the body. If the intent is to provide support, then the use of a touch with the hand is more likely to be correctly perceived than a hug or other form of touch.

Protective Touch

Protective touch is physical contact that is generally intended to provide physical or emotional support for the person initiating the touch and/or the person who is the intended recipient. Such physical contact may be spontaneous or intentional; in either case, however, it primarily serves to promote safety.

Examples of protective touch include physically restraining someone from engaging in self-harm, intervening to grab someone at risk for an accidental physical injury, and holding a person firmly when he is in the midst of an intense emotional experience with a quality of decompensating or "falling apart." Sometimes, a simple physical contact with a client can communicate the important message "I am here," providing the client with a felt sense of being cared for and protected.

Protective touch must sometimes be employed with an air of caution because it can be perceived as an aggressive act if offered at the wrong time, in the wrong situation, or to the wrong client. The intention of the therapist who is extending the offer of protective touch is less important than the client's ability to receive this level of physical contact. For example, grasping the wrist of a client who is about to punch himself may lead to the client's punching the psychotherapist instead.

Playful/Affectionate Touch

Playful/affectionate touch is used to reduce the seriousness of a situation. This type of touch frequently includes wrestling, tickling, punching, pinching, and bumping and often involves a mutual exchange of physical contact.

This type of touch is more likely to take place *between* clients in a group, family, or couples session. It can be modeled, however, by cotherapists during a couples or group session, at a moment in which the tension has become too great. Examples include the therapist who gives his cotherapist a playful, gentle kick to the shin combined with a smile and the therapist who affectionately reaches over to touch the arm of his cotherapist while modeling a tender or nurturing interchange.

Touch for Catharsis

Cathartic touch is physical contact that facilitates the release or expression of emotions. Such physical contact frequently uses a particular motion that may generate emotional expression. Contact is sometimes targeted to a specific area of the body that has been identified as a location for constricted emotions. In either case, the intended focus is to access emotions and trigger their release.

An example of cathartic touch is engaging with a client in a structured activity that involves some form of physical contact to catalyze the expression of anger. Another example is gently reaching out to touch the arm of a friend who is stoically resisting expressing feelings after having received some devastating news.

> *Pausing to apply this material:* Look back over the various forms of emotional/expressive touch, and determine which you have made use of as a psychotherapist and what impact they had on your relationships with your clients.

Aggressive Touch

Aggressive touch is physical contact that has a quality of agitation and that sometimes, but not always, results in a harmful outcome. Such physical contact may be impulsive in nature and is usually characterized by a pushing of limits or a disregard of boundaries and containment.

Sometimes, aggressive touch may have playful overtones, such as the rough-and-tumble, rolling-around-on-the-floor physical encounters that an adult caretaker might initiate with a child. Playful aggressive touch is sometimes used to reduce the seriousness of a situation and/or to qualify the aggression.

Examples of aggressive touch include the sudden and impulsive lunging of an arm to strike out and hit someone in response to a comment, the punches and head holds that are exchanged between two people when they are engaged in either a friendly or competitive wrestling encounter, and the shoving motion that is intended to push a person toward or away from another person or an object.

Psychotherapists need to validate for their clients that aggressive physical contact may sometimes be relevant within certain life contexts. We believe that psychotherapists have a responsibility to help clients find appropriate outlets to express aggressive physical energy. The use of aggressive touch within a psychotherapy setting, however, must be evaluated with care. Such forms of physical expression by clients are appropriate only after issues of safety and containment have been clearly established. Aggressive touch for therapeutic purposes is generally most appropriate when it is planned and structured.

Some examples of acceptable ways for a client to engage in aggressive touch include the use of punching bags; structured exercises that involve pushing, pulling, or physical resistance; hitting a soft but firm object with a fist, bat, tennis racket, or battaka; and throwing breakable objects within the confines of a contained environment, such as a recycling center. If aggressive touch takes place spontaneously between clients or between a client and therapist, the aggressive theme of the act ought to be made overt by the therapist and its meaning discussed.

> *Pausing to apply this material:* Have you or any of your clients been involved in aggressive touch within a session? If so, how did it affect you and the client?

Sensual Touch

Sensual touch is physical contact that is intended to gratify the senses. Although such physical contact may have erotic overtones, it is primarily intended for a purpose other than sexual stimulation. Examples of sensual touch include exchanging a warm and tender embrace with a trusted friend, engaging in a playful bout of tickling behavior, and gently caressing the body of one's partner in a way that has previously been identified as soothing but not sexually stimulating.

Because of the dangers that sensual touch may so easily be misinterpreted as implying sexual intentions, it is advisable not to use this level of touch directly within the context of a client–therapist relationship. It is often appropriate, however, to talk with a client about sensual aspects of relationships or to facilitate a client in expanding his capacity to experience the sensual dimension of life. It may be especially valuable to instruct members of a couple to be more sensual in their manner of relating to one another.

> *Pausing to apply this material:* How capable are you at providing information for clients on how to access sensual touch outside the therapeutic relationship? How concerned are you that such a discussion would lead to erotic energy between you and clients?

Sexual Touch

Sexual touch is physical contact that has overt or implied sexual overtones. This category of physical contact generally encompasses highly erotic touch that communicates sexual intent or interest. It is sometimes employed in a manner that is sexually provocative or stimulating. This type of touch is frequently directed toward the chest, pelvic, or buttock area of the body.

Context and accompanying nonverbal behaviors often influence this type of touch. Therefore, a general touch gesture, such as softly touching someone's arm, can have a nonsexual meaning if used in a public setting, whereas the same gesture can have a strongly erotic meaning if used in a private and intimate setting. Examples of sexual touch include direct physical contact to one's own or another person's genital area, caressing an area of one's partner's body that one knows to be one of his erogenous zones, and initiating a physical contact that has been previously linked with a particular sexual outcome.

There are no examples to clarify the application of sexual touch to therapy because sexual touch is forbidden in psychotherapy. This type of touch is *never* appropriate within the context of a therapeutic relationship and should *not be used under any circumstances* (see Chapter 13).

> *Pausing to apply this material:* Have you ever worked with a client who was sexually involved with a previous therapist? If so, what was the impact of that experience on the client?

▥ Appropriate Situations for Using Touch

In many specific situations, using touch as a therapeutic tool is highly appropriate. A few of the numerous possibilities are described below.

To Reorient a Client

Physical contact can help to reestablish or strengthen contact with reality for a client who has become overwhelmed by anxiety or who is experiencing a dissociative episode. In many cases, you can give a client verbal instructions to make physical contact with himself or with some object in his immediate environment. For example, you may encourage the client to "touch the fabric on the sofa on which you are sitting" or "touch your hand to your face to feel that you have a body." In other cases, you may want to establish interpersonal contact, such as asking the client to "let yourself feel my hand on your shoulder so that you can know that I am really here in the room with you right now."

Caution needs to be exercised, however. Physical sensations that accompany touch are easily susceptible to distortions when a client is in an altered state of consciousness. Therefore, before using touch to assist in reorienting a client, it is essential to have (a) a solid working rapport with that client, (b) a general working knowledge of how the client is likely to assimilate the subjective experience of touch, and (c) a previously established feedback loop that provides a mechanism to process any concerns that might arise surrounding the physical contact.

To Emphasize a Point

Touch or physical gestures can be a practical way to highlight something during an interaction or to focus someone's attention in a particular way. For example, placing a hand over your mouth may be a clear signal to convey a sense of surprise. In another context, that same gesture might communicate a request for silence. Gently touching a client's arm as the client reports a distressing incident may supplement any verbal expression of empathy and may highlight the extent to which you really do understand the client's feeling. In another context, gently touching a client's arm may serve instead as a cue to alert him that it is his turn or that something is occurring that requires attention.

Woodall and Folger (1985) studied the impact of the use of gestures on the recall of spoken material. They found that immediately after a conversation, participants were able to recall only 5% of the utterances that were not paired with gestures but could recall 11% of the material that was paired with "rhythmic motion—i.e., pounding, pointing, or chopping movements towards or away from the body" (p. 324). When the gestures were less generic—such as describing a person eating and making hand motions similar to those normally associated with eating—the recall rate was 34%. The power of the nongeneric gestures to act as memory triggers continued at a significant level even when the participants were retested after a week had passed since the conversation.

To Access Memories or Emotions

Touch has the capacity to awaken even the most deeply hidden and infantile human desires. Physical contact generally bypasses the internal mechanisms for cognitive processing and is experienced at a more emotional, and sometimes even preverbal, level. Therefore, touch may provide a bridge that links a client directly to some experience or feeling from another time or place. In addition to using touch intentionally for this purpose, you should remain attentive for any cues that suggest that unintended linkages to memories or emotions are also being experienced by a client. All these responses—unintended as well as intended—can become valuable in the therapy relationship.

An example of using touch to access memories or emotions is illustrated by a client who becomes intensely frightened by merely witnessing physical contact between yourself and another client within a group setting. Although such contact may have been fully consensual, the observing client might be triggered to remember all the ways that touch was used as preparation for subsequent physical or sexual abuse. This experience might be rich in therapeutic material to assist the client in accessing emotions surrounding the prior abuse as well as challenging the client to consider the possibility that touch does not always result in boundary violations.

To Communicate Empathy

Touch has the capacity to communicate acceptance and understanding. For example, on hearing a tragic story reported by a client, you might place a hand on your own heart and simply respond, "I am deeply touched as I have listened to what you are sharing with me." A gentle hand on the shoulder of a child client who is working on a difficult assignment—such as completing a testing task or drawing a picture—may sometimes be a nonverbal statement that "I understand how hard you are working right now."

Within the context of psychotherapy, touch can be especially effective for the client who feels "toxic" or "unlovable" or who is overwhelmed by feelings of self-loathing. Because many people have been conditioned as children to believe they are bad, dirty, or disgusting, it is important to be cognizant of how highly charged the mere suggestion of touch might be for some clients. In such instances, the intense emotional response surrounding an offer that touch could be available to a client may be a therapeutically corrective experience that is equally significant whether or not actual physical contact ever occurs. The *intention* or availability to touch may be a more important expression of empathy than an actual act of physical contact.

To Provide Safety or to Calm a Client

When used in the right situation at the right time, touch is an amazingly powerful adjunct to help in calming a client who is feeling overwhelmed by a distressing emotion. Frequently, touch in such a circumstance provides a vehicle to bypass a client's present defenses and offers the possibility of accessing the client's preverbal transference, thereby allowing an opportunity to comfort primitive emotions that may have become stirred by the distressing stimulus.

It is important to remain sensitive to how vulnerable a client may feel when he is in a state of feeling overwhelmed with emotions. In such circumstances, it is essential to solicit consent before making any level of direct contact with that client. In general, unanticipated touch is perceived negatively by most recipients. Furthermore, for some clients, abuse or trauma may be linked to previous experiences of feeling overwhelmed, such that the familiarity of those emotions may instinctively mobilize their hypervigilance in an effort to guard themselves against their (real or perceived) vulnerability. In such an instance, touch offered by even the most kind and well-intentioned therapist without first checking for consent risks triggering the client into an even more intense state of emotional distress. Unfortunately, a client may not verbalize his state of distress or may mask or internalize his feelings of vulnerability, leading the therapist to assess incorrectly that the client is responding in a positive manner to the touch.

Hand contact is one way to assist in calming a client. In this technique, you simply cover a client's hands gently by using one or both of your hands. You may add an accompanying smile or offer a verbal statement suggesting to the client that he is now "in good hands," thereby communicating an added dimension of reassurance. Or if ground rules for gaining permission have previously been negotiated, you may offer to sit next to a client, place your arms around the client's shoulder, and/or gently hold the client. When working with couples, families, or in a group setting, a sense of security can sometimes be transferred from another member to a client by asking a member who has previously been identified as an ally to employ any of these same touch activities that were described above.

To Assist in Enhancing Ego Strength

As we discussed in Chapters 1 and 2, research clearly indicates that touch deprivation during early infancy contributes to significant impairment in normal developmental processes. Therefore, for clients who have experienced severe deprivation during early childhood, touch may address the primitive void of tactile contact. For such a client, sitting next to him with an arm around his shoulder while discussing a topic, reading a story, or processing an experience may provide an opportunity for him to feel cared for, thereby allowing him to "soak up" nurturing feelings at an experiential, rather than a cognitive, level. The availability of nurturance from the therapist may provide "corrective experiences" that assist the client in repairing developmental stuck spots, thereby facilitating ego strengthening and enhancing positive self-esteem.

Some research supports a correlation between touch and positive self-esteem. Fromme et al. (1989) reported that comfort with touch often seems to reflect a person's openness to expressing intimate behavior and seems to reflect an active interpersonal style. Silverman et al. (1973) found that those persons who were evaluated as having high self-esteem tended to use more touch to communicate with their friends than did persons who were in a low self-esteem group. The higher self-esteem group also reported having an easier time touching others than did the latter group.

Other studies (Andersen, Andersen, & Lustig, 1987; Fromme et al., 1989) have found that persons with a high level of comfort with touch also tend to have higher levels of socialization, more effective interpersonal skills, greater levels of assertiveness, and lower levels of shyness and negative affective states such as depression and loneliness, compared with persons who have a low level of comfort with touch. Further research is needed with those who have low comfort with touch to determine if positive touch experiences would lead to improved social skills and self-esteem and to an increase in comfort with touch.

It seems probable that receiving touch at critical periods of need is generally processed by clients at the most primitive emotional level. Expressions of nurturing touch are likely to be internalized at the emotional level as a sense of interpersonal contact, thereby challenging—and helping to overcome—feelings of being alone in the world. Although this may be a valuable response for clients who have experienced much abandonment or rejection, some clients with this history may be startled by the reality that they are not alone. For example, a client who is still caught in unresolved transference dynamics with a destructive parent or guardian—resulting from abuse or neglect—may initially rebuff a therapist's efforts to make physical contact, perceiving such an overture as a threat of annihilation to the self.

The same is often true for the client who has internalized a deeply held negative self-image or who perceives himself to be a profoundly bad or evil person. If such a client can eventually risk receiving touch, the resulting experiences of physical contact may aid him in the process of individuating from the neglectful or abusive world with which he has remained fused, thereby helping him achieve a new understanding that his old feelings of unworthiness are no longer justified. As this client can accept feelings of being nurtured, he will most likely gain a more positive body image, with a resulting increase in ego strength.

To Change the Level of Intimacy

Physical contact provides a simple, but direct, tool for moving to a deeper level of intimacy. For example, extending a hand to offer a handshake generally moves contact with another person from the level of stranger to the level of acquaintance. Asking another person if he would like a hug is generally experienced as moving a relationship to an even deeper level of intimacy.

As discussed previously, touch has a powerful influence on changing the level of intimacy. Therefore, before initiating any physical contact that may affect the degree of intimacy, it is important to evaluate the degree to which a client has the ability to say no as well as to gauge the level of intimacy the client can tolerate. Touch is a useful adjunct in therapy only to the extent that such physical contact keeps pace with a client's ability to tolerate such an emotional experience.

The therapist's ability to tolerate intimacy is also an important factor to consider in determining whether touch is appropriate. The client does not bear all the responsibility for determining whether touch is appropriate within the context of the therapeutic relationship. For example, holding and comforting may sometimes precipitate a client's grieving process, which can be positive in facilitating that client's resolution of grief. Such a powerful release of emotions, however, may also move the client to a much deeper level of intimacy toward the therapist, which is fine if the therapist is in a position to receive such expressions of feelings. Shepherd (1979) warned the therapist to be clear about his abilities or limits for intimacy if he is moving toward employing physical touch within the therapy setting: "If the therapist is afraid of intimacy, avoids it, or is deprived of close relationships in his or her own life, then difficulties will surely follow" (p. 11).

For many people, intimacy implies sexuality. Therefore, there is an inherent danger that moving to a deeper level of intimacy within any therapeutic setting may introduce the dynamics of sexual tension between therapist and client. In the same regard, a client or therapist may become fearful or anxious about a possible increase in the level of closeness in the therapeutic relationship and may experience this emotional dilemma as sexual tension. It is always the therapist's responsibility to keep this clinical dynamic in mind and to ensure that it is dealt with in a therapeutic manner.

Assisting a client in distinguishing between emotional and sexual intimacy, however, can be a powerful learning experience. With this focus in mind, the ethical use of touch for purposes of exploring intimacy is an important aspect of a therapeutic relationship.

Dealing with the dynamics of intimacy is frequently an issue between two members of a couple, so it is easy to illustrate the use of touch to change the level of intimacy within the context of couples therapy. Instructing a client to engage in physical contact with his partner can be an effective tool to facilitate a decrease in tension or to move through an impasse. For example, asking both members of a couple if they would be willing to share a hug at the end of a particularly rancorous session might offer a strong nonverbal reminder of how important the relationship is to both of them, softening the tension between them and interjecting a sense of hope that the difficult emotions they have shared during the preceding hour have a purpose. Within the context of group therapy, deepening levels of intimacy can be observed as members evolve from their initial stance of no physical contact when they first join group to ever-increasing comfort with handshakes or hugs as a desirable behavior during greetings and/or departures.

As an Adjunct in Hypnosis

Touch can be a valuable adjunct in using hypnosis in therapy. For example, it may be helpful to gently touch the client's arm or to gently squeeze his hand to assist during the phase of the initial induction, to deepen a hypnotic trance, or to aid in terminating a trance. In some situations, physical contact—such as holding on to a client's hand—can provide a vehicle to "ground" that client in the here and now as he remains engaged in a hypnotic trance to explore material from another time or place.

Therapy itself, in reality, is basically a hypnotic experience, whether or not any techniques of formal hypnosis are employed. In your role as therapist, you actually begin the process of therapeutic induction each time you greet a client at the beginning of a session. Frequently, this induction begins with the ritual of touch, in which a handshake or a hug has become a predictable routine by which the client has come to understand "my time has just begun." As the client progresses into the therapy session, he becomes more receptive to his emotions, and, at a particular moment when he accesses a certain feeling, you may hand him a box of tissues, thereby encouraging him to progress more deeply into his emotions. At the end of the session, you may place your hands on the arm of your chair, a physical cue that time is about to expire. The client will probably follow your physical gestures toward closure, moving out of the therapeutic trance and beginning the process of reintegrating into the world outside the therapy office.

To Assist in Working With
Past Traumatic Experience

Touch has the potential power to activate the dynamics of regression. When undertaken within the framework of a planned and controlled therapeutic structure, physical contact can be employed to assist in triggering dissociated emotional responses that are otherwise problematic to access through a verbal modality. For example, a planned intervention to touch a client at a location that was the target of childhood abuse may facilitate efforts to revisit the trauma experience and provide therapeutic interventions that can assist in moving the client toward resolution of beliefs, behaviors, and/or emotions that have otherwise remained frozen in time.

Touch can also be an important adjunct to modulate or contain emotions during an abreactive experience. For example, you may extend a calm and steady hand to a client during a moment of overwhelming anxiety and suggest that he make contact if he needs support in grounding himself so that he can continue with the abreaction. Or you may gently take a client's hand and place it lightly on his abdomen while suggesting that he focus his attention on the nurturance and contentment this touch is able to offer. In circumstances during which a client may have regressed to an emotional state of infancy, you may need to assume a more active parental or protective role concerning functions to which the client may be temporarily unable to respond. For example, you may need to use a tissue to wipe the tears from a client's eyes or to wipe his runny nose—physical symptoms that may have been precipitated by the abreactive experience. This physical contact from you may provide a powerful healing experience for the client who never had a caring adult available to respond to him with nurturance during such a moment of emotional distress.

▓ Summary

Once a psychotherapist has accepted physical contact as a viable option to employ within a clinical setting, it is important to establish an ethical framework for permissible touch. Touch is a subjective experience, with context greatly influencing the range of meanings ascribed to physical contact. For elaboration, we have examined touch within the framework of functional categories. We have presented appropriate situations for using touch in psychotherapy, in preparation for Chapter 8, in which we will explore the guidelines for using touch in psychotherapy.

Chapter

Guidelines for Using
Touch in Psychotherapy

W hen the question is asked, "Is it ethical and appropriate to use touch as an adjunct to psychotherapy?" the answer must be that it depends on who the therapist is, who the client is, the nature of the therapeutic relationship, what has just transpired before the touch is to occur, the type of touch being considered, the therapist's intended meaning for the contact, the client's interpretation of the touch, whether permission for touch has been obtained in the past, and whether permission for the proposed touch has been given. This can be stated in a simpler fashion: Perhaps it is a question not of *whether* to use touch in the therapeutic relationship but rather of *when* and *how* to use touch. As Older (1982) pointed out, "Appropriate touch becomes inappropriate when given at the wrong time, in the wrong dose, or to the wrong person" (p. 241). This chapter will address the guidelines within which the ethical use of touch can actually be undertaken for psychotherapy.

Three factors are most significant in determining whether a touch will be experienced positively: The contact is appropriate to the situation, does not impose a greater level of intimacy than the client can tolerate, and does not communicate a negative message. Holroyd and Brodsky (1980) suggested several situations in which touching a client may be appropriate: with socially/emotionally immature clients; with clients who have a history of parental deprivation; with clients who are experiencing acute grief, depression, or distress; as a general greeting at the beginning of a session; and as a sign of session termination.

Wilson (1982) suggested that except for crisis intervention, a therapist should never touch a client in the introductory phase of treatment. To touch during the time when the therapeutic alliance has yet to be established prevents necessary trust from developing and leaves the client threatened and confused. Wilson further stated that touch may be appropriate during the working-through phase of therapy, when the client is using the therapeutic relationship to modify dysfunctional patterns of relating with others, as well as during the final, or termination, stage of the therapeutic relationship. It is essential that any psychotherapist who intends to use touch first have a basic understanding of the underlying motivations in using touch as an adjunct for healing with each specific client and in each particular situation.

Consent is a prerequisite for the use of touch in any therapeutic encounter. Once permission is gained for the use of touch, consent does not necessarily generalize to other situations in which touch could be used. Each situation is unique, and permission may need to be reconfirmed or renegotiated. Informed touch does not have to be mechanical touch. As with any therapeutic technique, the therapist must find a stylistic approach that allows for touch to become integrated into the therapeutic relationship with a sense of natural flow, balance, and graceful delivery.

The client who can identify and express some degree of ambivalence, apprehension, or fear when she first faces the prospect of a touch interaction should be supported for demonstrating the skills of striving to make a fully informed and mature decision about consenting to physical contact. The client who demonstrates a quality of reflective and conscious consent in response to the touch proposal is more likely a good candidate for therapeutic touch versus the client who consents to touch too quickly or too willingly. It is important that the therapist trust her own feelings about giving touch. If it does not seem right to engage in touch with a particular client—even if she has followed all the guidelines—it may be best not to do so.

Sanderson (1995) offered the following advice to underscore that touch should be used only if a therapist has previously explored this issue through her professional training:

> In general, therapists are better prepared to handle situations competently when they have been prepared to deal with an issue before it appears in their clinical practice. Education about touch is especially important since an unexamined practice of touch can so easily lead a therapist into serious difficulty. It would not be easy for therapists to intuit what appropriate touch with clients would be. (p. 256)

Touch, as with any therapeutic activity, should not be used by any therapist who views physical contact as practicing outside her area of professional competency or without first obtaining training or supervision. The governing bodies of most mental health professions—such as the American Psychological Association and the National Association of Social Workers—usually offer general guidelines concerning issues of professional competency. In addition, touch should not be used outside the checks and balances of continuing supervision/consultation, no matter how experienced the therapist may be.

Chapter 14 offers questions to ask in evaluating whether it is appropriate to use touch within the context of psychotherapy activities with clients. If, after considering these questions, the use of touch seems like a viable option to pursue in the therapy relationship, it is then time to define more clearly those circumstances in which the use of touch has clinical application. The multitude of pros and cons concerning the ethical use of touch in psychotherapy can be synthesized into the following general guidelines about when the use of touch is appropriate.

▥ When Is It Clinically Appropriate to Use Touch in Psychotherapy?

The Client Wants to Touch or to Be Touched

Because many clients may be uninformed about touch as a viable option within the context of therapy, the therapist may need to initially raise this issue. No matter who introduces the concept into the therapy process, however, the actual use of any type of touch becomes appropriate only once the client understands the clinical implications of touch and articulates a conscious desire for such a therapeutic intervention. The therapist needs to explore the meaning of touch with each client and gain insight into how each client perceives touch—what values, biases, and experiences each client brings to the present as she considers the use of touch.

The client's expectations are a critical factor in determining the appropriateness of touch. Expectations should fall within the range of what is actually possible within the therapy relationship; expectations that are either unrealistically high or low can precipitate dissociation, distortion, or negative transference for the client. Consideration must also be given to the client's past experiences with touch to evaluate whether the expressed desire for touch is consistent with the client's reported history. Touch that falls outside a client's existing abilities for tolerance may be experienced by the client as a boundary violation or may trigger resistance, fear, or negative transference.

A client's desire or comfort level with touch may vary throughout the course of therapy. The therapist must maintain an equal level of respect even if a client moves through the differing stages of not wanting touch, to wanting touch, and perhaps again away from wanting touch. The therapist should become familiar with how a client experiences touch by requesting that she verbalize her experiences both during and after physical contact occurs. Developing a map of verbal and nonverbal cues that indicate touch preferences and/or discomforts will provide an active feedback loop to monitor the client's experience, to identify inconsistencies between verbal and nonverbal responses, and to alert the therapist to sudden—and sometimes subtle—changes in affect. The therapist must always be willing to discontinue the use of any touch when the client communicates—verbally or nonverbally—any signs of hesitancy.

The Purpose of the Touch Is Clear

It is helpful to introduce clients to the concept of touch early in the therapeutic relationship. It is often beneficial to have a set of written guidelines to clarify the overall approach to therapy, to outline the boundaries of the therapy relationship, and to elaborate the basic rights and responsibilities for both therapist and client. It is easy to incorporate a statement pertaining to touch into such a document, which can then serve as a focus to investigate more about a client's history with touch and to educate a client about the options for using touch in therapy. For example, one of us (Struve) includes the following statement in the written guidelines that all members sign on entering one of his therapy groups:

> Touching in a supportive way (e.g., hugs or sitting closer to someone) is permitted and supported but only with permission from the other member(s) involved. You always have the right to say "no" to any requests that are made during sessions. You always have the right to question or challenge the group leaders.

Within the current litigious environment, some psychotherapists have chosen to avoid using any form of touch unless the patient has signed an informed consent form. Although we do not normally use such an informed consent form, we have made one available for those clinicians who see a need for written permission from clients (see Appendix 8.1). This consent form can be used as a part of the normal intake process during which other forms are signed or can be reserved for use after a therapeutic relationship has been developed and the use of touch is being considered. Because clients cannot relinquish their rights, even if an informed consent form is a part of the client's file, a malpractice suit can still be initiated. Although the consent form does document that the therapist and the client discussed the use of touch, it could be argued that clients are unable to give thoroughly informed consent. A form such as this may actually be used against a therapist in a malpractice suit as evidence that by utilizing such a form the therapist was aware that the use of touch is a controversial technique. The best defense against an angry client is the combination of a firm therapeutic relationship, clear clinical reasoning for the use of touch, client agreement with the use of touch, and thorough processing of the experience following the touch.

The purpose for any proposed use of touch must be clear before it is safe and appropriate to proceed with actually engaging in such physical contact. Touch merely for the sake of touching has too much ambiguity to be effective therapeutically. The therapist must be able to explain the touch proposal to the client in a manner that is clear, understandable, and relevant to the overall treatment objectives. It is also valuable to give consideration to how the touch may affect the transference process.

The Touch Is Clearly Intended
for the Client's Benefit

One of the first questions to ask is this: Who is likely to benefit from this? In all cases, the answer must be the client. If the touch is being considered for the therapist's needs rather than for the client's needs, it should not be used. The therapist must not have a personal investment in whether the client agrees to the proposed touch that is offered. Touch is therapeutic only if it is offered within the context of consent and only if the physical contact remains respectful of the client's dignity. The client needs to feel comfortable in saying no and to believe that she will not be subtly persuaded to go along with the proposal and that the therapist will not be disappointed. "No" must always mean *no*.

The Client Understands Concepts of Empowerment
and Has Demonstrated an Ability to Use Those
Concepts in Therapy

It is difficult to assess the true meaning of "yes" unless a client can demonstrate that "no" is an equally viable option. Therefore, it is useful to incorporate basic education about empowerment concepts into the therapy experience to ensure that client consent concerning the use of touch is grounded in understanding, not compliance. Touch is appropriate only when a client understands that her choice about who touches her and whom she touches is a fundamental right in the real world and not merely an abstract concept in some fantasy world.

Presenting the client with a written service contract or a set of guidelines during the intake phase of therapy can provide a useful forum to explore the rights and responsibilities of both therapist and client. For example, one of us (Struve) uses a therapy services agreement with clients that includes the following statement:

My therapist is committed to promoting the principles of empowerment to help me toward my goals for healing. My therapist views healing as a process, not an event.

This type of contractual agreement can be used as a bridge to provide basic education about the concepts of empowerment and to discuss the ways those concepts have application in the therapy.

Once the client has a working framework to understand empowerment, the therapist may do a number of things to demonstrate the application of these concepts to the use of touch. The therapist may (a) solicit verbal consent from the client each time before touch is used, until trust is sufficiently established to allow that checking may also occur nonverbally; (b) encourage the client to notice and verbalize touch boundaries, preferences, and any related feelings; (c) assist the client in establishing both verbal and nonverbal signals that clearly communicate "Stop" before engaging in any form of touch; and (d) implement several trial runs during the initial stages of using touch that allow the client to be in complete control concerning the structure of a touch exercise and/or the length of time a particular touch contact will last to allow the client an opportunity to experience the therapist's respect for her stated boundaries.

A concrete way to demonstrate commitment to empowerment-based principles of psychotherapy can be illustrated by inviting the client to discuss various options for how to implement a particular touch experiment. For example, the therapist might explore with a client the pros and cons and the meanings of whether to touch the client while she remains where she is sitting, having the client move to a position that is closer to the therapist, or using a third location in the room, thereby allowing the client the ability to retreat to her original place if she wants to.

The Therapist Has a Solid Knowledge Base About the Clinical Impact of Using Touch

Touch is appropriate to introduce into the therapy relationship once the therapist is adequately familiar with current research and clinical training about the efficacy of touch as a therapeutic technique. The therapist should have a philosophical framework that gives meaning to the use of touch within the context of her style of conducting therapy. Before venturing into using touch directly with clients, more than book knowledge is needed. A solid level of competency can be achieved only through active participation in educational and training workshops that have provided experiential opportunities to explore clinical issues related to the use of touch.

The Boundaries Governing the Use of Touch Are Clearly Understood by Both Client and Therapist

It should not be assumed that the framework of a therapy relationship inherently defines the boundaries for any touch that is to occur between therapist and client. Rather, time should be taken to identify and verbalize the specific boundaries that are to govern any use of touch in therapy before engaging in any physical contact. The therapist should build on the concepts of empowerment to educate and encourage each client about her rights to define and enforce boundaries related to touch. The therapist should also be clear in communicating that no touch will occur for any client between the belt line and the knees nor for female clients anywhere on the chest.

Enough Time Remains in the Therapy Session to Process the Touch Interaction

Sufficient time should remain in the therapy session to process the effects of any touch that is used. Although the time needed to accomplish this processing will vary, a rough estimate is to allow 10 to 15 minutes. Less time may be needed to process touch interactions as the therapy relationship progresses; it is also possible, however, that deeper levels of emotions may be accessed as physical contact becomes more familiar and as the client takes greater emotional risks in the therapy. Therefore, it is always important to allow enough time following the use of touch to address any feelings that are unexpectedly triggered.

The Therapist–Client Relationship Has Developed Sufficiently

Because touching another human being can be such an intimate experience, it should not occur before a safe and trusting relationship has been established. In other words, touch must be congruent with the level of intimacy that has been established in the therapeutic relationship. Therefore, it is usually inappropriate to touch a client during the introductory phase of therapy. Before touch is introduced into the therapy experience, the therapist–client relationship must have developed to a point at which trust is solid and communication is possible about whatever feelings arise in both the discussion and execution of any physical contact. The biggest danger in using touch prematurely is that physical contact might exceed the level of emotional intimacy that the client can tolerate.

The one exception to this general prohibition against using touch during the initial phase of a therapeutic encounter involves the potential value of using touch in a situation involving crisis intervention. Within the framework of crisis intervention, a physical contact, such as gently touching a client's arm or even firmly holding a client, may be a significant way to demonstrate acceptance and to encourage the rapid formation of a therapeutic alliance. This may be an important factor in helping a client regain a sense of security or establish a sense of hope. If therapy continues beyond the immediacy of the crisis situation, however, the therapist must refrain from using physical contact for a time to allow the therapy relationship to move through a more normal developmental phase in which trust is established on a different level from the crisis milieu.

Touch Can Be Offered to All Types of Clients

Touch must be available as a viable option for all clients with whom a therapist works, regardless of gender, cultural/ethnic heritage, age, physical attributes, or sexual orientation. In other words, touch as a therapeutic technique should not be used if it has a selective quality. This does not imply that touch must be applied globally to all clients but rather addresses the issue that the appropriate use or nonuse of touch responds to therapeutic needs rather than to individual personality traits. A propensity to restrict or to apply touch on the basis of any of the above-noted demographic groupings suggests a process of selective application that may be grounded more in personal motives than clinical judgment. For example, a heterosexual male therapist who will consider using touch only with white female heterosexual clients is likely to have an agenda that can be considered more personal than therapeutic in nature.

Although there is a need to strive for inclusion in the application of touch, it is also important to develop personal and client awareness that touch does not necessarily have universal application within the context of all cultural/ethnic traditions. The possibility always exists that the therapist and a client may not share the same cultural/ethnic heritage, in which case the therapist and the client may hold different norms regarding when, where, or how the use of touch is appropriate. A therapist who is clinically savvy realizes the therapeutic significance of checking out her own and her client's assumptions before acting on them.

Consultation Is Available and Used

In general, it is judicious to become familiar with the professional rules that govern the delivery of clinical services to clients. A therapist should never operate outside the parameters of her professional affiliation or the rules of any jurisdiction that regulates her work as a therapist. For example, the therapist should know the rules pertaining to the use of touch in therapy of the state licensing board, the laws of the state or local governing body, and/or the policies of any agency with which she is affiliated. A therapist may discover, however, that there are no such rules or policies that address the issue of touch. If policies do exist and if a therapist disagrees with any of the rules of these administrative bodies, she should pursue action to change them or be sure that she is familiar with the consequences if she consciously decides to violate any of them. It is also advisable to check the malpractice policy to become familiar with any clauses that relate to coverage for suits involving the use of nonsexual touch within the practice of psychotherapy.

In addition, it is extremely important to use the supportive services of consultation if a therapist is using touch in therapy with clients. Whether attending professional consultation or participating in peer supervision, the therapist should be in regular communication with colleagues with whom it is possible to be completely honest. It is critical to create a professional space in which to be safe and vulnerable. Consultation can be invaluable in identifying blind spots that affect clinical work, uncovering unrealized or unintended hidden agendas, and supporting efforts to acknowledge and work openly with clients if and when a therapist makes mistakes. It is also wise to enter information about any use of touch into the client's chart, including that permission was obtained. (See Appendix 8.2 for a sample of appropriate documentation.)

The Therapist Is Comfortable With the Touch

Some clients are quite adamant about their desire for touch, and many therapists believe they should be available in whatever way a client wants them to be. Permission, however, needs to be mutual. The therapist's boundaries concerning touch by a client also deserve to be respected. To be effective, the use of touch must be appropriate in relation to the therapist's own level of comfort concerning touching and being touched. Competency as a therapist is facilitated by learning about and listening to personal body signals. A therapist who seeks to provide good quality clinical services to her clients should not relinquish her right to respect her own boundaries.

If a client wants a hug and the therapist does not feel comfortable giving it, the therapist has an equal right to say no. In such circumstances, however, it is then the therapist's responsibility also to talk with the client about that decision and any feelings it may engender. As with any other therapeutic tool, touch must have congruency to be effective; using touch must be a genuine expression of feelings, beliefs, and attitudes within the existing context of the therapeutic relationship with any client with whom touch is used.

As with any situation in which interpersonal relationships develop, it is not unusual for attractions and affections to develop between a client and a therapist. Although such attractions are not inherently problematic to the therapy relationship, it is important for the therapist to monitor the use of touch within the confines of established limits to ensure that if she begins to experience any sexual arousal, then she will refrain from touch contact with the client.

In addition, a client may bring to therapy an inherent propensity to sexualize all touch. The therapist is *always* responsible for ensuring that a client's seduction is never consummated in the therapy relationship. Furthermore, the therapist is also responsible for maintaining a perspective on how sexualized touch may have emerged from the context of a particular client's life history. Ultimately, it is a difficult, and sometimes tricky, responsibility for the therapist to give the client nonshaming but nonetheless clear and firm feedback to help the client learn to distinguish between sexual and nonsexual options for touch.

It is equally important to identify the boundaries that help to clarify when it is not appropriate to use touch. Older (1982) identified certain types of clients with whom it may not be advisable to use touch: "Touch a paranoid and risk losing a tooth; touch a seductress and risk losing your license. Touch a violent patient with a short fuse and risk losing everything" (p. 201).

Bacorn and Dixon (1984) stressed the importance of not using touch merely to reduce the *therapist's* discomfort caused by witnessing a client experiencing pain. They likewise pointed out that touching to lessen a client's anxiety may prevent that client from gaining awareness and insight into important issues. Of course, this criticism can also be leveled at any therapeutic intervention, physical or verbal.

As we stated earlier in this chapter, there are a multitude of pros and cons concerning the ethical use of touch in psychotherapy. Therefore, it is equally useful to identify general guidelines about when the use of touch is inappropriate.

When Is It Clinically Advisable *Not* to Use Touch in Psychotherapy?

The Focus of Therapy Involves Sexual Content Prior to Touch

It is common for clients to explore sexual matters during their therapy. Using touch within the context of such interactions has a much higher risk for eliciting transference or countertransference dynamics that sexualize the quality of any physical contact that might occur. Therefore, it is generally unwise to use touch during or following the discussion of any type of sexual content. Touch is also dangerous if either the client or the therapist has experienced any degree of sexual arousal prior to the consideration of physical contact. Furthermore, it is the therapist's responsibility to interrupt and process any touch that leads to sexual arousal. We agree with the judgment of Holroyd and Brodsky (1985) that any therapist who continues to touch a client after it becomes known that such physical contact is sexually arousing is essentially engaging in deliberate sexual abuse.

A Risk of Violence Exists

It is generally an unwise or unsafe therapeutic intervention to use touch with a client who is inclined toward violence, who is feeling overwhelmed with rage, or who has a history of poor impulse control. If a therapist uses touch in such a situation, she runs the risk of becoming an unwitting target of the client's aggression. Therapy may be an intense experience for a client, catalyzing much stress, internal conflict, and anxiety—emotions that the client may have previously learned to cope with through anger or violence. In such situations, a client may be equally at risk for inflicting violence against herself as she is for posing a threat to the therapist.

A therapist should routinely include in the intake process a solid assessment to determine each client's propensity to respond aggressively to situations in which she experiences stress or conflict. Such an assessment is most valid if questions are posed to elicit specific behavioral replies rather than subjective interpretations. For example, the therapist can more accurately evaluate a client's potential for using violence by asking that client, "Have you ever hit another person?" or "How do you express your anger when you are faced with an overwhelmingly stressful situation?" than merely asking the client, "Do you ever resort to violence?" A client's previous history with impulse control is a significant factor in determining the degree of risk for violence. As a general rule, the more difficulty a person has in self-control, the greater the possibility that touch could serve as a trigger to release some aggressive behavioral impulse.

The Touch Occurs in Secret

The prevailing taboo against using touch in therapeutic settings, combined with the cultural tendency to sexualize most forms of touch, requires that any use of physical contact be generously accompanied by verbal discussion. For many clients, an air of ambiguity already surrounds the distinction between confidentiality and secrecy, such that any overtones of "hiding" by the therapist will most likely be interpreted by the client as secretive. A general guideline is never to engage in any physical contact with a client that a therapist would in any way discontinue if she were being observed through a two-way mirror. Another general guideline is to refrain from any touch that the therapist does not feel comfortable with the client's discussing outside the therapy setting or any touch that she feels has overtones of being misinterpreted by others if it were disclosed outside the context of therapy.

The Therapist Doubts the Client's Ability to Say No

Exploitation is sometimes a subjective experience. It is generally helpful to assume that any circumstance in which a client does not feel solidly empowered with the ability to say no has the potential to be interpreted—either consciously or unconsciously—as an exploitive encounter by that client. Therefore, it is essential that concepts of empowerment be discussed in therapy before initiating any overtures of using physical touch and that the client has previously demonstrated an ability to verbalize *no* as an option within the therapy relationship. The therapist must always remember the power inherent in the therapeutic role, such that in some situations and with some clients, even a subtle request has the potential of being experienced by a client as manipulative or coercive. In such cases, the experience of the client in processing the request for touch is paramount over the therapist's intentions in offering that touch.

The Therapist Has Been Manipulated or Coerced Into the Touch

Exploitation has the potential to be a two-way street within the context of any healing relationship. Sometimes, a client brings to the therapy setting a strong bias that physical contact must be employed for the therapeutic relationship to have meaning. In other cases, a client may demonstrate such a high degree of touch deprivation that the therapist is drawn to use physical contact to "soothe" that client in ways that enable her to avoid a certain level of pain, rather than helping her move through the depths of the pain. It is generally inappropriate to use touch in a situation in which the client is merely attempting to use that physical contact to gratify infantile needs.

It is important to trust intuitive and gut-level reactions about being manipulated or coerced. Sometimes, it may be hard to identify or verbalize this dynamic when it is present in the therapeutic relationship. Touch is generally inappropriate unless the therapist can identify how such physical contact is consistent with overall treatment goals or specific clinical strategies.

The Use of Touch Is Clinically Inappropriate

A client may have certain diagnostic presentations in response to which touch may be a risky proposition. For example, it is generally unwise to engage in physical contact with a client who has a history of paranoia or sociopathic behavior or who exhibits seductive traits. It is also unwise to use touch during certain phases of a client's therapy. For example, touch may be dangerously distorted or misinterpreted in certain circumstances, such as when a client is experiencing a dissociative episode or encountering a psychotic break.

The Touch Is Used to Replace Verbal Therapy

Touch must always be used within the larger context of the therapy experience. From this perspective, touch must be an adjunct, not a replacement, for talk therapy. The therapist should avoid using touch in situations in which such physical contact facilitates a client's efforts to avoid feelings, when the client is manipulating the therapist into supporting a helpless stance for her, or when physical comfort assists a client in dissociating cognitive awareness about tensions or conflicts that underlie an emotional encounter.

The Client Does Not Want to Touch or Be Touched

Some clients may simply feel uncomfortable with touch, and some clients may go through phases in their therapy during which they are inclined to refrain from touch. A client should not have to justify a request not to be touched. This does not imply that the therapist will refrain from processing the therapeutic significance of the client's stance in not wanting to touch or be touched, but it is a prerequisite to using touch in therapy to adopt a stance of unconditional acceptance whenever a client states the preference not to touch or be touched.

The Therapist Is Not Comfortable Using Touch

Not all therapists feel comfortable using touch, and touch may be inappropriate for certain therapists at certain times. Touch is not a natural personality match for all therapists. In general, those clinicians for whom the use of touch in therapy is an appropriate match are probably those individuals who are comfortable with their own bodies, their own sexuality, with touching, and with being touched.

It is also possible for therapists to cycle through periods in which physical contact may not be congruent with their own emotional disposition. For example, a therapist who is a survivor of physical or sexual abuse may need to restrict her use of touch when she is feeling particularly vulnerable or fragile because of issues that are occurring in her personal therapy. Or a therapist may need to refrain from touch if she is aware of feeling hostile or sexual toward a client. In general, it is not helpful for a therapist to pretend to be comfortable with touch; using touch in such circumstances will usually be perceived by the client as insincere. Such a false expression may risk the consequence of replicating an earlier traumatic experience, invalidating a client's perception of reality, or increasing—rather than lowering—a client's anxiety.

Countertransference is an important dynamic for a therapist to monitor in helping to maintain a perspective on the comfort level for using touch. Sanderson (1995) offered the clinical insight that countertransference is occurring when the therapist is "minimizing, rationalizing, or glorifying the use of touch with clients" (p. 71). Sanderson further stated that "being terrified to touch clients can also be countertransference" (p. 142).

Finally, although it is important to acknowledge that using touch may complicate the transferential dynamics within a therapeutic relationship, it is equally relevant to highlight that *not* using touch in therapy may sometimes complicate the transference relationship. The therapist who chooses not to employ touch when such an intervention has the potential to facilitate therapeutic progress is just as accountable to claims of exercising poor clinical judgment as is the therapist whose touch interferes with therapeutic goals. Older (1982) underscored this point by commenting that "touching is not a technique; not-touching is a technique" (p. 203).

▓ Summary

This chapter has provided guidelines to assist in the process of evaluating the appropriateness of using touch with clients within the clinical setting. We have stressed the need for personal and professional discretion in determining the use of any form of touch with clients.

Appendix 8.1
Model Informed Consent Form

Although we do not normally use such a signed informed consent form as a part of our client files, some psychotherapists have expressed a desire for such a form. Therefore, we have developed the following model of such a consent form for those clinicians who may see a need for written permission. As with other clinical information that is included in this book, we want to express our concerns that methods and techniques not be used just because they are available. Rather, the stage of therapy, the nature of the therapist–client relationship, the dynamics of each particular client, the style of the therapist, and the context for using this information must be carefully evaluated before determining whether it is appropriate to apply this material within an actual clinical setting.

This form can be used as a part of the normal intake process during which other forms are signed. It can also be used after a therapeutic relationship has been established and the use of touch is being considered. Therapists are advised to consult with a lawyer about the laws that govern their particular jurisdiction before using this form if they are seeking informed consent as a preventive step to avoid future litigation.

Informed Consent for the Use of Touch in Psychotherapy

Physical contact between human beings can have significant effects on those involved. Research has indicated that in certain situations, and under specific circumstances, touch can be a useful adjunct to psychotherapy (which is primarily focused on verbal interactions between the client and the therapist). One study found that one third of the psychotherapists surveyed reported using some form of touch with their clients.

Before you consider including touch as a part of your psychotherapy, you ought to be aware of some of the possible effects. There are several possible positive effects of touch between the psychotherapist and the client: It can lead to a reduction of anxiety, increase the level of trust, increase the client's awareness of emotions and physical sensation, and improve the client's ability to discuss difficult topics.

It is also possible that the use of touch can lead to an increase in anxiety, a reduction of the trust level, a triggering of unpleasant memories or emotions, or a fear of the touch becoming sexual.

It is unethical and illegal for psychotherapists to have sexual contact with their clients, in the office and elsewhere. Sexual contact is defined as touching or kissing of the genital area, groin, inner thigh, buttock, or breast or of the clothing covering any of these body parts. Requests for this type of activity are also considered inappropriate.

If you decide to include the ethical use of touch as a part of your psychotherapy, you are free at any time, for any reason, to withdraw this permission, without fear of punishment.

Even if you grant permission for the use of ethical touch, the psychotherapist retains the right to not use touch if it appears not to fit with the treatment goals, does not facilitate your psychological growth, or is otherwise not in your best interest.

I/We, the understated, have read and understand the material above and hereby grant permission for the following type(s) of touch to be offered if the psychotherapist deems appropriate (check all that apply):

_____ Handshake

_____ Hand on shoulder

_____ Hand-holding

_____ Hugs

_____ Holding

_____ Other (Describe) _____

_____

Client's signature _____ Date____/____/____

Client's name printed _____

Client's signature _____ Date____/____/____

Client's name printed _____

This form may be copied without obtaining permission from the authors or the publisher. It is provided only as an example and can be modified to better fit the population with which the clinician is working. *It is not intended as legal advice.* Clinicians and/or administrators should consult with an attorney to ensure that this form meets the requirement under which the clinician is practicing.

Appendix 8.2

Documentation of Touch in Client Records

Because the use of any touch is currently a controversial subject, we are often asked how we document in client files when touch is used. We suggest that session notes contain at least the following information:

What type of touch was offered

The client's reaction to the offer

Whether touch took place

How the client reacted to the touch

The clinician may also wish to note the reason for choosing to use touch as a treatment technique (e.g., what treatment goal was being addressed).

Although it seems important to acknowledge the use of touch in the file, it seems equally wise to avoid overdocumenting the event in a defensive manner. In other words, treat the use of touch in a similar fashion to that of any other treatment technique.

Here are some examples of session notes.

Client was able to cry about the ending of his marriage. He declined the offer of the therapist offering physical comforting in the form of a hand on his shoulder, stating he "was not really comfortable with that touchy-feely stuff."

Client was able to make progress on her ability to be more empathic to others by holding the hand of another group member who was upset by learning that she was not accepted into graduate school.

Client followed through on agreement to read a letter to the man who sexually abused him. He began to weep and requested that I sit beside him and hold his hand while he read the letter. He reported that the touch made it easier for him to continue the difficult task of reading the letter aloud.

The client completed the abreaction planned last week. I offered to hug him following our processing the abreaction. He accepted the hug and reported he found it comforting.

In an individual session, the client requested that I hold her, as she had seen me do with another client during group therapy. I told her I was not willing to do this since we had spent the first half of the session discussing her recent romantic fantasy, which included me.

Client attended intake session. As she left the session, she requested a hug. I informed her that I was unwilling to fulfill her request since we had met only an hour ago. She seemed disappointed but agreed to discuss it next week.

Client worked on his fear of touch by having me sit beside him with my hand on his shoulder for two minutes. He reported that he feared that eventually I would try to have sex with him "just like all the men in my childhood." I reminded him of our contract that no sexual contact would take place and that I would be responsible to maintain that boundary. I reminded him that he was free to modify his treatment plan if he thought the goal was inappropriate or if we were moving at too rapid a rate. He said that he thought that "no matter what pace we do this touch stuff, it will be scary" and that he wants to continue according to plan. We will discuss in the next session how the use of touch today affected him in the hours following the session.

Chapter 9

A Continuum of Touch

Webster's *New Universal Unabridged Dictionary* (McKechnie, 1983) has 59 definitions listed under *touch*. The definitions that likely come to mind for most people are "to put the hand, finger, or other part of the body on, so as to feel; to perceive by the sense of feeling" and "to bring [something] into contact with [something else]" (p. 1928). In considering the use of touch in a clinical setting, however, it is best to think of the term *touch* as a broader concept than merely skin-to-skin contact. *Webster's* also lists the following definitions: "to arouse an emotion in, especially one of sympathy, gratitude, etc." and "an impression received as if by touching; a mental response; a slight emotion" (p. 1929).

Within the framework of psychotherapy, touch can be conceptualized as existing on a continuum that begins with the language of touch metaphors and continues until actual physical contact is experienced, with much room for variation in between these points. A therapist has a range of touch techniques available for responding to clients. The intensity of a client's response to touch at any point along the contin-

159

uum is idiosyncratic. What in one client may produce little or no response can, in another client, be experienced as overwhelming.

A therapist ought not to value the ability to touch a client physically as more valuable than the ability to touch a client metaphorically. In other words, the goal is to assist a client therapeutically, not to see how much physical contact can be tolerated.

The continuum we will provide begins with language and behaviors that subconsciously act as a form of touch. We then describe techniques that involve actual physical contact between the psychotherapist and the client, including placing a hand on the client, holding the client's hand, hugging, and, finally, holding the client.

▓ Language as Touch

> I remember how, when I was seven, we passed a plot of opened morning glories. She pointed at them. "That's the way you'll feel inside the first time a boy you love touches you."
>
> Later we passed the same flowers closed into tight little twists. "And that," she said, "is how you'll feel inside the first time a boy you don't love touches you." (Kadohata, 1989, p. 38)

The importance of touch is reflected in the very language we use to communicate with one another. Montagu (1971) noted that the *Oxford English Dictionary* included 14 columns under the entry for *touch*.

Katz (1989) pointed out that the Latin verbs *percipere* (perceive) and *comprehendere* (understand) refer to understanding through use of the hand. He also noted how there are numerous current "linguistic expressions derived from the tactile-motor sphere, particularly the activity of the touching hand. When we wish to indicate that we have mastered some facts of a practical or theoretical nature, we say that we have grasped them" (pp. 238-239). The word *tact*, which has come to mean "a sensitive skill in dealing with people," is derived from the Latin *tactus*, or "touch" and the French *tangere*, "to delicately touch" (McKechnie, 1983, p. 1856).

A vast array of the words that pervade our daily language directly or indirectly reflect meanings related to touch (Peloquin, 1989; Thayer, 1982). For example, the metaphor of being touched (as in the expression

"Your predicament touches me") conveys a meaning of significant connectedness. We reach out to others or lend a hand. We inquire, "How did that grab you?" We try to get a grip. People who get along with others have the human touch. A person who is hypersensitive is touchy. Delicate situations must be handled carefully, even to the point of requiring kid gloves. We try to put the finishing touch on a situation. We sometimes step back and adopt a hands-off policy. When loved ones travel, we encourage them to keep in touch.

The preceding discussion highlights how extensively language is influenced by concerns about touch. Within the context of these numerous expressions that make reference to touch, many possibilities are available to "connect" with another person through the use and expansion of touch metaphors. For example, a client who is upset and complaining but "can't get a handle on what is bothering him" has provided the therapist with an opportunity to use a touch metaphor:

Therapist: If you could get a hold on what is bothering you, what might you grab onto?

Client: I would grab onto a raft. I feel like I'm adrift in a storm, and there is nothing to cling to.

Therapist: So help seems out of reach?

Client: Yes.

Therapist: Who could you reach out to?

Client: I don't know if anyone is there, and even if there were, they would just push me away.

In seconds, through the use of metaphor, what was unclear has taken form: The client has a sense of helplessness or isolation. These issues then become the focus of the therapy session.

Let us now look at a similar example, but in more detail. Here, the therapist uses a touch metaphor to facilitate a client's efforts to explore his experience:

Client: Something is bothering me, but I'm really out of touch with whatever it is.

Therapist: So you can't put your finger on it.

Client: No, I'm stumbling around in the dark, just bumping into things.

Therapist: You are reaching out, groping, but finding nothing.

Client: I feel really lost.

Therapist: Would you like someone to take you by the hand and point you in the right direction?

Client: Yeah, but nobody is there.

Therapist: If you were to hold your hand out, who would you like to take it and help you find your way?

Talking about touch as an imaginary event helps the client experience the possibility of touch without actually touching physically. This can be further enhanced by the therapist's prefacing a statement with the suggestion "Can you now imagine . . ," which becomes clear as this example continues:

Client: I always wanted my father to give me some direction.

Therapist: Can you now imagine what it would be like if you held out your hand to find that your father was there to take it and lead you forward?

Client: [*Beginning to cry*] He never did touch me when he was alive.

Therapist: Imagine now [*Increasing the suggestion*] that he is actually holding your hand this moment.

Client: [*Crying increases*] All I can imagine is him pushing me away.

Therapist: [*At this point, the therapist must decide if it would be more therapeutic to have the client attempt to imagine a different relationship with his father or to introduce the possibility of another person who could provide what he needs.*] On the other hand, who else might you reach out to?

Client: I can imagine you being there.

Therapist: And what am I doing?

Client: You are holding my hand.

Therapist: And then what happens?

Client: I don't feel so lost and alone anymore.

This client was able to respond to and maintain the metaphorical language that led him to his previously blocked emotions so he was no longer "out of touch" as his original statement suggested.

The use of touch as metaphor and touch in imagination does not require the same guidelines and permission that using physical touch does. This is because talk is tacitly agreed to when a client enters psychotherapy, whereas touch as a therapeutic tool is usually not a recognized and agreed-on treatment modality. In contrast, in many other types of professional–client relationships, the use of touch is taken as part of the treatment. For example, a person does not go to the dentist without expecting that the dentist will examine his mouth with his hands. What makes the examination safe is the rigorous adherence to a specific protocol. The client knows what to expect. It is unlikely that a dentist would ask permission to put his hand in a patient's mouth. Permission is simply taken for granted. In psychotherapy, however—in which touch is not part of the normal protocol—it is extremely important to gain permission prior to using touch.

Self-Touch

Most of us tend to live in the world as if our bodies were surrounded by invisible fences that help regulate the distances between ourselves and others, to achieve a sense of safety and comfort. Visible displays of self-touching behaviors can sometimes reveal a person's readiness or availability for an increased level of personal involvement. For example, personal behaviors such as fiddling with one's hair, adjusting one's clothing, or stroking one's body may be external cues intended— directly or indirectly—to communicate that a person is concerned with his personal appearance and attractiveness. This may be a person's way of expressing a desire for an increased level of personal interaction with the recipient of those cues. Allowing access to one's personal body with touch is generally viewed as a final stage in dissolving the distance between people.

Not all touch that occurs in therapy is between a therapist and a client. People who are experiencing strong emotions frequently touch themselves, for example, the laugh that is expressed with a slap of the knee, the grief-stricken wringing of the hands, and holding oneself when in fear. Numerous cultures make use of stones or beads (e.g., worry stones and rosaries) that are fingered to reduce anxiety or to otherwise comfort the owner (Montagu, 1971). An attentive therapist can frequently use these self-touching responses as cues regarding internal feelings a client may be experiencing. A therapist can heighten a client's self-awareness of this behavior merely by making an observation of it, for example, "Your hand is over your mouth." Interpreting the behavior or asking a client to do so distances the client from the actual experience and places him in the cognitive realm. By calling attention to the self-touch, without interpreting it, a client focuses awareness on his body; this in itself increases the likelihood of more emotional content.

Goldberg and Rosenthal's (1986) research, although on job applicants, may still provide psychotherapists useful information when observing self-touching behaviors in clients. They found that participants touched their hair, face, and arm more in an informal setting—a chat—than they did in what was designed to be a more formal and stressful situation—an interview. Therefore, when a psychotherapist begins to notice that a client is engaging in these types of self-touching behavior, it may be appropriate to assume that the client is becoming more comfortable with the therapy setting and is becoming less concerned that his actions are going to be censored or criticized. Not all self-touching behaviors, however, are indicators of an increase in comfort. For example, Ekman and Friesen (1977) reported that some types of self-touching "increase with psychological discomfort or anxiety" (p. 363).

Henley (1977) reported that "feminine" women are more likely than "feminist" women to engage in self-touch behaviors, particularly hair touching. Scheflen (1973) suggested that for American women, hair touching is employed when they wish to be viewed as attractive or when they are being seductive. Under such circumstances, hair touching mandates that the therapist ought to avoid having physical contact with that client, focusing instead on an inquiry into the client's emotions and thoughts. Because self-touch can be conscious, planned, spontaneous, or outside a client's awareness, the meaning of any specific behavior can be varied. Clients who were sexually abused as children often resort to seductive-like behaviors when feeling frightened or shameful. Clients who were physically abused as children sometimes exhibit self-destructive behaviors—such as digging into their skin with a pen, soda can tab, or their own fingernails—while discussing a painful or stressful topic.

▩ Touch by Proxy

This category of touch also does not involve direct physical contact between the therapist and client. Rather, it is the symbolic touch that takes place between two people through the use of an object or a third person.

An example is holding out the tissue box for a client who begins to cry during a therapy session. As the client takes the box, there is a moment when both therapist and client are touching the box together. This is a slightly more intimate gesture than placing the tissue box next to the client. Another, even more intimate variation on this would be for the therapist to remove a tissue from the box and offer it to the client. Again, as the client takes the tissue, assuming that he does, there is a moment when the therapist and client touch the tissue together. The implied support offered by this action is considerably greater than verbally stating, "The box of tissues is on the table if you want one."

A therapist may also touch himself, intending to offer some message to the client. For example, a client who finishes telling a painful recounting of a childhood experience with little emotional expression might benefit from a therapist who places his hand over his heart while saying, "That is a heartbreaking story, and it touches me deeply."

In witnessing touch, a client observes others touching and being touched. Obviously, this needs to happen in a group or other therapy setting with others besides the therapist and a single client. As a client witnesses touch, he may also be imagining what it would be like if he were in the position of the one either receiving or giving touch, which allows him to anticipate what this experience might entail prior to deciding to participate. This also provides modeling of the behavior and may reduce anxiety associated with actually participating in a similar experience.

It is helpful to decorate the therapy office with "touchable" objects, such as blankets, pillows, stuffed animals, kush balls, and trinkets that are available for clients to pick up and touch. Such inanimate objects can be used in several valuable ways. For example, a therapist may himself hold a stuffed animal or inanimate object, with the client as witness. This demonstration of touch by the therapist can communicate comfort or concern, which the client may experience as himself being comforted.

Clients can be invited to touch the stuffed animals or inanimate objects that are available throughout the therapist's office. Clients can also be encouraged to bring to the therapy sessions an object of their own or a favorite stuffed animal. In times of discomfort, the client may touch his familiar object or stuffed animal for comfort. Sometimes, such contact behavior by the client may reflect an indication that he desires to be touched. The therapist may also provide opportunities for a client to take a stuffed animal or inanimate object home, facilitating the use of transitional objects as the client broadens the boundaries of therapeutic safety and acquires an enhanced sense of his own ego development.

A photograph or other representation—such as a drawing, school report card, or valued object of a client—can be touched or held in a manner that promotes a sense of comfort and security for a client. As with the stuffed animal, the client may not be consciously aware of the reason that he is experiencing the feeling of being comforted, but nonetheless experiences a reduction in the anxiety otherwise often associated with touch.

Observing how a client handles such objects may provide cues as to how he views touch. We have also found it useful to have a client bring photographs of himself touching or being touched or illustrations from magazines that can facilitate his efforts to describe what he feels as he views images that portray different types of touch.

Each person has a "personal space," the area around his body that he considers "his." The size of this area depends on the person's cultural background. When presenting workshops, we often notice how the participants choose which chairs to occupy. Those who arrive together and apparently know one another sit at the same table and arrange their chairs and personal belongings, such as coffee cups, notepads, and coats, closer together than those participants who attend without knowing other persons.

Other examples of the unspoken rules of personal space include how to stand in an elevator or the sequence in which urinals are occupied in a men's rest room. When three strangers ride in an elevator, they tend to divide the space into thirds. When one person leaves the elevator, the two who remain usually then automatically divide the space into two equal sections and relocate where they are standing. Proper men's room etiquette demands that if there are three urinals and two men, they will each choose to stand with an empty urinal between them. Nobody ever verbally explains these rules; they are simply acquired nonverbally through the influences of cultural socialization.

Hall (1963) suggested that when working with Americans, four distinct interpersonal distances should be kept in mind: public (more than 12 feet), social (12 feet), personal (1.5 to 4 feet), and intimate (less than 1.5 feet). On the basis of these distances, psychotherapy tends to fall within the range of the personal to intimate zones.

Given that each person has a sense of personal space, it follows that entering that space is a form of touching the person. The act of a therapist's placing his foot on the floor near where a client has previously placed his foot can be seen as a form of touch. For example, a client who is hypervigilant and easily frightened by hand gestures may be much more comfortable when the therapist emphasizes a point by tapping his foot on the floor rather than by using hand movements.

In discussions with our clients, we have found that it is a more intimate experience for a client if both the therapist and the client are sitting on a couch than when they sit beside one another on separate chairs. This perception remains even if a therapist is physically farther away from the client when sitting on the couch than when sitting closer to the client in separate chairs. Because the furniture on which a client sits is viewed as an extension of that client's body, the act of touching the arm or back of the chair or sofa is symbolic of touching the client himself. Such touching ought to be treated as such by a therapist and done only with intention and caution.

▥ Physical Touch

Actual physical skin-to-skin contact also has many levels of intensity and variations in application. This sense of "physical positioning" begins with how to—or not to—engage a client at the first meeting. Although in America, most situations of greeting between men call for a handshake, it is an important question to consider whether the automatic extension of a hand by a therapist without knowing how this will be received by a client is already a breach of boundaries between that therapist and the client. It would certainly be difficult for a client to refuse this initial handshake even if he were uncomfortable with it. One way of circumventing this dilemma is to wait until the client offers his hand, thereby increasing the certainty that the client is willingly engaging in this custom. At the same time, it must be equally acknowledged that assuming a wait-and-see stance could appear to a new client as a sign of aloofness or even rejection, as we mentioned in our discussion of the effects of withholding touch. Although we do not want to belabor the point, this clinical dilemma illustrates how difficult these decisions concerning touch really are and how much room there is for misinterpretation.

If a client initiates a handshake on meeting a therapist, much can be learned from this seemingly simple ritual. For example, the therapist can begin to assess that client's comfort with touch. Does the client grasp the therapist's hand firmly and warmly, or is his grip the classic "dead fish" handshake? Does the client wait for the therapist to end the handshake, or does he determine how long it continues? Does the client withdraw from the contact slowly or rapidly yank the hand back? Does the client grasp the therapist's hand with both of his hands and cling long after the appropriate length of contact for a first meeting? All these behaviors can be attended to and used as data as the clinical impression begins to take form.

It is our practice always to allow a client to determine if a handshake is to take place and to determine the duration of that contact, unless it becomes excessively long, in which case we stop the contact. This behavior by a therapist sends a nonverbal signal to the client that the client has a choice whether touch is a part of the psychotherapeutic relationship.

The issue of culture must also be taken into account when attempting to determine the meaning of a client's behavior (see Chapter 5). For example, Sue and Sue (1981) noted that people from Latin American countries tend to "shake hands more vigorously, frequently, and for a longer period of time" (p. 55) than do persons from North America. Moitoza (1982) noted that for clients with a Portuguese background, touch is an important method of communication:

Physical touching between men is common, especially during conversation. They may interlock arms or put one arm around the other's waist while discussing a particularly important point, or, when sitting down, they may touch each other's hands or knees so as to emphasize their point. A male therapist may reciprocate these gestures but only if they are initiated by the male family head. Women, too, frequently touch and kiss each other, but again, the therapist should avoid touching, or in many cases, even sitting next to a family member of the opposite sex. (p. 427)

The Laying on of Hands

Although this phrase has religious connotations for many people, it is a useful way to remember to avoid patting or stroking a client when using touch in psychotherapy. Patting can promote two undesired reactions in the client. First, patting is often perceived as a signal to suppress emotions, a nonverbal method of saying, "There, there, honey, don't cry." Second, many persons perceive patting as demeaning, a method of putting people in their place. Peloquin (1989) noted that when an adult is patted on the hand, cheek, knee, thigh, or buttock, it is a sexual gesture—although the football player who pats his teammate on the buttock after a touchdown may disagree. A pat on the head is condescending, whereas a pat on the back is used to signify condolence or congratulations.

Although stroking can be a way of soothing another person, it is often associated with caressing and sexual arousal and thus should be avoided. When a therapist has physical contact with a client, it is best for the therapist merely to place his hand on the client and avoid any movement. This reduces the likelihood that the touch will be misinterpreted.

Hand-Holding

A common expression for giving comfort is hand-holding. During group therapy, a client may silently offer a hand to another member who is expressing pain. This simple act can wordlessly speak volumes. When this same instance of contact takes place between a therapist and a client, however, it carries with it more transferential issues than when it takes place between two clients, so it must be done with more caution. We suggest that a therapist not take a client's hand but rather offer his own hand, palm up, so that the client's hand can be placed on the therapist's hand. In this position, the therapist's hand is not on top of the client's, and the client is more likely to see that he can easily end the touch when he so desires. Again, therapists must be alert for cultural differences. For example, Sue and Sue (1981) reminded therapists that for clients of the Islamic faith and those from Asian counties, the left hand is associated with the process of bodily elimination and therefore considered unclean. Consequently, the well-intentioned offer of physical contact by a therapist with the left hand to a client with this ethnic heritage could easily be viewed as offensive.

When a therapist offers to hold the hand of a client, it is important to ensure that he is in a physical position to maintain the contact without undue muscle strain. For example, if the therapist is seated in a position that requires extending his arm and supporting the *combined* weight of his own and the client's arm, the therapist will rapidly tire. The client will be aware of the physical tension in the therapist's arm and may seek to end the physical contact to prevent further physical discomfort for the therapist. This premature ending of the touch prevents the client from obtaining the benefits of the touch and ends up reversing the roles of the client and therapist. The client is no longer focused on himself but has become focused on the therapist's experience and changes his stance to meet the perceived needs of the therapist. Therefore, when a therapist offers a hand to a client, it is better to move the therapist's chair—or otherwise change position—to comfortably support the client's hand for as long as appropriate.

We have found it useful for the therapist to place his forearm on his leg or on the arm of a chair for support prior to making his hand available for a client. During the physical contact between a therapist's hand and the hand of the client, the therapist ought to notice if the client is actually allowing the therapist to support/hold the client's hand, or if the client is subconsciously holding back from accepting the touch. Are the client's arm muscles relaxed so that his hand is actually resting on the palm of the therapist's hand, or is his arm holding the hand away from the touch? All this is information for fruitful discussion. The client probably is unaware of such subtle cues whether or not the touch is being fully accepted.

In moments of great grief or other emotional distress, a therapist may wish to use both hands to hold a client's hand. This can be a supportive gesture, often used by clergy persons. It is as if two hands offer twice the support of a single hand. Although it can be more effective, it can also be more threatening because usually the client's hand is supported from below by one of the therapist's hands, while the therapist's other hand is on top of the client's hand. Being literally surrounded physically by an authority figure can be quite threatening for many clients.

Hugging

Webster defined *hug* as "to put the arms around and hold closely and fondly" (McKechnie, 1983, p. 883). However, as Schoener and Luepker (1996) noted when discussing the use of hugs in psychotherapy, one must better define what is meant by the term. We suggest that, when hugging, the therapist's hand rest on the upper back of the client near the shoulder blades, and the hands remain motionless, avoid stroking or patting.

As with any form of touch, it is useful to observe how clients behave during a hug. Many people are frightened of hugging because of the direct bodily contact and because being face-to-face is too similar to sexual acts. Some clients exhibit the "A-frame hug," in which the two people hugging place their arms around one another but stand so far apart that they must lean forward so that only their upper chests come into contact. The wide distance between their lower bodies assures them—and anyone watching—that the touch has no sexual undertones. Some of those uncomfortable with hugging—particularly men—will slap one another on the back, sometimes to the point of pounding on each other. They seem to think that if pain is involved in the hug, then they are not enjoying it "too much" and the hug is clearly not sexual. Others will embrace but hold their breath and dissociate so that they are not experiencing the hug but merely enduring it. All these behaviors can be noted and their meanings discussed with clients.

It is common for clients who attend 12-step-based mutual help groups such as Alcoholics Anonymous or who have completed chemical dependency treatment to view exchanging a hug at the end of a session as appropriate. Many of these groups use hugs as part of the ritual for ending group meetings. As with any form of touch, it is useful for the psychotherapist to have a clear policy on such contact prior to being faced with the situation. Because one of us (Hunter) began his career as a chemical dependency treatment provider and frequently receives referrals from members of mutual help groups, he routinely is faced with new clients who expect to receive a hug at the termination of the first session. Although obviously a proponent of the use of touch in psychotherapy, he believes that any contact between psychotherapist and client ought to be done consciously and purposely. Therefore, he usually declines any offer or request for a hug at the end of the first session. He explains to the client that although touch may be an aspect of the therapeutic relationship, he is not comfortable with such contact immediately.

Some clients are offended by this perceived rejection, so a therapist must plan for time at the end of the session to allow an opportunity for the client and therapist to discuss the client's reaction to the therapist's refusal to take part in a hug. Although some clients are hurt by the therapist's response, others are greatly relieved. If they have just completed a month to 6 months of treatment in a setting in which they were encouraged to hug strangers simply because they shared a history of drug abuse, they may have learned to hug without thinking about what it could mean to them or others. Hugging may have become automatic, engaged in merely from habit. As a result, these clients may have begun to dissociate emotional aspects of their experience during such instances of nonnegotiable/nonconsensual physical contact. A therapist's willingness not to hug until a significant relationship has formed provides a model for clients to evaluate the role that hugging and other forms of touch will play in the future.

Our final word about hugging within the context of psychotherapy is this: It is important that hugging occur within the context of the therapeutic benefits to the client and that such a clinical intervention not be undertaken to address the emotional needs of the therapist. An example of the use of touch for the therapist's needs versus the client's needs involves a situation in which the therapist initiates a hug at the end of a session as a demonstration of proof that the client still accepts the therapist even though the session that day was painful or as reas-

surance that no therapeutic break occurred as a result of difficult feedback the therapist gave to the client.

Holding

Perhaps the most intimate form of touch that is appropriate in the
therapeutic setting is when a therapist holds a client. Such an act is likely
to trigger intense transference—and possibly countertransference—so
it must be done only with a clear purpose in mind. Ideally, if possible,
the holding of a client ought to be done by a person other than the
therapist. This can be accomplished most easily in a group therapy
session or in couples therapy. It can be an influential experience for a
client to observe another group member holding a third member. For
example, it may be the first time that a client has witnessed a man
physically comforting another man or a female and male touching
without being sexual. In such cases, it is vital for the therapist to elicit
the responses not only of the clients who directly experienced the touch
but also of those clients who observed it taking place.

Hollender (1970) identified four factors that may lead to the desire
to be held (none of which seem particularly positive):

1. *Depression:* Although it is common for depressed people to
   avoid contact with others, largely because of their shame, others have a strong desire to be held or cuddled.
2. *Anxiety:* The embrace of another's arm can give the anxious
   or fearful person a sense of security.
3. *Anger:* Most people avoid body contact when angry themselves
   or when in the presence of an angry person, but an angry
   exchange brings some people emotionally closer, and they then
   desire to hold one another.
4. *Misuse of self:* For persons whose self-worth relies extensively
   on the validation of others, being held is sometimes seen as a
   sign of acceptance.

We believe that clients in the last category are unlikely to be appropriate
candidates for the ethical use of touch in psychotherapy. These people
are often described as extremely needy, and even therapists who are

usually comfortable providing holding with their clients recoil from holding them. A therapist's description in this type of encounter frequently is, "I'm afraid they will suck me dry. It is as if I can't give them enough."

Being held appears to be a highly desirable experience. Malmquist, Kiresuk, and Spano (1966) studied women who had already had three or more children out of wedlock and found that 65% of them had begun having intercourse prior to the age of 12 but reported that they did not find sex satisfying. These women did report, however, that sex was the price they paid to be held. Hollender (1970) noted that when participants were unable to obtain physical comforting or holding, they turned to other forms of bodily stimulation, including rocking, holding an inanimate object, eating, smoking, masturbation, or holding their own children. Clinicians who work with clients who are compulsive overeaters, compulsive masturbators, or drug addicts will no doubt confirm our observation that people who do not have access to some*one* often settle for some*thing*.

The difference between being held and exchanging a hug is the positioning of the client's arms. When a client is being held, the therapist's arms are around the client's shoulders, and the client's head is supported by the therapist's shoulder. If the client's arms are around the therapist's body, then the contact has become a hug, and the dynamics have changed. A hug is something that is exchanged, whereas being held is something one person gives to another. Clients who are uncomfortable receiving nurturing will often attempt to turn being held into a hug. They must be educated to distinguish the difference in these physical acts as well as encouraged to process their emotional response to receiving nurturing contact.

When working with couples who report a lack of physical intimacy in their relationship, or who only touch one another while being sexual, the therapist may find it useful to ask them to hold one another during the session so their behavior can be observed. If either person appears stiff, this can be pointed out to the client and its meaning discussed. In some cases, a therapist may wish to direct the couple—or even demonstrate to them—how to hold one another. We have found videotaping useful in helping clients observe how they interact physically. The couple and the therapist can review the videotape and discuss what thought and emotions were taking place while the members of the couple were touching one another.

▨ The Importance of Observing a Client's Breathing

Whenever observing a client involved in physical contact with another client or with a therapist, it is useful to observe the client's breathing. If a client stops breathing during the physical contact, it is most commonly a sign of fear and/or dissociation. At this point, a therapist can bring this to the client's attention verbally, for example, by commenting, "You're not breathing. What are you feeling and thinking?" A therapist may also merely say "Breathe," thereby reminding the client to remain present during the touch experience. The same thing may be accomplished if the therapist exhales louder than normal to subconsciously remind the client to breath. In a group therapy setting, a therapist should be aware of which clients hold their breath while they are observing other group members having physical contact, so that their reactions to witnessing the touch can be processed.

We have found it extremely valuable to inform our clients about our practice of observing them for signs of holding their breath. As male therapists, it is particularly important to explain this stance to female clients, who may observe us looking at their chests or the chests of other clients and misinterpret our behavior as sexual or voyeuristic. It is better to explain the purpose of this behavior than to "get caught" doing it and then try to explain the reasoning. We merely state, "When many people become frightened or dissociate, they hold their breath. One of the things I can do to help you make the changes you have stated you wish to make is to point out when you are holding your breath so you can be more aware of what you might be feeling at the moment." Most clients find this a reasonable explanation.

Because it can be extremely threatening for a female client to have a male therapist glance at her chest, it may prove useful to spend some time discussing breathing and to demonstrate the difference between shallow chest breathing—the type done when persons are frightened— and deeper belly breathing that comes from the diaphragm and is associated with relaxation. This can be accomplished if the therapist turns 90 degrees to the client and places one hand on his chest and the other hand on his belly. When he inhales while demonstrating shallow chest breathing, the hand on his chest rises higher than the hand on his belly. When demonstrating deep breathing, the hand on his belly rises higher than the hand on the chest. (Try this now, and see for yourself.) Most clients will spontaneously place their own hands on their chest and diaphragm to experience the difference. This also gives the client permission to look at the therapist's body during the demonstration. When the client duplicates the action, the therapist's observation is usually less threatening than if the therapist were looking at the client's chest under normal circumstances.

▩ Summary

The psychotherapist who is able to effectively use a variety of tools to facilitate the progress of treatment has an advantage over the psychotherapist who is master of but a few tools. The use of touch is best thought of as a group of tools, not merely a single tool. Conceptualizing touch along a continuum enables the ethical psychotherapist to use the least intrusive technique to obtain the desired goal.

10

Specific Techniques and Case Examples Involving the Use of Touch

We begin this chapter on the practical application of touch within psychotherapy by describing two specific techniques: timed touch and supervised massage. Although these techniques could be used as experiential learning exercises with trainees or practicing psychotherapists, they will be presented here as techniques for use with psychotherapy clients.

▦ Timed Touch

The timed touch[1] technique can be used when working with a couple or as a part of group therapy. One of us (Hunter) has used it in couples communication retreats for several years. The majority of the retreat participants have found it a useful and rewarding experience. It is common for the participants to experience profound emotional reactions as a result of taking part in the exercise. The most common reactions are shame (particularly body-centered shame, e.g., "No one would want to touch me, I am gross"); fear ("What if the touch turns sexual, and he won't stop when I tell him to quit?"); joy ("I have never been so free to enjoy being touched before!"); and gratitude ("I am so grateful you have stayed in our relationship, even when I was afraid to be touched by you").

The structure of this technique involves a dyad that takes turns giving and receiving 3 minutes of touch. The guidelines involve the person being touched giving the person doing the touching continual feedback and direction. The therapist observes the behavior of the persons involved in the exercise and times it, calling out the time at 1-minute intervals. At some point during the 3 minutes, the person being touched is to direct the other person to end all physical contact. After a moment, the person is to again invite the physical contact to resume and continues with the directions as to the type of touch desired and feedback as to how well the person doing the touching is following the directions.

Three areas of the body may be used for this exercise: the face, the feet, or the hands. The area used depends on the comfort level of the participants. In most cases, Hunter prefers to limit the exercise to the hands. Once the 3 minutes have elapsed, the roles are reversed so that the person who was being touched is now the person doing the touching. The same guidelines as before are used. Following this 3-minute period, the participants discuss their emotional and cognitive reactions to the exercise.

This exercise can provide useful information to the participants and to the therapist concerning the participants' comfort level with (a) participating in nonsexual physical contact, (b) giving directives to another, (c) receiving directives from another, (d) saying "stop" to someone who is touching their body, and (e) hearing "stop" from someone they are touching.

In addition, the therapist can observe the style of feedback. For example, does the client give feedback in negative language, such as "Not so hard!" or in a more positive fashion, such as "I like it better when you massage my hand softly"? For some clients, this exercise provides them with their first experience of nonsexual and/or nonviolent touch. Others have never had the opportunity to say what they enjoy or to safely tell someone to stop touching their body. It can be a powerful moment when they say "stop," and their request is honored. We have witnessed clients burst into tears at these times, exclaiming, "I never thought I had the right to decide when someone touches my body!"

This exercise is useful for couples who are having difficulties with their sexual relationship but are hesitant to describe their sexual interactions in any detail so the therapist can get a clear picture of how they behave. By observing how they act during this exercise, the therapist can make assumptions on their style of interacting in the bedroom. For some couples, it is the first time they have ever been verbal when having physical contact, and this paves the way for them to begin talking while being sexual.

▩ Supervised Massage

The controversy concerning the use of touch with psychotherapy clients is perhaps at its greatest when the clients have been convicted of a sexual offense. The staff of the Personal/Social Awareness Program, a program designed to treat adolescent sex offenders, believe that "healthy, consensual, non-genital touch is central in the treatment of adolescent youth who have committed sex offenses" (Lutz & Willcox, 1994).[2]

Sex offenders are notorious for their lack of understanding of or blatant disregard for appropriate boundaries regarding physical contact. Therefore, any effort to rehabilitate sex offenders must include a dramatic change in attitudes and behaviors related to touch. Toward that treatment goal, the participants in the Personal/Social Awareness Program are involved six times per year in a highly structured activity that allows them to experience supervised massage. The experience takes place in a large room with all members of the program present. Those who do not take part in touching or being touched observe and report on their reactions to witnessing the touching.

As an illustration, we offer a brief description of the purpose and guidelines of this exercise. We invite you to imagine what impact this type of experience might have on you if you were a client in this type of treatment program.

The program proposes several purposes for the use of touch in the treatment program:

1. To practice respecting another person's physical boundaries and limits on touch
2. To practice clearly communicating personal limits to another person
3. To facilitate an increase in awareness of emotions and physical sensations
4. To increase the ability to recall past experiences of touch, whether nurturing or abusive
5. To reduce homophobia
6. To learn that physical contact does not have to lead to sexual arousal and that if arousal takes place, it does not have to lead to sexual activity

To enhance safety in the use of touch, the program provides the following rules to guide the participants.

1. Everyone has the right to choose, at any time in the process, not to engage in the exercise.
2. The participants choose whom they touch and who touches them.
3. All participants remain in the room for the duration of the exercise.
4. At least two therapists are available at all times.
5. Touch to the hands, feet, back, or head may take place, but no touch may occur between the belt line and the knees. The buttocks, thighs, and genitals are off-limits.
6. Participants may ask therapists to touch them, but therapists are not to ask to touch clients.
7. Therapists do not touch clients during individual private sessions.

This protocol follows the guidelines that we proposed in earlier chapters. The key to making this a useful experience for the participants is the opportunity to have a choice about what takes place, to not be alone when the touch is taking place, and to openly talk about the experience and the thoughts and emotions it triggered. All these characteristics of the setting are in sharp contrast to the lack of choice, isolation, and secrecy found in sexually abusive situations. Such a highly structured protocol could be used for client populations other than adolescent sex offenders and could also be used with trainees or experienced psychotherapists.

▥ Case Examples

Our discussion will now focus on some case examples that illustrate the practical application of ethical touch in the clinical setting. Much of the literature related to the use of touch in psychotherapy is extremely vague as to how to use touch effectively. For example, Fromm-Reichmann (1959) offered directives for the use of touch, including *touch reassuringly*. Furthermore, it has often been suggested that the therapist be thrifty with the expression of any physical contact (noted in Aguilera, 1967).

A variety of examples for using touch in therapeutic settings have been included throughout this book as illustrations for issues and clinical dynamics that have been presented. In this section, we will provide several examples that elaborate more details about how touch can be used in actual treatment settings.

As we have previously stated, any use of touch is appropriate and effective only within the specific context of a particular therapeutic relationship. The case examples included in this chapter are ethical because the use of touch is consistent with the clinical style of the therapist, is undertaken with the consent of the client, and has therapeutic relevance within the context of the existing process between therapist and client. Therefore, these case examples are offered for illustration and should not be considered recipes for touch interventions that can be randomly applied to clients. Details—such as names—have been altered to protect client confidentiality.

The Tattoo

In this example, the client is an adult male who—during an individual session—spontaneously begins to describe his body-focused shame related to a tattoo on his upper arm. The therapist makes use of touch as a method for helping the client reframe the shame experience and identify its origins, thereby facilitating the client's expression of emotion and reevaluation of himself as worthy of physical contact and emotional acceptance.

When working with a client who has a high degree of shame associated with some aspect of the body, or who has experienced a trauma to a specific part of the body, it is usually preferable to introduce touch to some other portion of the body to establish a relationship of trust with the client's conscious and unconscious mind. In this particular case, the client and the therapist have been meeting weekly for several months. Permission for other touch has been given in a prior session. This session is already in progress. The client is seated across from the therapist; both are seated on chairs.

> *Client:* I noticed that I felt very self-conscious when I was changing clothes at the health club. [Self-conscious *is a term clients frequently use to indicate shame.*]
>
> *Therapist:* What were you telling yourself?
>
> *Client:* It just seemed that everyone was looking at me.
>
> *Therapist:* And thinking . . . ?
>
> *Client:* That there is something wrong with me.
>
> *Therapist:* Wrong? In what way?
>
> *Client:* In lots of ways. They could see that I'm no good.
>
> *Therapist:* So you were feeling shameful. How could they see that you're no good? [*The therapist labels the experience as shame, while not attempting to change the client's experience.*]
>
> *Client:* Well, for one thing, when I have my shirt off, they can all see my ugly tattoo.
>
> *Therapist:* What's ugly about it?
>
> *Client:* Well, when I did it, I was looking in a mirror. So I tattooed some of the letters of my name backwards. It looks sloppy, and everyone can see that I'm stupid. [*Client begins to rub his arm through his shirt.*]
>
> *Therapist:* When did you tattoo yourself?
>
> *Client:* When I was an adolescent. I did it with a friend.

Therapist: What would you like from me?

[*The therapist brings the shame experience into the room by focusing on the here and now and the therapeutic relationship. Because the tattoo is merely a metaphor for the client's shame, the therapist does not directly ask to see the tattoo but rather offers her permission for the client to determine how much of his shame he will expose. In other words, the therapist's actions are saying, "I will not expose you; you will determine how much of yourself to disclose. You are in charge. I am but a witness."*]

Client: Do you want to see it?

Therapist: How would you feel showing it to me? [*The therapist gives the client the opportunity to imagine showing the tattoo without having to commit to actually showing it.*]

Client: I would feel frightened.

Therapist: Frightened of . . . ?

Client: Your reaction.

Therapist: You are afraid that I will . . . ?

Client: Be disgusted. [*Another clue that this is a shame response*]

Therapist: So you're afraid that I would change my view of you. [*Implying that the therapist already has a positive view of the client. The client and the therapist are covertly discussing if their relationship is strong enough to tolerate the introduction of what the client fears is dangerous material. The client believes that the therapist's view of him is based solely on what the client has consciously disclosed, so that giving this new material risks the destruction of the relationship.*]

Client: I guess this is about shame. When I shower in the gym, I always make sure to keep the arm with the tattoo to the wall so nobody can see it. [*Notice the depersonalization in the use of the term* the arm, *rather than* my arm—*another clue that the client is currently experiencing shame.*] Would you be willing to look at it?

Therapist: Yes.

Client: Well . . . here goes. [*Rolls up sleeve. Fortunately, the tattoo is on the client's arm and not his buttock or some other less accessible area. Were it on a more personal area of his body, then the use of touch would be inappropriate. In such a case, the therapist would have to use touch in a symbolic fashion, for example, having the client draw the tattoo so the therapist could touch the image of the tattoo.*]

Therapist: You're right. The letters are backwards. [*Providing an emotionally nonreactive response; merely stating what is already known*] How are you feeling about my looking? [*Moving eyes from tattoo to the client's eyes*]

Client: [*Avoiding eye contact*] Pretty ashamed. [*Quietly*]

Therapist: What is it that you think I see? [*Focusing on the shameful self-talk rather than the tattoo itself*]

Client: Are you angry at me? [*Softly*]

Therapist: What would I be angry about?

Client: That I did such a dumb thing. [*The therapist begins to mirror the client by rubbing her own arm in a similar fashion.*]

Therapist: Where did you learn that? [*Seeking the origins of the shame*]

Client: That's what my mother told me. She said that this proves I didn't have any brains, just like my father. They had broken up by then, and she is always bad-mouthing him. [*The client is speaking in the present tense, showing that he is reexperiencing the shaming event rather than merely recalling it.*] That really hurt. [*Begins to tear*] I hate that she did that. I get so angry at her for comparing me to him. [*Voice rising*] I think I did it to piss her off. I was drinking a lot and skipping school. I was doing a lot of things to show her I was angry. But that was another thing I got shamed for, being angry. She looked at me with so much disgust whenever I was angry. I think she really hated me. [*His shame preventing him from being able to stay angry for long.*]

Therapist: So this tattoo is really a reminder of all that, and you think that everyone views you the way your mother did, with disgust?

Client: Yeah, I never really thought of it like that, but I think that's really true.

Therapist: I am touched that you would allow me to see this. [*Meaning both the tattoo and the shame and introducing the concept of touch by using the term*] I see that you keep rubbing your arm. How does it feel?

Client: It feels hot and tingly.

Therapist: Is it red from your rubbing it? [*Leaning closer. Therapist is touching the client by touching his personal space.*] The area all around it is red. [*Using her finger to point as another form of touch. At this point, the client raises his arm so that it nearly touches the therapist's finger as she is gesturing, a possible indication that the client is comfortable with the current level of contact and that further touch may be introduced.*]

Therapist: I'm wondering what it would be like for you if I actually touched your tattoo? [*Again, offering the opportunity for the client to imagine something prior to experiencing it*]

Client: What, do you mean touch it?

Therapist: Is there some way that I could touch you that would be helpful to you at this moment?

Client: Could you touch it in a way that would make it go away? [*Chuckling and reducing the tension of the moment*]

Therapist: The tattoo or the shame? [*Smiling*]

Client: [*Smiling*] Both.

Therapist: How 'bout we try working on the shame. Is there some way that I could touch you that would be helpful to you at this moment? [*Reorienting the client to the fear-producing moment*]

Client: [*Tearing again and looking away*] Would you put your hand on it? [*Sounding more like a request than a further negotiation*]

Therapist: [*Slowly places hand on tattoo*] It is hot. [*Providing an emotionally nonreactive response. Merely stating what is already known. In Gestalt therapy, this is known as an external awareness statement; in hypnotherapy, it is termed a pace statement.*]

Client: Would you rub it?

Therapist: Like you were doing?

Client: Yes. [*Begins to openly cry*] I feel like you are touching my pain. [*This is the moment when the healing of the shame is beginning. By allowing the therapist to touch the symbol and source of his pain, he challenges the belief that he is disgusting and unworthy of a relationship. His willingness to expose his core of shame in a safe relationship allows the emergence of a belief in his own worth and ability to care for himself.]*

Therapist: I wish there had been someone there for you when you were hurt.

Client: Me, too. But I'm glad I can get this now. It feels healing.

Therapist: Tell me when you want me to stop.

Client: [*After another minute*] I think I'm ready to stop. [*As therapist removes her hand, client continues to stare at tattoo.*]

Therapist: Let's process this. What did you learn from this experience? [*It is important to have enough time in the session to process what happened during the experience.*]

The preceding is a poignant example of the use of touch within a single psychotherapy session. Whenever such an intense event takes place, the psychotherapist ought to continue the discussion of its impact in the next session. The following is a portion of the subsequent session with this client:

Therapist: Now that a week has gone by, how are things different for you?

Client: Well, I noticed when I went to the health club this week and took off my shirt, I didn't feel as shameful. I still noticed what other people were doing, but it didn't seem as though everyone was looking at me. I also noticed another guy's tattoo and wondered what his story was. [*The therapist has followed up on the earlier learning, and the client is describing how the therapeutic experience is generalizing outside the office.*]

The Heart Transplant

This next case example involves a male therapist and a client who is an adult gay male. His presenting problem is that he is a member of a fundamentalist church that believes that homosexuality is sinful. He is experiencing great fear that he will be damned to hell because he has been living with another man in a lover relationship for several years. He has attempted to end this relationship with his lover but has always returned to the relationship. He views his situation as a double bind: He must choose between his lover and God, both of whom he loves deeply. As a result of his conflict, he has developed a major depression, is underemployed, and periodically is sexual with strangers in public rest rooms, putting himself at risk for sexually transmitted diseases and possible arrest.

The first section of this vignette is taken from a session that took place after 2 months of weekly individual sessions. During the first month, he described—with flattened affect—his family and relationship history and current symptoms. In the sessions of the second month, he exerted a great deal of energy providing the therapist with biblical and religious materials showing homosexuality to be an unnatural and sinful condition that could be cured through the use of prayer. In addition to being homosexual, the client viewed himself to be further flawed by his unwillingness to leave his "sinful fornicating sodomy relationship so that Jesus could cure him" of his homosexuality.

The transcript begins after the first 15 minutes of the session have passed. The client is sitting on a sofa facing the therapist, who is sitting on a chair:

> *Client:* I'm depressed as ever. I don't know what to do. [*Placing hand over his heart*]
>
> *Therapist:* You still believe that you have no choice.
>
> *Client:* I don't believe I have no choice, I know I have no choice. The word of God is quite clear on this matter. We have been over this before. Oh, I wish I could do what's right. [*Placing his hand over his heart again and sighing*]
>
> *Therapist:* You keep touching your heart. [*Placing his hand over his heart, attempting to focus the client on the sensations within his own body*]
>
> *Client:* What does that mean?
>
> *Therapist:* [*Shrugs shoulders*]
>
> *Client:* Well, I certainly don't know what it means either.

Therapist: Have you read any of *Embodiment* (Nelson, 1978) yet?

Client: No. I started to, but it makes me too depressed.

Therapist: Depressed or anxious?

Client: Both. [*Placing both hands over his heart and sighing*]

Therapist: You are torn between two men that you love.

Client: Who do you mean?

Therapist: Do you not love both God and [lover's name]?

Client: You know I do. But I shouldn't. I should love God more than [lover's name]. Why can't I do what God wants me to do? [*Tugging on his shirt over his heart*]

Therapist: Your love is so great, yet you suffer with a broken heart.

Client: Yes, that describes it exactly. My heart is breaking. [*Beginning to tear*]

Therapist: [*Again placing his own hand over his heart*] I am touched by how strongly you love. [*Slowly moving his hand from his heart and moving 6 inches toward the client, symbolically touching the client*]

Client: I want to tear my heart out. [*Crying, clutching at his shirt, and pulling*] I can't stand to live like this anymore.

Therapist: I'm wondering what it would be like for you if I were to touch you? [*This is a premature introduction of physical contact. Although the therapist has used the word* touched, *mirrored the client's self-touch, and symbolically touched the client, the client has not responded in a manner that suggests that additional touch is appropriate, as the reader will see. Perhaps the therapist is frustrated after 2 months with little progress or is uncomfortable with the client's level of despair.*]

Client: No! Don't! [*Pushing himself back against the sofa and throwing his arms up*]

Therapist: [*Leaning back slowly, to increase the space between the client and himself*] I would never touch you without your permission.

Client: I'm sorry. I didn't mean to yell. I hope I didn't offend you. I just thought you were going to touch me. [*A sign of a shameful individual is apologizing for setting reasonable limits.*]

Therapist: I am not offended or angry. I think it is wonderful that you know when you don't want to be touched and that you were able to tell me so.

Client: I just didn't want you to be hurt.

Therapist: Hurt?

Client: By touching me.

Therapist: How could I be hurt by touching you?

Client: [*Long silence*] I don't want you to risk yourself by getting too close to me. [*Shame often leads to grandiosity. He believes he is so bad that he is a danger to others, as if his shamefulness is contagious.*]

Therapist: You are afraid that if I touched you, it would lead to sex? [*He does not yet understand what the client is implying.*] I want to remind you that I never have any sexual contact with any of my clients. [*This was discussed in the initial session as a part of defining the expectations of the therapeutic relationship.*]

Client: No. I'm not afraid we would have sex.

Therapist: [*Puzzled look*]

Client: I don't want you to go to hell, too.

Therapist: You are afraid that if I were to touch you, I, too, would become as bad as you think you are.

Client: I know it sounds crazy, but I don't want you to risk it.

Therapist: I am grateful that you care enough about me to want me to be safe. [*Reframing the client's action as positive*] I understand that you don't want me to touch you today, and I won't. I just want you to know that if someone ever wanted a nonsexual comforting touch, this is a place where it is available. [*Using depersonalized language to reduce the tension*]

Client: Well, now that we've got that all taken care of, maybe I could tell you about how my week went. [*The session continues, focusing on day-to-day events.*]

The client returns in 2 weeks. He begins the session describing an event at his place of employment. The seating arrangement is the same as the previous session.

Client: Were you serious when you said that you would be willing to touch me? [*Not looking at the therapist*]

Therapist: Yes.

Client: You could go to hell for eternity.

Therapist: Perhaps. But I'm willing to bet my soul that if I touched you, not only would I not go to hell, but you would get better. [*The therapist is using the language style of the client. He is also planting a suggestion that the client will benefit from the intervention.*]

Client: Well, I appreciate that you would be willing to do it, but I really don't want you to.

Therapist: You are always in charge of when you want to be touched and when you do not want to be touched. [*Supporting the client's right to set limits*]

The session continues, focusing on other issues. Several sessions later and a few minutes into the current session:

Client: I have been thinking about the idea of you touching me.

Therapist: And how do you feel as you imagine me touching you?

Client: I feel afraid.

Therapist: I wonder what your fear is telling you.

Client: It is telling me that what I am thinking about could be very powerful.

Therapist: You have been hurt by the way some people have touched you in the past.

Client: Yes, that's true. But I'm wondering if I couldn't be helped by being touched, too.

Therapist: I wonder as well.

Client: Do you still believe that you wouldn't be hurt by touching me?

Therapist: I still believe.

Client: How would it look?

Therapist: How do you imagine it happening?

Client: I imagine you touching my broken heart.

Therapist: And then?

Client: I imagine that my hurt goes away.

Therapist: Perhaps in the long run, but not at first. [*Wanting to reduce the client's expectation that a single experience of touch has the power to eliminate years of shame*]

Client: Maybe that is what I am afraid of, that it will hurt as well as help.

Therapist: That you will have big feelings?

Client: Very big.

Therapist: You have had big feelings before in this room. [*Reminding client of past successes*]

Client: And it didn't kill me.

Therapist: Nor me. [*Assuring the client that the therapist can comfortably tolerate the expression of emotions*]

Client: Where would you be if you did touch me?

Therapist: Where would you want me to be? [*Giving the client the responsibility for determining the course of the touch experience*]

Client: I would want you sitting beside me.

Therapist: And . . . ?

Client: I would want you to put your hand on my chest where my heart is. [*Moving from imagining touch to directing a touch experience*]

Therapist: Are you asking me or describing a thought?

Client: If you are sure it is safe.

Therapist: I am sure that my soul is safe and that I will not attempt to sexualize the touch.

Client: I know you won't hurt me.

Therapist: Tell me when you are ready.

Client: I am ready to have you sit beside me.

Therapist: [*Moving to the sofa and sitting beside the client*] Are you breathing?

Client: More or less.

Therapist: When you are breathing regularly, that will be a sign that you can consider moving to the next step.

Client: [*After a period of time*] I am back in my body now. You can touch me now.

Therapist: In a moment, I will place my hand in front of you. If it seems right for you, then you can use your hand and bring my hand as close to your chest as seems right to you. You can stop at any time. How does that sound?

Client: OK.

Therapist: Remember to keep breathing. [*Placing hand approximately 18 inches from the client's chest, palm toward the client*]

Client: OK. [*Staring at the therapist's hand*]

Therapist: You have all the time you require.

Client: I know. [*After approximately 1 minute, the client takes the therapist's hand and begins slowly to move it closer to his chest. When the distance between the therapist's hand and the client's chest becomes about 5 inches, the client begins to shake.*]

Therapist: You are shaking.

Client: I am getting so hot. [*Beads of sweat beginning to form on his forehead*]

Therapist: You are beginning to sweat.

Client: I don't want to stop.

Therapist: You have all the time you require. [*Exhaling loudly to covertly remind the client to continue breathing regularly and deeply*]

Client: [*As the therapist's hand comes within an inch of the client's chest, he closes his eyes tightly—as if bracing for something. As the therapist's hand comes in contact with the client's chest, his head falls back, and he begins to weep and sob loudly. His other hand comes up and presses the therapist's and his own hand tightly to his chest.*] Oh my God. I hurt so much. God help me.

Therapist: Invite your God into your heart. [*Discussions were held in earlier sessions that the God of his parents may not be the God of his understanding.*]

Client: [*Weeping*] God, mend my heart. Make me whole again. Give me peace from this pain. [*Several minutes pass while the client's crying lessens.*]

Therapist: I wonder what is happening in there.

Client: [*Softly*] I don't feel so empty anymore.

Therapist: Take all the time required to fill yourself with comfort.

Client: [*Several minutes pass, and the client gently rocks back and forth. His grip on the therapist's hand loosens.*] Thank you.

Therapist: Thank you for trusting. [*The therapist does not say who the agent of trust is, leaving it open that it could be the therapist and/or that the client was able to trust himself.*]

Client: I did good.

Therapist: You were very brave. When you are ready to have me remove my hand, let me know by letting go and I will sit back so that we can process how you have changed as a result of what you have done. [*The client squeezes the therapist's hand and then releases it. The therapist slowly withdraws his hand and sits back on the sofa. At this point, the therapist may wish to ask the client where he wants the therapist to sit while they discuss the impact of the touch experience. Some clients prefer the therapist to remain sitting close, while others need to reduce the intimacy by having the therapist move back to his original seat.*]

Client: I feel different.

Therapist: Different?

Client: Like I am whole, filled up. I like it.

Therapist: I'm glad.

Client: Will I always feel like this from now on?

Therapist: No. But now you know one more way to fill yourself and to let others into your life.

Client: Damn. I want to always feel this way. [*Laughing*]

Therapist: What did you experience?

Client: God told me that I am OK just the way I am. That He loves me and that I can love myself.

Therapist: You can love yourself. [*Reinforcing the message*]

Following the above session, the client reported a reduction in his depressive symptoms and a lessening of his impulses to become involved in anonymous sexual encounters in public toilets. He and his lover began to touch one another in nonsexual ways, something they had not previously done at any time in their relationship.

Several weeks after the above session, a friend of the client who was also in a therapeutic relationship with the same therapist asked if she could also have "a heart transplant." It seems that the first client had described his touch experience to the second client, who then wished to make a similar event a part of her therapy. At first, the therapist was unwilling to repeat the touch experience, imagining himself before the state licensing board of his profession, attempting to explain how he justified placing his hand on the chest of a female client. So that the client might benefit from something that she saw as desirable, however, he modified the technique.

The client described her shame as "a large, dense, hard, dark mass in her chest surrounding her heart." This prevented it (her heart) from fully connecting with anyone, including herself. The therapist sat next to the client on the sofa, and rather than have his hand on her chest, he placed his hand on his own chest. He invited her to place her hand on her chest and, when she was ready, to take his free hand with her other hand. He then made the suggestion that their hands formed a "circuit from heart to heart," whereby she could begin to experience what she needed.

Role Plays

The following case example is used to illustrate the way in which touch can be incorporated into a therapeutic role play to help a client access and express an emotion, such as anger. "Terry" was extremely passive in therapy and rarely had any agenda for himself. He would wait for the therapist to initiate the therapy session and would go in whatever direction was provided. Terry entered therapy following a separation from his wife. His wife had left the marriage with no explanation to Terry of why she was leaving. Following her departure, Terry became quite depressed.

During his early therapy sessions, Terry became frightened and tearful whenever he talked about his past but had difficulty acknowledging these feelings, although they were evident to the therapist. It became apparent that his wife's leaving triggered anger related to the abandonment he experienced from his mother and reminded him of his childhood powerlessness to do anything in his own behalf. Terry had been physically abused for several years by his mother, and he began to describe the incidents of physical abuse that had been inflicted on him by his mother. His memory included his mother pulling him by his arm from a position on the floor in the living room of the house in which he grew up. She would pull him outside and take him into the garage, where she then held him by putting her arm around his waist as he bent over facing the floor so his back was exposed to her. She would then pull up his shirt and pull down his pants. After he was exposed in this way, she would take a wooden dowel and hit him repeatedly on his back and buttocks. This is where the memory stopped. Terry had no idea what prompted his mother to pull him outside and hit him and no idea what happened after she was through.

When Terry talked about this, his voice was soft and he showed no emotion. He mentioned that his recall of the event seemed as though he were an observer, rather than a participant. This behavior had generalized in such a way that Terry dissociated whenever he believed he was threatened and/or saw himself as powerless to act in his own behalf. He had only the abuse memory to guide his present actions, and he did what had been his protection in the past, that is, he used dissociation as a primary coping response.

The task in helping Terry to access, express, and resolve his feelings was to enable him to experience as fully as possible a recall of the abusive event and provide him the opportunity to behave differently. The initial therapy sessions were spent going through the memories that Terry had of his mother abusing him. Each time, the memory was told, there was more detail and more emotion identified. Through the telling and retelling of his story, the therapist learned what happened and how Terry was still frozen in his ability to act in his own behalf. Through this information gathering, the therapeutic relationship was formed, and a plan was developed for a role play.

Terry's story began with the memory of himself sitting in front of the television in the family living room. His mother would come into the living room and grab his arm and pull him up from the floor. In the retelling of this incident, the therapist inquired about where on Terry's arm his mother would grab him and how hard she would pull. This information was useful in planning the role play because it was important to create as much of the actual past experience in the present as possible.

Terry acknowledged that he felt lost much of the time and would like to be able to take more initiative. He agreed that the difficulty he had in doing so may be connected to the abuse he experienced as a child. At this point, the therapeutic process of role play was explained to him.

> *Therapist:* It seems to me that much of the powerlessness you feel now might be the result of how threatened you were as a child and that there was no one available to help you. You reacted in the only way that seemed available. You disconnected from the pain both physically and emotionally and waited until it was over. That may be why you remember the abuse that happened in the garage as though you were an observer and not a participant. Even now, you seem to take the role of observer in what happens to you and find it impossible to do anything different to protect yourself. Does that make sense to you?
>
> *Terry:* Well, yeah, I guess so.
>
> *Therapist:* I would like to propose something that might help you to experience yourself as powerful. Would you be interested in hearing it?
>
> *Terry:* Sure.
>
> *Therapist:* We've been over what occurred in the garage a number of times, and it seems as though you have a pretty good idea of what happened, at least a certain segment of it. I would like to propose that we explore that actual past event here in my office. It would go like this: You would be sitting on the floor as if you were watching television like you were at the point you remember. I would pretend to be your mother and come into the room and grab you by the wrist and begin to pull you up and away from the TV. Your job is to pay attention to how you feel and notice your reaction. If at any time you want to stop, you only need to say "cease," and I will immediately stop. Do you believe that?

Terry: I think so, but I'm not sure that I would be able to tell you to stop.

Therapist: I understand. That's what you couldn't do when your mother was pulling you. You were a child and were powerless to stop your mom. That fear is still with you now, and what might help would be for you to have the experience of the grownup part of you being able to protect the child. Do you believe that if you couldn't tell me to stop that I would stop at some point anyway?

Terry: I think so. I don't think you would do what my mother did to me. I think I'm really afraid of my own fear.

Therapist: I think that's right, and you can make the decision about when and how you are going to attend to your fear. If we don't work on it the way I just suggested, we can find another way. Will you think about it during the next week, and we can talk about this again the next time we meet?

Terry: OK.

At the next session, this client begins to discuss his thoughts concerning the suggestion of experiencing a role play.

Terry: I have been thinking about your suggestion that we explore an incident during which my mother abused me. Your idea makes sense. I would like to try it. What do I have to do?

Therapist: You don't *have* to do anything [*smiling*], but you might decide to re-create the situation to the point where you have more access to what you were originally thinking and feeling. And then you could have a new, more desirable ending to the event.

Terry: I would like to experience standing up to my mother and telling her she can't hit me anymore.

Therapist: Describe the sequence of events in detail.

Terry: I am sitting cross-legged on the floor. She comes into the room . . .

Therapist: From which direction? [*Encouraging him to be as detailed as possible*]

Terry: She comes from behind and from the left. [*His left shoulder raising slightly as if he is already experiencing her approach*] Then she grabs my arm and . . .

Therapist: Which arm?

Terry: My left arm. And tries to haul me to my feet while she is yelling at me.

Therapist: What is she saying? [*Using the present tense*]

Terry: [*Eyes narrowing, head cocked, as if listening*] She is yelling. She is calling me "a little shit." And telling me that she's had enough of me, and all the problems I cause her. [*Also speaking in the present tense*]

Therapist: What are you doing?

Terry: I am going limp. [*Holding his left arm up*] I hope if she has trouble getting me to my feet, she won't be able to get me into the garage.

Therapist: Are you saying anything?

Terry: No, I just look at the floor and hope she goes away.

Therapist: What happens next?

Terry: She manages to yank me to my feet and drag me to the garage. [*His face takes on a pained look*]

Therapist: Is that where you want it to change?

Terry: No. I want to know what she did to me. I want to know why I am so afraid.

Therapist: I wonder what it would be like for you if we were to re-create the events you fully recall in slow motion? What if I were to play you, and you showed me how your mother pulled you to your feet?

After an agreement is reached, the therapist sits on the floor as directed by the client. Terry slowly approaches her, verbally describing the actions as he makes them. After he re-creates the event with the therapist, they agree to switch roles: Terry sits on the floor, and the therapist re-creates the actions of very slowly pulling Terry to his feet. No yelling takes place. The participants are still in the planning stage and discussing their movements and touch as therapist and client, not as mother and child. Once the therapist has pulled the client to his feet, Terry begins to describe more images and directs the therapist:

> *Terry:* Pull on my arm, like you are dragging me out of the room. [*The therapist slowly pulls on the client's arm, but does not walk or otherwise move.*] I'm feeling afraid. [*He begins to bend at the waist.*]
>
> *Therapist:* You are bending at the waist.
>
> *Terry:* It seems like the right thing to do. [*He continues to bend.*] Put your arm around my waist. [*The therapist does so.*] Now raise your other arm up like you were going to hit me. [*The therapist very slowly lifts her arm, while continuing to keep her other arm around the client's waist.*] Yes, I can just imagine it. I was bent over, and she was hitting me with that wooden pole. She was screaming, she was crazy mad. I was crying and begging her to stop, but she just kept hitting me. [*Notice, he has switched to the past tense. He is describing an event rather than reliving it.*] No wonder I'm so afraid. I couldn't do anything to stop her. It hurt so much.
>
> *Therapist:* If you could change things, how would it be different? [*Beginning to focus on the modifying of the cognitions, as she releases her grip*]
>
> *Terry:* I would like tell her to stop before she ever gets me into the garage. [*Rising*]
>
> *Therapist:* Describe it to me.
>
> *Terry:* I would be sitting and she would come in, just like she always did, but when she yanked me to my feet, I would pull away from her and demand that she leave me alone.
>
> *Therapist:* If we were to do a role play, would you want her to stop immediately or to put up some resistance?
>
> *Terry:* I would want you to resist at first, but then back off. [*Already imaging the cognitive reframe*]
>
> *Therapist:* What type of resistance?
>
> *Terry:* The first time I attempt to pull away, don't let me, make me work for it.

> *Therapist:* So I pull you to your feet. You begin to resist. I continue to attempt to pull you to the garage, but then you break free. Then what?
>
> *Terry:* Then I tell you—I mean her—to leave me alone.
>
> *Therapist:* You can be as mad as you want, and yell, but you won't hit me or anything in my office. And if either of us wants it to stop, we just say "cease" and everything stops immediately. Agreed?
>
> *Terry:* Agreed.

At this point, the client sits on the floor. The therapist, who had moved slowly in the planning stage of the role play, now storms up to Terry and grabs his arm as she had been instructed. Terry reacts just as he did in the past. The therapist feels Terry going limp and yells, "This time it can be different, Terry!" As Terry begins to resist, the therapist begins to scream, "You little shit!" Terry jumps to his feet and yanks his arm from the grip of the therapist. Terry begins to yell, "How dare you beat me? It's not my fault you're a drunk! You can't ever hit me again! You touch me again and I'll call the police! I'm big now! You can't hurt my body anymore! I'm strong! I'm an adult!"

The therapist backs away from the client, giving him room to use his arms to express his anger.

> *Therapist:* [*Staying in role for the moment*] You're right, Terry. It's your body, and you can decide who touches it and how. You are strong. I won't ever hit you again.
>
> *Client:* [*At this moment, begins to smile*] I was angry wasn't I? It felt good.

The therapist indicates the role play is ended by stating that she is no longer in the role of the client's mother—but is his psychotherapist—and further reinforces this message by moving to a different location in the room. They spend the remainder of the session processing what was learned during the role play and how these lessons can be generalized to other situations. Terry reported that for the first time in his life, he was able to stand up for himself and express anger. He was amazed to learn that he was able to experience himself as powerful, yet nobody—including himself—was injured. In subsequent sessions, he and the therapist continued to discuss ways Terry could stand up for himself and be assertive without being aggressive.

This example demonstrates how a client's recall of memory and emotion is facilitated by the use of touch and how a client is able to experience a different, more desirable, ending to an event that the client may have continued to re-create repeatedly in his life.

The recall of memory—particularly when related to a history of abuse—is controversial. The purpose of this text is to focus on the ethical uses of touch in psychotherapy, *not* to debate the literature on memory. A brief discussion of the dynamics of memory recall, however, is useful to provide a generic framework in which to evaluate the clinical effectiveness of this vignette.

Memory, both content that is normal and that which is highly emotionally charged, is a complex phenomenon that is not well understood. There are currently more than 20 proposed theories of memory (Hammond et al., 1995). A number of committees have been formed to address the believability of traumatic abuse. Lawsuits have proliferated to challenge alleged memories that have been accessed through a variety of therapeutic approaches.

The American Psychiatric Association (1994b) issued a report on delayed memory that included this statement:

Children and adolescents who have been abused cope with the trauma by using a variety of psychological mechanisms. In some instances, these coping mechanisms result in a lack of conscious awareness of the abuse for varying periods of time. Conscious thoughts and feelings stemming from the abuse may emerge at a later date. (p. 26)

The American Medical Association Council on Scientific Affairs (1994) reported on memory and childhood abuse and concluded that "the AMA considers recovered memories of childhood sexual abuse to be of uncertain authenticity, which should be subject to external verification" (p. 4). But this same report also stated, in a less frequently quoted passage, that "other research indicates that some survivors of abuse do not remember, at least temporarily, having been abused. . . . In short, empirical evidence can be cited for both sides of the argument" (p. 3).

The American Society of Clinical Hypnosis (Hammond et al., 1995) stated that

> research focused on malleability of normal memory teaches us that there is potential for inaccuracy of recall of details, whether or not enhancement procedures have been used, so that the total accuracy of a memory cannot be claimed or assumed unless the memory is corroborated by independent sources and methods. At the same time, however, other simulation and autobiographical memory research has shown that there is often considerable accuracy of memory, especially in the recall of emotional/traumatic events. Thus, it seems imperative for professionals to take a balanced view of memory and not become influenced by extreme positions that represent an over-generalization from studies of normal, unstressed memory pro-cess. (p. 4)

It is not our purpose here to defend either side of the repressed memory debate. We believe that it is not the function of a therapist to determine the degree to which cognitions that are accessed in therapy are fully accurate or distorted. We subscribe to the stance that it is the client's subjective experience of historical events that determines the direction for the therapeutic exploration.

▥ Summary

This chapter has focused on several examples that demonstrate the direct clinical application of different forms of touch. These examples illustrate the variety of ways that a clinician may use touch, as well as highlight the degree to which the ethical use of touch involves a collabo-rative effort between helper and helpee.

※ Notes

1. Timed touch is not an exercise we developed ourselves. Unfortunately, we cannot recall who first introduced us to this technique, so we cannot give credit where credit is due.

2. The information in this section on the policy for teaching appropriate touch has been provided by the staff of the Personal/Social Awareness Program, Lutheran Social Services, Minneapolis, MN. Used with permission.

Chapter 11

The Use of Touch
in Various Modalities
and With Specific Populations

This chapter will elaborate the particular value in using touch in three distinct modalities of therapy: couples, family, and group therapy. We will also briefly discuss the use of touch with clients who are survivors of childhood trauma to illustrate the application of touch to the needs of specific client populations. We have chosen to use trauma survivors for purposes of illustration, not because there is anything exceptional about using touch with this population but rather because an extensive amount of our clinical experience has involved working with this client population. By focusing on trauma survivors, we hope to stimulate consideration of ways that touch can be applied to clinical work with a wider variety of special client populations.

It is beyond the scope of this book, and our expertise, to attempt to discuss the possible use of touch with every type of client. We hope that this presentation will encourage clinicians who work with other client populations and special issues to share their experiences in professional publications.

Although it is important to consider the relevance of touch in working with complex clinical issues, it is essential to also consider the ways that touch might be counterproductive in response to any specific focus in the therapy. As we have stated previously, if the choice to use touch emerges from sound and reasonable clinical judgment, we encourage the consideration of ways that touch may have ethical application within the focus of particular clinical work. The guidelines that have been provided throughout the book can be used to make informed ethical decisions about individual clients within clinical settings.

▦ Working With Couples

Touch can be a valuable tool for working with couples as a vehicle for assessing interpersonal dynamics between the two members of a couple and/or as a method for strategic interventions to modify structural dysfunctions in the relationship. Valuable data concerning how the members of a couple relate to one another can be obtained by the attentive psychotherapist who simply observes how each person physically interacts prior to, during, and following a session. For example, it is useful to notice such things as these:

Do the two persons sit near one another in the waiting room?

If they arrive separately, do they touch when they greet?

What degree of physical proximity do they maintain with each other during the actual session?

Are their physical interactions consistent with the content of their verbal statements, or are there noticeable incongruities between verbal and nonverbal responses?

Does one member of the couple offer touch to the other member to reinforce a position of power and control? As an expression of appeasement? As a form of comforting during painful disclosures? If so, how comfortable does each appear to be when touching and being touched in any of or all these circumstances?

> Do the members of the couple routinely offer or accept touch as they are leaving the session?
>
> Is touch included in any way in the "good-bye" that occurs between the couple if they are leaving from the session by using separate forms of transportation?

Although no touch is involved between therapist and clients in any of the preceding questions, merely observing the couple regarding these touch dynamics can provide feedback that is rich in quality and substantial in quantity. Like any observation intended for assessment, any conclusions that are formulated as to the meaning of particular actions must rely on more than one occurrence of those behaviors.

As the therapy progresses, the therapist may decide to call the couple's attention to their use—or nonuse—of touch, or lack thereof, and invite them to discuss their understanding of the role that physical contact plays in their relationship. The current role of touch can be contrasted with the past, as well as discussing how the couple would like to see touch function in the future. By discussing touch dynamics in this way, the couple may increase their awareness of how they each brought differing cultural norms about touch to their relationship, they may discover ways in which gender has influenced their styles of using touch, and/or they may disclose more to their partner about how previous incidents of boundary violations involving touch (incidents that may have occurred prior to the relationship, during the relationship, or both) affect their current comfort level with touch in the relationship.

An example of how observing touch can provide valuable information for a therapist and can lead to a strategic intervention is illustrated by the couple who entered the office arm in arm and sat on a couch holding hands with their bodies touching. Merely watching them suggested that they were happy newlyweds. Their words, however, were not congruent with their actions. Once they began to talk, they both described a marriage of two decades that had been filled with loneliness, sadness, hurt, and fear. Even as they spewed out bitter accusations toward one another and repeatedly mentioned divorce, their bodies remained intertwined.

On the basis of feedback from observing the physical contacts between the two members of this couple during several sessions, the psychotherapist formulated an assumption that this unusual behavior was a physical representation of the primary problem in their relationship: They were too dependent on one another. In other words, their enmeshment prevented them from getting their needs met as individuals.

During one of their subsequent sessions, the therapist suggested, without explaining the reasoning, that they relocate to separate pieces of furniture. They reluctantly did so. The effect was immediate. They both reported a curious sense of relief combined with fear. When asked to elaborate, they reported that their fear was that the other partner would abandon the marriage and that the relief was the result of realizing that if the marriage ended, they could stop hurting each other on a daily basis.

With little prompting, they began to discuss what each would do if the marriage did end. As a result of seeing that each of them would survive the end of the marriage, their fear was reduced.

By the end of the session, they had agreed to sleep in separate rooms until the next session (2 weeks hence). As they left the session, they each shook the therapist's hand, something they had never done before, even though they had already attended several sessions. From the therapist's office window, it was observed that neither member of the couple touched the other as they parted in separate cars.

During the next few sessions, they spontaneously sat apart and discussed their respective commitments to stay married to one another while they were also more candid in expressing their desires for increased freedom to do things separately. They negotiated a weekly schedule whereby each of them had a night out without the other (which they had never done since they had begun dating), and they rearranged their home so that each of them had a physical space to decorate and use privately.

Although some couples have an excess of touch in their relationship, other couples have the opposite problem: They are unable to touch. When describing the elements that create a context that is conducive for effective communication, Weeks and Treat (1992) mentioned touch as one factor, noting, "Touching, if only hand to hand, or fingertip to fingertip can create even more intensity in the experience" (p. 130).

An example of this is illustrated by the couple who claimed to love one another deeply and stated their feelings eloquently, yet each of them reported not believing the other "really meant" the frequent pronouncements of affection. They were asked to demonstrate such an exchange. They did so, and although the words and voice tone were appropriate, their bodies were held in stiff postures. When queried, both of them reported the usual disbelief of the other's sincerity.

At this point, the therapist encouraged them to repeat the statements but to lean forward. They did so and cautiously reported that "it sounded different this time." Then they were asked to place one hand on the arm of the other's chair and repeat the statements. Again, they reported that their partner sounded more sincere. They were invited to hold one another's hand during the next repetition. At this point, they realized what had been missing from their exchanges. They spontaneously took one another's face gently in their hands and again proclaimed their love. The session ended with them holding hands, laughing and exclaiming that they now believed the other's words.

In addition to being aware of how the members of a couple interact physically with one another, the therapist will benefit from observing client-to-therapist and therapist-to-client physical interactions. Weeks and Treat (1992) noted the importance of maintaining balanced interventions:

> Touch, if perceived to be appropriate by the therapist, should be of the same quality and nature with both partners. For instance, if the therapist shakes the hand of the husband, she or he should probably do the same with the wife. A hug offered to one partner and not to the other can create issues of injustice and feelings of alienation. Touch, in general, should emerge out of the feelings of the session and the needs of the client. When done as a habit, touch can communicate a superficial intimacy likened to a marital couple who give each other a peek on the cheek every morning. (p. 43)

As this quote emphasizes, many instances of differential touch interactions between a therapist and members of a couple emerge from contrasting norms related to gender. It is important that the therapist be aware of how his own value biases about gender may influence his therapeutic use of touch with a couple. It is equally important for the therapist to notice the cultural and gender norms that operate between the members of the couple. The therapist will need to exercise clinical judgment on when his role is merely to observe these norms, when the couple can benefit from his naming and labeling those norms, and when it is clinically appropriate to make therapeutic interventions that attempt to modify those norms.

As we have discussed in earlier chapters, the norms about touch can vary widely and may be highly subjective in nature. Therefore, it is essential that the therapist be familiar with the normative biases that emerge from his own values, beliefs, and experiences. Only by doing so can he hope to identify and work with blind spots that may influence the therapy process with couples.

For example, many male therapists may fail to notice the subtle ways that some men use gestures or physical contact to communicate messages of power and control during interactions with their partner. A therapist who subscribes to traditional norms of masculinity and femininity will probably interpret many of these nonverbal touch cues as "expected" behaviors that fall within the framework of a "normal" marriage, thereby minimizing or perhaps even failing to notice the element of gender dominance. A therapist who observes a couple from the paradigm of gender equality, however, may notice these same gestures of physical contact as reflecting control or abuse dynamics that have previously been disguised or kept secret but that may be a significant underlying factor that contributes to the dysfunctions about which the couple has requested therapy.

Another example is illustrated by the differing cultural norms concerning "permissible" displays of affection between partners in a same-gender, as compared with an opposite-gender, couple. The therapist who is not familiar with gay and lesbian culture or who has a heterosexist bias will probably not expect the same level of physical contact between two members of a same-gender couple during therapy sessions as he would between members of an opposite-gender couple in the same session. On the other hand, the therapist who is more knowledgeable and accepting of same-gender relationships will probably process touch interactions that reflect distancing maneuvers or dynamics of overenmeshment in the same way that he would if an opposite-gender couple exhibited those same physical interactions.

Being a gay or gay-friendly therapist does not ensure freedom from heterosexist biases concerning acceptable norms for touch within same-gender couples.

Many therapists believe that it is important to maintain a balance in the number and type of interventions that are directed toward each member of a couple. The therapist, however, should not touch one member of a couple merely because the other member was touched during that session. In some cases, it may be clinically appropriate to touch only one member of a couple or to touch one member more than the other.

The therapist must be aware to avoid using touch in a way that encourages transference toward himself as a good partner in contrast to the bad or deficient partner. Ultimately, any touch that is used by a therapist within the context of couples therapy should be focused toward the therapeutic goal of strengthening the positive bonds between the two members of the couple.

▨ Working With Families

Many of the same questions that were identified for the couples therapist can be used by the family therapist:

Do the members of the family sit near one another in the waiting room?

If they arrive separately, do they touch when they greet?

How do they sit in the actual session?

Do they interact physically when they interact verbally?

Does anyone offer touch to the other members as a form of comforting during painful disclosures? If so, how comfortable does each appear to be when touching and being touched?

Do the family members touch as they are leaving the session?

Do they use touch as they part if they are leaving using separate forms of transportation?

Additional questions that are relevant for families include these:

Is touch allowed by only one gender?

Does touch cross the generational boundaries? If so, does it move both directions, or does it occur only one way?

Do any members of the family use touch for control or containment? If so, how can such physical interventions be evaluated along the continuum of nonabusive to abusive touch?

How is touch refused and requested?

How are refusals and requests responded to?

As with any technique that is powerful with an individual or couple, touch can be a useful therapeutic tool within the framework of family therapy. Moursund (1985) articulated the following observations about the use of touch in family therapy:

> A final note on the general tone of family sessions: touching helps! Dysfunctional family members may seldom touch each other. When they do, the touch has negative connotations, it is either punishing or smothering. Families need to relearn the value of positive touching. The therapist can model a stroke or pat or supportive hug, and encourage members to give and accept similar touching with each other. Members also need to learn when and how to reject touching, how to maintain distance when they want to be separate. (p. 212)

Touch can be used to create distance and set limits between family members. Weeks and Treat (1992) identified touch as a way of "cutting down on the number of insults or physical attacks" (p. 172) that are exchanged between difficult children during family sessions. Touch can also be a valuable method for containment and safety, as when a parent firmly intervenes to stop a child who is about to tip over a dangerous or valuable object in the therapist's office.

Many people who grow up with negative experiences with touch become parents who are afraid or ill equipped to use touch with their children. Parents who were abused as children may have developed a belief that all touch is hurtful; therefore, they may assume that avoiding all physical contact with their children demonstrates their love for them, oblivious of the neglectful dynamics of this style of parenting. In contrast, some parents who subscribe to physical methods for disciplining their children may lack an understanding of developmental issues concerning the ways in which children are different from adults; consequently, these parents may minimize the strength or heftiness of a physical intervention that is administered by an adult for disciplining or punishing a child, ignoring the abusive quality that results from the (intentional or unintentional) forcefulness of the touch. The therapist who is skilled in using touch in ways that are positive and nurturing can be a powerful role model to demonstrate that affectionate touch can be benign or nonhurtful and that such physical contact does not have to lead to a catastrophic ending.

An example of the use of touch in a family therapy setting is the case of a family that was referred for therapy by an adolescent male's chemical dependency counselor. The first session consisted entirely of information gathering and was of low emotional intensity. Therefore, the therapist was surprised at the end of the session, as the family was about to leave, when the son put his arms out as if to embrace the therapist. Before the physical contact was actually completed, however, the therapist carefully and compassionately stated, "I'm not comfortable hugging people until I get to know them better."

The family stopped silently in their tracks. The therapist asked them what they were thinking and feeling, and they all reported that they thought they were supposed to want to touch people. "When we attend the sessions at the treatment center, everybody hugs everybody else," they noted. During their brief involvement with treatment, they had already come to believe that they were supposed to be comfortable hugging people. Because they were uncomfortable hugging strangers, they had assumed that they must be dysfunctional. The mother stated further, "Even if I was uncomfortable, I never would have had the guts to refuse to give someone something they wanted."

Touch, of course, became the focus of the next session. The family identified two goals: becoming more comfortable with touch exchanged between family members and friends and becoming comfortable declining touch from people they did not know well.

Several sessions later, when the son was expressing hurt and sadness related to his relationship with his father, the father asked his son if he would like to be touched. The son nodded. The father sat next to the young man and stiffly put his arm around the back of the sofa.

"Would you like to increase the intensity?" the therapist asked. They both nodded, and the therapist moved to be near them, placing the father's arm around the son's shoulder. "More?" the therapist inquired. They nodded again. The son was directed to let his head rest on the father's shoulder. The boy's body was stiff, however. "You are not experiencing the touch," the therapist noted. "Let me show you how you look," the therapist said as he mirrored the boy's body. As the boy became aware of how he was holding his body, he began to relax his muscles. He began to cry as he allowed himself to be held and comforted by his father. As the therapist looked at the wife, he noticed that she was crying, too. When she was asked what meaning the tears held for her, she reported that she was envious of her son because her husband never touched her except when he was being sexual with her. Increasing nonsexual touch between the spouses was added to the treatment plan.

That the touch occurred during the session seems vital to the positive outcome. Had the father and son been assigned to practice touching at home, the experience likely would have been stiff and unrewarding. Because the therapist was able to observe them touching, however, he could coach them so that their experience was more positive, one that they would be more likely to repeat outside the office setting. In this case, touch was used to reduce the psychological distance within the family.

▦ Group Psychotherapy

Most of the research on touch has focused on individuals and dyads. Little research or literature addresses the use of touch within the context of psychotherapy groups. The limited research that is available, however, does support touch as a beneficial component for psychotherapy groups. Edwards (1984) found that female and male adults who took part in group therapy during a 6-week period that included handholding, arms around shoulders, and cathartic and supportive touch when expressing emotions reported an increase in levels of being cared for and seeing touch as playful and as a form of celebration. Participants also reported being more free to release emotions than they had been prior to attending the group. These positive changes were noted even in those participants who reported that touch was generally viewed as threatening. Only 1 of the 69 participants found the touch to be significantly sexually arousing.

Dies and Greenberg (1976) reported positive results from the use of touch in their research involving female and male undergraduates who had been divided into four-person groups. Their study was designed to examine the effects of varying levels of touch between members in all-male, all-female, and mixed-gender groups. Groups were structured to encourage either no touch, moderate touch, or high touch among the members. This was accomplished by varying degrees of encouragement and/or instructions regarding how to use touch to enhance positive feedback.

The results of their study indicated that physical contact between group members was not a naturally occurring phenomenon. They discovered that none of the participants made any physical contact with other members in the no-touch groups—that is, groups in which no encouragement or instructions were given regarding the use of touch—whether the group was all female, all male, or mixed gender. The frequency of touch in the moderate-touch groups—that is, groups in which general encouragement and instructions were given regarding the use of touch—was slightly higher than the no-touch groups, with all-female and mixed-gender groups exhibiting more frequent use of touch than all-male groups. Touch was used with considerably greater frequency in high-touch groups—that is, groups in which strong encouragement and specific instructions were given regarding the use of touch—for all three of the gender constellations.

The group modality allows the opportunity for peer support and peer challenge, a milieu in which a client can imagine and "invite" new behaviors—such as giving or receiving touch—and receive feedback about the impact of those behaviors on himself and others. A group setting is perhaps the safest environment in which the therapist can use touch because there are as many witnesses to the touch as there are group members. Therefore, a coleader or other participants are present to monitor ground rules for safety and/or to address any distortions or misperceptions that unexpectedly emerge from the touch experience. In addition, other group members are available to assist in the touch techniques and to add an interactive dimension that is not available in individual therapy.

It is important that the therapist be attentive to how the use of touch within the context of a therapy group affects all group members, not just the members who are directly involved in any exchanges of physical contact. Frequently, nonparticipating members may have intense feelings about touch or may be triggered by the mere suggestion that touch may occur within the proceedings of the group. Therefore, any negotiation about how and when touch is to occur should be cross-checked with all members of the group, and time should be allocated to process the reactions of both observing and participating members following any touch interactions that occur in a group session.

Some group members will be inclined toward a higher level of comfort with touch or will bring to the group prior experiences with using touch as a natural response to emotional expressions by others. It is the responsibility of the therapist to establish a milieu in which all touch that occurs is consenting and in which all members become conscious of how their use of touch affects their peers. Consequently, the therapist may need to make gentle, firm, and nonjudgmental interventions to limit the automatic—and perhaps seemingly unconscious—response of some members who may reach out to touch the arm, leg, or shoulder of a peer who is expressing strong feelings such as grief, distress, or pain. As Schoener and Luepker (1996) noted,

> Frequently group therapists indicate that they announce that no client should feel compelled to hug and that anyone who doesn't want to hug or be hugged should simply indicate this to others in the group. However, there is obviously group pressure to conform in most groups, and the question remains as to how difficult it would be to refuse a hug or refuse to hug. (p. 381)

The therapist must be alert for signs that a client is uncomfortable giving or receiving touch but is unable to say so, and intervene prior to any physical contact taking place. Some of the most productive personal growth related to touch takes place when, perhaps for the first time in the client's life, touch is declined.

▓ Working With Survivors of Childhood Trauma

The appropriate and ethical use of touch with survivor clients can be invaluable in helping them heal and recover from their trauma experiences. At the same time, using touch with this client population can be a precarious proposition, to say the least. Most trauma survivors will feel an intense sense of vulnerability at the mere suggestion of touch, more so within the intimate setting of a therapy relationship. The feelings of survivor clients must always be respected, and no physical contact should even be considered until and unless an adequate foundation of client safety and empowerment has been established.

Maintaining professional boundaries is a prerequisite to successful clinical work with survivor clients. Therefore, a therapist must take the time that is needed to explain his boundaries and procedures in a way that is understandable to the survivor client. It is generally helpful to have ground rules in written form because many survivors are highly dissociative and have difficulty retaining verbal information in stressful situations such as an initial interview. It is also helpful to state clearly and openly that the therapist accepts responsibility for ensuring that there will be no sexual contact between therapist and client.

Clients who have been physically or sexually abused may respond to anxiety by attempting to use threatening or seductive behaviors. For many survivor clients, this is an unconscious process but nevertheless a potentially volatile response to the intimacy that therapy poses for them. Clients who have experienced boundary violations as inevitable once a certain level of intimacy is achieved may seek to initiate familiar behaviors that reflect their efforts to gain control. They may attempt to decrease their anxiety and fear either by moving into a defensive stance or by pushing the therapist to "get it over with." These client stances, in addition to reflecting their probable fear of saying no, help explain why survivors are at greater risk for being revictimized.

There is a high frequency of dissociative responses with survivor clients. The therapist who is not already familiar with the dynamics of dissociation should become acquainted with this area of clinical concern before attempting to use touch with any survivor client. It is likely that a survivor client will dissociate during some segment of any touch contact between himself and the therapist. The most common cues to dissociation in such a therapeutic transaction include the therapist's noticing how a client begins to breathe in a shallow manner or may hold his breath completely and the therapist's noticing his own feeling that the client is not present and/or that he is beginning to feel spacey himself. (See Steele & Colrain, 1990, for an extensive list of dissociative signs.)

Some clients were able to survive their abuse only by dissociating from their emotions: Disconnecting from their own bodies during the abuse may have been the only way survivors could endure the experience, and forgetting what happened afterwards may have seemed like the only available option for regaining a sense of control. Therefore, many survivor clients may encounter difficulty experiencing pleasurable or comforting sensations from even gentle and nurturing touch until they are able to unlearn automatic dissociative responses to physical contact. Once they are able to begin receiving the physical sensations that accompany touch, survivors often describe their experience as painful, even when the touch is soft and gentle. It is important for the therapist to receive frequent and specific feedback in the form of the survivor client's description of his physical sensations as any touch interactions proceed. For example, a survivor may often experience a gentle hand placed on his shoulder as indistinguishable from a sharp slap to that same area of the body. The client can relearn to assimilate sensory data about physical contact only if they are processed concretely and with an intense focus on reality-testing feedback loops.

The survivor client who is able to experience touch as other than painful may then react with considerable ambivalence and/or shame. A decrease in his dissociative response to the touch he receives in therapy may trigger an increased awareness of ways in which he felt sexually aroused or experienced sexual pleasure during actual incidents of abuse. This will often trigger a crisis of confusion, resulting from his ambivalence about whether it is acceptable to experience physical pleasure. He may also discover the extent to which his avoidance of physical pleasure represents an underlying coping response that has allowed him to tolerate intense feelings of shame. As he struggles to allow himself to experience positive sensations related to touch, the sense that something is intrinsically wrong with him may intensify and/or he may more actively resist physical contact because he feels untouchable or toxic.

Because physical and sexual assault involve the negative use of touch—both types of abuse are violations of appropriate boundaries of the victim's body—many people consider touch to be totally inappropriate with these clients. We believe, however, that a client will have great difficulty in fully recovering from this trauma if only verbal or cognitive approaches to therapy are used. Rather, we advocate that therapeutic efforts to help a client heal from touch-related wounds ultimately ought to include experiential approaches that directly access the body and that provide the client with real-life opportunities to feel nonabusive touch. Healing is unlikely to occur if this positive and appropriate touch remains only an idea or intellectual concept.

Some survivors of trauma learn to adapt to their abuse experiences by dissociating physical sensations connected to their bodies. Using such a coping strategy persistently through extended periods sometimes results in the client's adapting a more global stance of not feeling anything about his body. Therefore, it is sometimes necessary for a client to become reacquainted with his own body. Visualization exercises can be helpful in guiding the client through a process of reconnecting with his body. Such a visualization can teach the client where in his body feelings might be found as well as teaching him the language about how to describe body sensations.

▦ Summary

This chapter has provided a focus on the relevance of using touch within the framework of couples, family, and group psychotherapy. We have also examined the application of touch with clients who are survivors of childhood trauma, such as physical and sexual abuse, to illustrate the importance of using touch with special client populations.

We realize this material is only a beginning for a dialogue that needs to be greatly expanded. We hope this, and the preceding, chapter will catalyze many additional efforts to disseminate case material that illustrates the uses of touch in a variety of clinical settings.

Chapter **12**

The Use of Bodyworkers
as an Adjunct to Psychotherapy

One method of providing psychotherapy clients with a safe experience of touch is to make referrals to credentialed body workers. This is effective in cases in which the psychotherapist is theoretically opposed to the use of touch by psychotherapists or is personally uncomfortable using touch or when it is in the client's best interest to obtain a greater level or a different type of touch than is appropriate for a psychotherapist to provide. For the purposes of this chapter, the word *bodyworker* will be used to describe massage therapists, physical therapists, and other professionals whose training has primarily focused on the physical body of the client. The term *psychotherapist* will continue to be used when describing the role of those whose clinical training is primarily focused on the mind/emotions of the client.

▓ Advantages

Bodywork can be a powerful adjunct to psychotherapy. Benjamin (1995a) noted the advantages of including bodywork with psychotherapy when he wrote that this combination of approaches can create a safe place for the experience of non-abusive, non-sexual touch, and can help survivors reconnect with their bodies. Massage can also help survivors regain control of their bodies as they practice setting limits and choosing where they wish to be touched. (p. 28)

Bodywork helps a client see both the body and touch as positive, rather than something dangerous, painful, or disgusting. A client's body image tends to improve as a result of bodywork, as does her ability to access emotions. Because touch serves to trigger memory recall, as described in earlier chapters of this book, bodywork can help a client fill in the gaps in her life story. Many persons who experienced trauma find it disturbing that they lack an integrated narrative of their past and wish to access more memory through the use of bodywork.

Benjamin (1995a), himself a bodyworker, made use of Herman's (1992) three-stage model, which consists of establishing safety, recalling and mourning, and reconnecting. He suggested that bodywork can be helpful, for different reasons, at each stage of recovery.

Stage 1: Establishing Safety

In the early stage of recovery, the client is learning to set psychological boundaries with the psychotherapist by determining what will be disclosed, to what degree of detail, and with what level of emotional expression. Once a psychological foundation of safety has been established with the psychotherapist, a client at this phase of recovery may benefit from bodywork as an adjunct to the psychotherapy.

The bodywork setting can allow the client to experience, perhaps for the first time, nonsexual touch from another human. The client can experience setting limits with the bodyworker and having those limits respected. The psychotherapist may wish to help the client set up an agenda prior to the first bodywork session, which includes what will be worn, what part(s) of the body will be touched, how the touching is to be given (e.g., no motion, only gentle squeezing), and a preplanned directive to the bodyworker that clearly establishes a mutually agreed-on ground rule for how to cease all physical contact (e.g., "After 5 minutes, I will tell her to stop touching me even if I'm not afraid, just to see how she reacts to it").

It is usually at this stage of recovery that the issue of the gender of the bodyworker is of the greatest concern to the client. Sexual orientation is frequently an issue. Often a heterosexual man experiences a difficult double bind: He is afraid of being touched by another male, but he is equally fearful of getting an erection in the presence of a female bodyworker. Not surprisingly, a client who is an abuse survivor is often afraid to meet with a bodyworker who is of the same gender as the person(s) who abused her in the past. On the other hand, a gay or lesbian client may be reluctant to see a bodyworker of the same gender because of fears of erotic transference and/or countertransference.

For these and a variety of other possible concerns, it is vital to the success of the referral that the nature of any fears be processed and addressed prior to the client's first meeting with the bodyworker. The psychotherapist cannot assume that the bodyworker will address this issue to the satisfaction of the client. The psychotherapist must also assess the degree to which information sharing and treatment coordination needs to be established with the bodyworker as a part of the referral process.

When first introducing the idea of a referral to a bodyworker, the psychotherapist ought to be alert for physical symptoms in the client that suggest fear or shame. Clients will often say that they are open to meeting with a bodyworker when they have no intention of following through on the referral. Sometimes, they may even end the psychotherapeutic relationship because such a suggestion engenders such a degree of fear.

One aspect of making this type of referral is to adequately prepare a client for the experience of working with another person whose training and techniques are different from those she may have become familiar with during psychotherapy. The psychotherapist can facilitate a client's development of safety by describing in detail the therapeutic reasoning for making the referral, the philosophical and process framework of bodywork, the background of the particular bodyworker to whom the referral is made, and the physical environment of the bodyworker's office. Naturally, to do some of this level of information sharing, it is necessary for the psychotherapist to have met the body-worker and visited the site. Ideally, the psychotherapist ought to have actually experienced some form of bodywork from the bodyworker and may wish to disclose this experience to the client. We have found that a comment as simple as, "When I had a massage from (bodyworker's name), I found her to be very respectful," can have a profound impact on reducing a client's fear.

Stage 2: Remembrance and Mourning

Stage 2 of Benjamin's (1995a, 1995b) version of Herman's (1992) model involves accessing previously fragmented, disguised, or uncon-scious memories. This can take place only if a client has developed a sense of safety with both the psychotherapist and the bodyworker. The physical contact between the bodyworker and the client can facilitate her client's accessing cognitive and emotional material that may never have become available if only psychotherapy had been employed. At this stage, it is helpful, if the psychotherapist and bodyworker are not providing concurrent services, for the client to schedule the psychother-apy session immediately after the bodywork session so that the emo-tions and memories brought forth can be processed.

Stage 3: Reconnection

In Herman's (1992) third stage, a client has the sense of a complete intact self. For example, a number of symptoms are characteristically present for people who suffer post-traumatic stress disorder (American Psychiatric Association, 1994a), including numbing of general respon-siveness, feelings of detachment or estrangement from others, sense of foreshortened future, and exaggerated startle response. Many of these symptoms should have become greatly reduced by this stage, which makes it feasible for a client not only to be able to tolerate bodywork sessions but actually to look forward to them for the relaxation and pleasant sensations that may be experienced. At this stage, the psycho-therapist and bodyworker can greatly reduce the frequency of discus-sion, needing only periodic updates or discussions when the client has an unexpected reaction to the bodywork.

▓ Psychotherapists' Concerns

Four common concerns beset most psychotherapists when they consider the possibility of using bodyworkers. First is the general lack of knowledge concerning the types of bodywork that are available.

Second is the fear that bodyworkers do not have adequate ethical guidelines that will provide safety and protection for their clients. Appendix 12.1 provides an example of a code of ethics that not only demonstrates that bodyworkers subscribe to guidelines but also is more precise than many of the existing codes similar to those that govern psychotherapists.

Third, some psychotherapists fear that bodyworkers will attempt to engage in psychotherapy with clients. Such actions would be unethical, if not illegal. Ethical treatment providers of all disciples understand that they are not to practice outside their area of competency and training. We have found that the bodyworkers with whom we have associated are open to collaborating with psychotherapists and coordinating who is responsible for which aspects of the client's treatment. Such a cooperative working relationship, however, is possible only if issues are discussed openly and directly as colleagues. We have found that it is helpful to make it clear from the beginning of the referral process that the psychotherapist functions in the role of case manager. Therefore, the referral goes more smoothly, and the results are more rewarding if it is mutually understood at the beginning that the psychotherapist is charged with the responsibility for overseeing and coordinating the client's treatment.

A fourth fear expressed by psychotherapists concerning the referral of clients to bodyworkers focuses on the perception that the bodyworker may not have an understanding of the inability of some clients, particularly those who have been physically or sexually abused, to set limits with a person in authority. For example, a bodyworker might assume that because a client did not speak during the bodywork session, she had no objections to the touch that was provided. In such a case, the bodyworker might be shocked later to learn that the client had been terrified but was helpless to object.

Many psychotherapists have little or no training in the dynamics and effects of trauma on humans, so it is not at all surprising that most bodyworkers might lack an understanding of these issues. We have found it helpful to suggest that the uninformed bodyworker benefit from reading such material as that included in this book, the first dozen pages of Chapter 6 in *Abused Boys* (Hunter, 1990), and/or Chapters 1, 2, and 4 of *Adults Molested as Children* (Bear & Dimock, 1988). With this background, bodyworkers are much more sensitive to the issues faced by a client who is involved in psychotherapy because of a history of trauma.

▧ Questions to Ask a Bodyworker Prior to Making a Referral

Because it is not unusual for persons to seek the services of a bodyworker for massage prior to ever meeting with a psychotherapist, it is quite possible that it will be the bodyworker who makes the referral to the psychotherapist rather than vice versa. We have numerous clients who were originally referred to us by their bodyworkers who either were aware of having a history of sexual abuse but did not expect to have a flashback while being massaged or did not recall a traumatic event until experiencing bodywork.

When considering using a particular bodyworker as a referral source, we have found the following questions helpful. Whenever possible, we like to see the site at which the bodywork takes place and have the bodyworker visit our office. The following questions are also useful to give to clients who are considering accepting a referral to a bodyworker. The very asking of the questions begins to form the relationship and reinforces that the client is the consumer of the service and has the right to ask questions.

> What is your educational background?
>
> What certification(s) or license(s) do you hold?
>
> In what professional organization(s) do you hold membership?
>
> Do you maintain professional insurance?
>
> Do you believe it is unethical to engage in any sexual conduct or activities with clients?
>
> Have any ethical complaints ever been filed against you? If so, what was the outcome of the complaint?

What services do you consider yourself qualified to deliver?

With what type of client(s) do you work best?

With what type of client(s) do you have difficulty?

How much clothing is a client expected to remove?

Do you leave the room while a client is removing clothing?

Do you ask a client at the beginning of each session where the client does *not* wish to be touched that day?

What do you do if a client begins to cry while being touched?

While interviewing a potential bodyworker, the psychotherapist must assess whether the bodyworker understands that a client with a history of sexual abuse has different needs than a client who does not have such a history. Bailey (1992) noted four common assumptions that a bodyworker must be able to question—rather than take for granted— to successfully interact with survivors of sexual abuse:

1. People are comfortable removing their clothes to be touched.
2. People are comfortable lying on their back or facedown.
3. Touch is inherently relaxing.
4. Passively receiving touch is comforting.

Anyone who has experience with clients who have been sexually abused will realize that they often find any of these four situations terrifying. The bodyworker ought to be aware of the possibility of spontaneous age regression during which an adult client can feel, think, and even behave as if a child. The bodyworker should be familiar with methods of helping a disturbed client become less upset and dissoci- ated, for example, having the client sit up, name objects in the room, and focus on breathing or even ending the session prior to the scheduled time.

When making a referral, the psychotherapist, after obtaining the client's permission, may wish to warn the bodyworker of potential problem areas. For example, if a client commonly dissociates, the body- worker will need to be alert for subtle signs of dissociation, such as shallow breathing, holding the breath, becoming more tense, and "freez- ing," in which case a client may not be able to set limits or ask that the touch be stopped. If a client has a great deal of body shame—because of obesity or scars from self-mutilation or physical abuse—the psychotherapist may wish to alert the bodyworker prior to the first session. If a client has a history of acting seductively in response to fear or shame, the psychotherapist may wish to inform the bodyworker of this dynamic and discuss how it will be handled if it takes place.

▓ Arrangements

Because of the powerful effect bodywork often has on a client, it is useful, particularly in the early stages of treatment, for the bodyworker and psychotherapist to discuss the treatment plan, the role of each treatment provider, and the client's progress. Normally, telephone consultation is preferable to written reports for two reasons. First, written reports tend to take too long to get from one provider to the other. Second, most bodyworkers are not trained to prepare the type of reports that psychotherapists desire. When making a referral to a bodyworker, we prefer to make arrangements to have the bodyworker and the client each contact us on the day of the first few bodywork sessions. Once the relationship between a client and a bodyworker is better established, the contact can be reduced in frequency. Initial contact is particularly important with a bodyworker with whom the psychotherapist has not had a long history.

The exchange of signed forms granting permission to disclose confidential material should be taken care of prior to a client's first contact with the bodyworker. This allows a psychotherapist to discuss the reasons for the referral with the bodyworker and the bodyworker to contact the psychotherapist with information on the response of the client to the bodywork.

Timms and Connors (1990, 1992) described the advantages of concurrent services provided by a psychotherapist and bodyworker. If such arrangements cannot be made, then the psychotherapist may wish to invite the bodyworker to use a room in the psychotherapist's suite or office building so the client has a sense of being on safe ground. The psychotherapist can also have phone contact with the client just prior to, just after, or even during the bodywork session. Regardless of the arrangements, the best results are usually obtained when the psychotherapy sessions and bodywork sessions are held within a few hours of one another.

▓ Summary

This chapter has advocated for the clinical advantages of employing bodywork as a viable adjunct to psychotherapy. For many clients, encouraging a collaborative relationship between bodywork and psychotherapy can enhance the quality of their therapeutic treatment. A variety of approaches to bodywork have been surveyed, and guidelines/questions have been included to facilitate the process of developing effective working relationships between psychotherapist and bodyworker.

Appendix 12.1

Excerpts From the Ethical Code of the Massachusetts Association of Body-Centered and Body-Oriented Psychotherapist and Counseling Bodyworkers

We specifically inform the client[s] about their rights involved in any decision regarding the use of touch in therapy, and their right to refuse touch at any time. We also understand that a client may have difficulty recognizing and/or expressing his/her need to refuse touch. Therefore we strive to be sensitive to the client's spoken and unspoken cues regarding touch.

The client has the right to refuse or terminate at any time any touch on the part of the therapist. The client has the right to say "no" and is the final arbiter of touch.

Under no circumstances do we engage in sexual activities with our clients. This includes acting upon sexual impulses with clients whether by means of gesture, words, innuendo, or quality of touch.

Under no circumstances do we engage in sexual activities with our clients. Because of the nature of the therapeutic relationship, we recognize that the act of terminating therapy does not automatically change that relationship. Thus sex with clients following termination is strongly discouraged and is generally unacceptable. (Schultz, 1992, p. 5)

Materials and Training Aids

The material included in Part III is not positioned here because it is any less important. Rather, these two chapters are placed in the final part because each will be better assimilated within the context of the material already presented in Parts I and II.

Part III focuses on information that is self-exploratory in its nature. Portions of this part are intended to assess and/or stir your personal and professional growth.

We encourage you to approach the material in Part III from the perspective of training and growth. If used effectively, these chapters can help you to deepen your own command of using touch ethically within a framework of solid and effective psychotherapy. In addition, much of the material contained in Part III provides opportunities for experiential learning that can enhance your level of personal understanding and professional competence.

We encourage you to use Part III for course work and/or clinical training. We hope the material that is presented in these chapters will stimulate others to develop additional training tools.

Chapter 13

Erotic Issues Within the
Psychotherapy Relationship

The psychotherapy professions have, in effect, imposed a moratorium on all forms of touch because of the actual or potential boundary violations of a few clinicians. The improper and unethical use of any technique should be the cause for an indictment not of the technique itself but merely of the clinician who misused it. Undeniably, some therapists overcharge their clients or commit insurance fraud, yet no one expects the majority of psychotherapists to stop charging for their services or to cease filing legitimate insurance claims.

Rather than promoting an environment supportive of scientific study, the field of mental health has rigidly subscribed to a paradigm that simply equates all forms of touch as synonymous with erotic contact. Historically, the standard way to deal with this topic has been through avoidance. Although psychotherapy professionals acknowledge that erotic touch is inappropriate and unethical within the setting of psychotherapy, clinical training programs and continuing education seminars routinely fail to address the complex dimensions of this topic in any significant way. The extreme cases in which a therapist has violated professional standards and has become sexual with a client are cited as examples of unethical behavior, but little attention is focused on helping clinicians understand the intricacies of how such encounters between therapist and client come to be and, most important, the degree to which any therapist may have personal vulnerabilities for an erotic transgression with a client. An environment that encourages more open debate would be especially helpful for the professional who is just starting training or a career as a psychotherapist.

Although we recognize that sexual contact has no place within an ethical therapeutic relationship, we do believe that discussion of erotic transference and countertransference is useful to gain a more thorough understanding of the operational boundaries between appropriate and inappropriate physical contact. Without reservation, we support a climate that fosters open discussion of issues related to erotic transference and countertransference and that promotes a greater discernment of nonerotic and erotic forms of touch.

The therapeutic relationships that psychotherapists establish with clients will be more clinically solid if the decision not to engage in any type of erotic touch reflects personal processes of thoughtful deliberation (subscribing to ethical standards that have personal meaning) rather than compliant obedience (adhering to established professional standards regardless of whether those ethical guidelines have personal meaning). In the end, there is a qualitative difference in the type of therapeutic relationship that is formed when a psychotherapist approaches clients from a deeply held conviction that erotic touch is ethically inappropriate and when a psychotherapist is merely adaptively compliant in obedience to professional codes that prohibit erotic touch.

We hope that your consideration of the material presented in this chapter will be thought-provoking and that your deepened awareness of the issues surrounding erotic touch will enhance your professional abilities to employ touch in ways that are clinically appropriate and ethical. If you provide teaching or supervision to clinicians, we encourage you to consider including discussions of this issue as a way to enhance the depth of training and consultation you are providing. If you are a student or supervisee, we invite you to challenge your teacher(s) or supervisor(s) to expand discussions of this issue to provide more opportunities for you to delve into this important area of your clinical work.

We encourage you to deliberate this issue not only in reference to your desire to refrain from behaviors that are defined as off-limits but also to increase the depth of your personal and professional understanding of the multitude of considerations that surround the dynamics of erotic touch. By reading this chapter, we hope that you will move beyond a one-dimensional stance whereby erotic touch is merely defined as "that behavior that I am not supposed to do."

■ Professional Standards Regulating Erotic Touch Between Psychotherapists and Clients

Concern about erotic touch has a long history within the traditions of the helping professions. Sexual contact between helper and helpee has been discouraged since recorded time. The Hippocratic oath, an ethical code that was established in ancient Greece and is often still displayed in the offices of modern-day physicians, includes the sentence, "In every house where I come, I will enter only the good of my patients, keeping myself far from all intentional ill-doing and all seduction, and especially from the pleasures of love with women and men" (*Dorland's Medical Dictionary*, 1974, p. 715).

Physical contact of a sexual nature is specifically prohibited by the ethical codes of most professional organizations in the fields of mental health. For example, the American Psychiatric Association and the National Association of Social Workers both explicitly prohibit sexual contact between therapist and client (Committee on Women in Psychology, 1989). The American Psychoanalytic Association (1983) is unambiguous in its position statement: "Sexual relationships between analyst and patient are antithetical to treatment and unacceptable under any circumstances. Any sexual activity with a patient constitutes a violation of this principle of ethics" (p. 5).

The American Psychological Association's *Ethical Principles of Psychologists* (1981) clearly prohibits sexual contact between the psychologist and the client. Principle 7, titled Professional Relationships, states,

Psychologists do not exploit their professional relationships with clients, supervisees, students, employees, or research participants sexually or otherwise. Psychologists do not condone or engage in sexual harassment. Sexual harassment is defined as deliberate or repeated comments, gestures, or physical contacts of a sexual nature that are unwanted by the recipient. (p. 9)

Principle 6, Welfare of the Consumer, is to the point: "Sexual intimacies with clients are unethical" (p. 9).

Appendix 13.1 offers a summary of existing prohibitions to erotic contact as stated in the professional codes for the American Association for Counseling and Development, the American Association of Marriage and Family Therapists, the American Group Psychotherapy Association, the American Psychiatric Association, the American Psychological Association, and the National Association of Social Workers.

▓ Research on Professional Conduct Regarding Erotic Touch

Considering how clearly the professional codes prohibit erotic contact with clients, one would think that such behavior would be almost nonexistent. Sadly, despite these clear statements, sexual contact between psychotherapists and clients continues at an alarming rate.

Research studies reveal that erotic contact between psychotherapist and client is not necessarily rare. Pope, Keith-Spiegel, and Tabachnick (1986) reported that allegations of sexual misconduct are the most frequently filed ethical complaint. During the first 20 months that the Minnesota Department of Health's Office of Mental Health Practice was in existence, 40% of the complaints that were filed alleged that sexual contact had taken place between a therapist and client (Marshall, 1992). Furthermore, research (Bouhoutsos, 1984; Pope & Bouhoutsos, 1986) indicates that only about 5% of clients who could file complaints actually do so.

An alarmingly large number of the psychiatrists who were participants in Kardener, Fuller, and Mensh's (1973) research admitted that they were erotically involved with patients. When asked if they believed that erotic contact with a patient may be beneficial to that patient, 3%

responded affirmatively, whereas a total of 5% of the participants reported they occasionally or rarely took part in such contact with patients—such as manual or oral stimulation of the genitals or kissing— and 4% noted that this included intercourse. Of those who engaged in sexual intercourse, 79% had done so with five or fewer patients. Of the participants, 9% thought such behavior was better kept out of the office setting. Explanations for this contact—offered by the respondees themselves—included

> improves sexual maladjustment, helps patients' recognition of their sexual status (especially in the depressed, middle-aged female who feels undesirable), teaches sexual anatomy, discloses areas of sexual blocking, helps them experience being with a normal sex partner, demonstrates there is no physical cause for absence of libido, relieves frustration in widow or divorcee who hasn't yet re-engaged in dating, makes the therapy go faster and deeper, and increases dreams. (p. 1079)

Such justifications are similar to Wagner's (1972) finding in which 25% of the medical students surveyed reported that sexual intercourse with patients was appropriate "under the right circumstances," which included the physician's being "genuine and authentic."

Psychiatrists are not the only mental health professionals who become sexually involved with patients. Surveys of psychologists, clinical social workers, and psychiatrists indicated that members of these different professional disciplines engage in sexual contact with their patients at relatively equivalent rates (e.g., Borys & Pope, 1989).

Those who are violating the ethical codes are not necessarily those psychotherapists who are practicing on the fringe. As Pope (1990b) noted,

> They are well represented among the most prominent and respected mental health professionals. Cases involving therapists publicly reported to have engaged in sexual behaviors with their patients have included those who have served as faculty at the most prestigious universities (including those with APA-approved training programs), psychology licensing board chair, state psychological association ethics committee

chair, psychoanalytic training institute director, state psychiatric association president, prominent media psychologist, chief psychiatrist at a prominent psychiatric hospital, and chief psychiatrist at a state correctional facility. (p. 233)

Unfortunately, when attempting to prevent erotic contact between psychotherapists and their clients, merely forbidding it appears to be inadequate. Therapists who had sexual contact with clients knew they were violating professional codes. For example, social workers who had offended with clients were more likely to have undergone personal therapy as well as have met the additional requirements for inclusion in the National Academy of Certified Social Workers than were nonoffending social workers (Gechtman, 1989). Offending therapists who have undergone rehabilitation efforts have not shown high recovery rates, with recidivism rates reaching 80% (California Department of Consumer Affairs, 1990; Holroyd & Brodsky, 1977; Pope, 1989).

During the last 20 years, considerable research has documented the negative effects of sexual exploitation of clients by various professional groups. Regardless of when the sexual contact took place, even posttermination, a large body of the prevailing research has determined that clients were negatively affected by the experience (Brown, 1984; Feldman-Summers & Jones, 1984; Pope, 1990a; Sonne, Meyer, Borys, & Marshall, 1985; Sonne & Pope, 1991; Taylor & Wagner, 1976). To describe the effects of sexual contact with therapists on clients, Pope and Bouhoutsos (1986) coined the phrase "therapist–client sex syndrome" (p. 5). They drew comparisons to post-traumatic stress disorder and also noted similarities to aspects of the borderline (and histrionic) personality disorder. The symptoms include ambivalence; guilt; a sense of isolation; a sense of emptiness; cognitive dysfunction; identity and boundary disturbances; inability to trust others; conflicts with dependence, control, and power; sexual confusion; lability of mood; suppressed rage; and an increased risk of suicide.

Williams (1990) pointed out that although the research on the effects of therapist–client sexual contact is "fraught with insurmountable validity problems," we still need to take action. He wrote,

I doubt that our attitudes and laws regarding rape and incest were shaped by a careful review of the research literature. We should feel free to sanction therapists who become sexually involved with present or former patients simply on the basis of our understanding of the meaning of the actions themselves, regardless of our data base concerning outcomes. (pp. 420-421)

Pope (1990a) was in agreement with Williams when he noted the numerous ethical sanctions that have routinely been imposed without the benefit of a body of systematic research investigations showing definitively that harm occurs from the acts. As examples, he offered the sanctions imposed on therapists who violate confidentiality; fail to obtain informed consent; or misrepresent their competence, training, or experience. He commented that even if an act is harmless, in some cases society still has a responsibility to prohibit that act when the harm that may result is severe. "For example, the proposition that only a small minority of the instances in which an individual drives while intoxicated result in actual harm (i.e. the driver hits someone or something) in no way invalidates the laws and sanctions against driving while intoxicated" (p. 422).

Problematic Behaviors Exhibited by Psychotherapists Prior to Erotic Contact With Clients

We believe that there are guideposts along the way that can alert the psychotherapist to concerns that his erotic feelings are moving in a dangerous direction. Careful attention to these signs can help the mature psychotherapist predict possible trouble spots in the therapeutic relationship and undertake appropriate limit-setting interventions.

Sexual contact between a psychotherapist and a client is best thought of as a process rather than an event. Usually, nonerotic problematic behaviors precede erotic contact between therapist and client (Brock, n.d.; Keith-Spiegel & Koocher, 1985; Slovut, 1992). Gutheil and Gabbard (1993) described this process as "a slippery slope" in which there is an "increasing intrusion into the patient's space" (p. 188). Their work will be used as a basis for examining the factors that could eventually lead to boundary violations that, if not contained, could then lead to erotic touch with a client.

Time

Time is a boundary that defines and contains the therapeutic relationship. Just as something is amiss in the relationship if the client has a pattern of arriving for sessions later than the appointed time or requesting to end sessions prior to the time scheduled, so, too, it is a signal of trouble when the psychotherapist seeks to start sessions with a client earlier than scheduled or continually exceeds the allotted time. Routinely scheduling a particular client at the end of a workday or at a time when other staff are unlikely to be on the premises should also be noted as a potential danger signal.

Money

Despite the number of psychotherapists who hate to acknowledge it, psychotherapy is a business: One individual provides a service to another individual, couple, or family, for a fee. Whether that fee comes directly out of the pocket of the client or is paid by an insurance company or a government agency, the psychotherapist is compensated for services provided. As soon as the psychotherapist stops collecting financial compensation, the dynamics in the relationship shift, and the client is at risk for being pressured—overtly or covertly—to compensate the psychotherapist in some other manner. It is also important that a therapist not accept expensive gifts or numerous gifts from a client.

Clothing

When a therapist changes the style of clothing worn when seeing one client from the type of clothing worn with other clients, it is a sign the relationship has begun to move into the realm of therapeutic decay. An example of this is the therapist who decides how to dress on a particular day on the basis of what clients are scheduled for sessions that day. A psychotherapist who chooses not to set a limit with a client who is wearing overly revealing or sexually provocative clothing to sessions is equally at risk for jeopardizing the therapeutic relationship. A therapist who removes any item of clothing—including jewelry and shoes, or even loosening a tie—during a therapy session may contribute to boundary confusion for the client and may unwittingly undermine that client's sense of safety.

Language

When a therapist and client begin to engage in sexually suggestive jokes or eroticized language, then psychotherapy has begun to digress. When the therapist becomes sexually stimulated by a client's description of sexual behaviors or thoughts but fails to set limits, there is reason to suspect some underlying dysfunction in the therapeutic relationship. Because so much of everyday jargon and so many of the commonplace jokes that are exchanged within Western culture involve sexual innuendo, however, routine communication is vulnerable to sexual undertones. This danger may be particularly acute for practitioners who subscribe to traditional values regarding gender definitions and divisions.

It is always a danger signal if a therapist refers to a client by a pet name. Context and the manner of delivery determine whether a therapist's comments about a client's attractiveness and remarks about a client's body are therapeutically appropriate or alarm signals for erotic countertransference. The therapist who sexually or romantically fantasizes about a client during or after sessions—whether masturbating to these thoughts or not—is at high risk for entering the realm of a boundary violation.

Self-Disclosure

A therapist who discloses current personal information to a client to solicit advice or to get relief from personal emotional problems is violating the therapeutic contract by reversing the role in the psychotherapist–client relationship. Self-disclosure should always focus on already resolved problems. The therapist who begins to discuss current problems with a client must be attentive to what motivations underlie such self-disclosures. The blurring of roles in one area can be the precursor that allows for easier slippage of roles in another aspect of the relationship.

A related concern is the therapist who fails to engage in appropriate levels of self-disclosure within supervisory settings, who avoids supervision completely, or who overlooks consultation for selected clients. For example, the therapist who determines not to bring a client to supervision or consultation because "others would not understand this client as I do" is positioning himself for an accident waiting to happen.

Place

Differences in psychotherapeutic ideologies make violations in this category complex to determine. Gutheil and Gabbard (1993) illustrated this point when they wrote, "It would not be a boundary violation for a behaviorist, under certain circumstances, to accompany a patient in a car, to an elevator, to an airplane, or even to a public rest room [in the treatment of paruresis, the fear of urinating in a public rest room]" (p. 192). It likely would be a boundary violation, however, for a treatment provider who uses psychoanalysis to attempt to treat a patient in these same settings.

In general, transacting therapy activities in nontraditional settings is reason for concern. For example, meeting clients for coffee, meals, or other forms of socialization can easily lead to confusion in the therapeutic relationship. A therapist who has prior awareness that his personal life overlaps with that of a client should negotiate *in advance* the boundaries and ground rules that will govern their contact outside the therapy setting. Unplanned contact should be responded to conservatively, with utmost respect for the therapeutic dimension of the relationship and from a stance that the therapy relationship must *always* be given priority over social protocols.

Simon (1989) noted a progression in changes of place with psychotherapists who became sexual with their clients: First, they met outside the office, then at an establishment that served alcoholic beverages. Then an evening meal was shared. At subsequent meetings, they went to a movie or a social event, and finally there was sexual intercourse.

It is equally important to establish a therapeutic environment for the physical setting within which therapy sessions are conducted. The office that is furnished in an unbusinesslike manner or has a too-intimate atmosphere may be an incubator for an erotic transgression.

Physical Contact

Ethical therapeutic interventions involving touch are generated from a stance of conscious awareness. Any physical contact that is employed during therapy without a clear and intentional purpose must be viewed with suspicion. The therapist who makes physical contact with a client randomly or impulsively is unlikely to be operating from a truly ethical motivation. Physical contact that is not fully conscious in its formulation may insidiously undermine the clarity of boundaries that is essential to the therapeutic relationship.

Although we do seek to promote clarity, we do not support the rigidity that Gutheil and Gabbard (1993) advocated when they offered the following commentary to illustrate problematic behavior concerning the issue of physical contact.

> From the view point of current risk-management principles, a handshake is about the limit of social physical contact at this time. Of course a patient who attempts a hug in the last session after 7 years of intense, intensive, and successful therapy should probably not be hurled across the room. (p. 195)

Although we urge all practitioners to be respectful of the delicate and volatile implications when using physical contact in therapy, we believe that problematic behaviors will inherently be avoided if such interventions are initiated with a conscious awareness to context and intentionality.

Inappropriate Therapeutic Relationships
That Can Lead to Inappropriate Touch

On the basis of existing literature (Schoener & Gonsiorek, 1988; Schoener, Milrom, Luepker, & Conroe, 1989), nine common types of inappropriate psychotherapeutic relationships appear to create an increased risk for inappropriate touch between therapist and client.

Sexual Touch as Therapy. The therapist determines that the client's presenting problem is the result of sexual inhibitions and prescribes sexual contact with the therapist as the treatment of choice.

Using Therapy as a Container Within Which to Help a Client Learn How to Love. The therapist tells the client that the term *transference* refers to the ability of the client to learn to become a mature loving person by transferring affection and love onto the therapist. A detailed example of this thinking can be found in McCartney (1966). He wrote,

> Psychoanalysis is an attempt to help the patient gain insight into psychosexual development, and to gain full adult hetero-sexuality. In order to gain this emotional maturity, the patient must find an active relationship in the living presence, for without this reality relationship, the patient can never ade-quately fulfill the demands that adaptation requires and the patient will therefore remain in a life of phantasy. The therapist, thus being a vessel of expression, cannot put restraints upon the patient that would appear to be demanded by moral and social standards. (p. 234)

Dr. McCartney reported that a high percentage of his female clients found it "necessary" to engage in sexual contact with him as a part of their treatment. He termed this dynamic *overt transference* and placed the responsibility for the behavior squarely on the shoulders of his clients. In his words,

> Of the adult women in analysis, 30 per cent expressed some form of Overt Transference, such as sitting on the analyst's lap, holding his hand, hugging or kissing him. About 10 per cent found it necessary to act-out extremely, such as mutual undress-ing, genital manipulation or coitus. (p. 236)

He not only believed his behavior was appropriate but claimed that the majority of his patients benefited, when he concluded, "For the last twenty years, I have allowed full overt expression. Of the female pa-tients who underwent psychoanalytic therapy about 75 per cent made good adjustments" (p. 236).

Closeness Between Same-Gender Persons Is "Different." The therapist tells the client that unlike sexual contact between men and women, sexual contact between people of the same gender is not exploitive.

Exploring Sexual Identity. Examples of this category include the therapist who attempts to "cure" a client of homosexuality by engaging in sexual contact with that client and the therapist who helps a client to "come out" as a gay man by initiating sexual contact with him. The same can be said for the therapist who engages in sexual conduct with a young and inexperienced client with the justification that he is initiating that client into the sexual world by providing a "rite of passage" experience within the safety of a therapeutic relationship.

The Fatal Attraction. The therapist and client develop an intense sexual relationship from the initial session. This leads to stormy encounters and blackmail by the client, who threatens to destroy the reputation of the therapist if the relationship is ended.

Romance. The therapist and client insist that they have fallen in love. Some of these relationships result in marriage. We can think of no circumstance in which a romantic relationship is valid or healthy if any prior therapist–client relationship has existed. Although licensing boards excuse, professional organizations ignore, and colleagues forgive such transgressions, we believe that tolerance of such behavior within the field of mental health is one of the contributing factors that undermine credibility about the possibility that touch can be employed in ethical ways by psychotherapists.

Brief Loss of Control. The therapist—due to situational circumstances—initiates or accepts sexual contact with a client.

Bonding. The therapist tells the client that the presenting problems require the use of regressive techniques for that client to be "reparented." Unfortunately, the reparenting also involves sexual contact, which clearly constitutes an incest dynamic.

Nurturance. Nurturance is similar to the previously noted bonding relationship, except the sexual contact is presented as a form of nurturing for the client's benefit. An example is the client who was encouraged to take part in mock breast-feeding with the therapist.

▓ Clinical Considerations Regarding Erotic Issues as a Variable in Psychotherapy

Two tenets create the basic foundations of our framework for discussing this issue. First is our clear stance that nonerotic touch is a category of physical contact distinct from erotic touch. We do not adhere to traditional views that consider these types of touch as synonymous. Second, we perceive a distinct and defined difference between the dynamics of erotic transference/countertransference and actual behaviors that constitute erotic touch. We believe that the clinical dynamics of transference and countertransference are responded to in different ways than are considerations of specific behaviors.

Legal and professional codes of ethical conduct tend to define erotic touch both by intent and by specific acts. Holroyd and Brodsky's (1977) definition of erotic touch focused on the intent to arouse or satisfy sexual desire. The Minnesota State Legislature (Statute 148A, 1986) defines sexual contact as sexual intercourse; cunnilingus; fellatio; anal intercourse; any intrusion, however slight, into the genital or anal openings of the person's body; or kissing of the genital area, groin, inner thigh, buttock, breast, or of the clothing covering any of these body parts. Requests for this type of activity are also considered sexual contact (Bisbing, Jorgenson, & Sutherland, 1995). Most other states define sexual contact in nearly the same language (e.g., Georgia Statute 16-6-5.1, 1994). For an in-depth examination of the legal issues related to mental and pastoral counseling, see Bisging, Jorgenson, and Sutherland (1995).

The erotic spectrum on the touch continuum is characterized by a transition from emotional to overtly sexual energy. The dynamics of eroticism range from a faint emotional stirring, moving further toward more defined sensual/sexual feelings, onward toward powerful sexual fantasies, and eventually leading to overpowering urges to satisfy seemingly uncontained sexual feelings. It is essential to identify *in advance* some of the warning signals to which the ethical psychotherapist must be alert.

The issue of erotic transference and countertransference within the setting of psychotherapy is not as simple as "Don't allow it to happen." What makes the process of psychotherapy so complicated is the reality that successfully achieving intimacy within the context of a therapist–client relationship may naturally elicit some level of erotic feelings for either therapist and client and that those feelings—when dealt with in a clinically responsible and ethically contained manner—can actually facilitate, rather than impede, the therapeutic process. In other words, the experienced clinician accepts that clients sometimes fall in love with their therapist and that psychotherapists are real human beings who can sometimes develop a particular fondness toward a client (Freud, 1915/1983). Taylor and Wagner (1976) noted, "It is not uncommon for the therapist and client to develop feelings of sexual attraction and to have sexual fantasies about the other" (p. 593). Dujovne (1983) also viewed erotic energy as "fairly common products of therapy" (p. 242) and explained its existence by noting, "The sex act is the prototype of intimacy, a physical, bodily interaction that lends itself to the expression of early emotional issues which precede genital development" (p. 246).

From this perspective, it is important that any psychotherapist who seeks to use touch with clients develop a working command that allows him to address this energy in ways that are appropriate and ethical. Just as nonerotic touch need not lead to erotic touch, the existence of erotic energy within the therapeutic relationship does not necessarily lead to sexual contact between the individuals. The presence of erotic energy may be a metaphor for nonsexual issues. It is the therapist's (and client's) misunderstanding of this dynamic that can lead to inappropriate physical contact between therapist and client. Regardless of a client's desire for sexual contact, a therapist must not be available to the client for such an act, just as it would be inappropriate for a therapist to permit acts of violence from a client merely because the client strongly desired to be aggressive (Dujovne, 1983).

Transference and Countertransference

Understanding the complexities of erotic transference and counter-transference requires that the therapist first have a basic comprehension of the dynamics of transference and countertransference. Wilson and Lindy (1994) offered the following definition of transference: "The process and behaviors by which a client relates to the therapist in a manner similar to that in past relationships with significant others" (p. 27). In essence, the client engages current-day figures in historically significant emotional experiences. As the client attempts to make sense of his strong feelings within the context of his here-and-now experience, he usually focuses the area of greatest conflict and meaning on the therapist as the apparent cause for this emotional energy.

Transference is characteristically an unconscious process, although the client probably has some degree of conscious awareness of his intense emotions. Generally, the client is less alert to his historical context, which is the more probable source of this relational transference. Most experienced psychotherapists realize that the necessary therapeutic task in this situation is to facilitate the client's process toward making the unconscious conscious.

Countertransference originally emerged as a clinical construct in writings by Freud (1915/1983). A more contemporary definition of countertransference, provided by Pearlman and Saakvitne (1995), has relevance to our discussion of erotic touch:

> Our definition of countertransference includes two components: (1) the affective, ideational, and physical responses a therapist has to her client, his clinical material, transference, and reenactments, and (2) the therapist's conscious and unconscious defenses against the affects, intrapsychic conflicts, and associations aroused by the former. All of a client's responses and our responses to the client arise in the context of our role and professional identity as therapist, the unique nature of the therapeutic relationship, and our own personal histories. (p. 23)

As with transference, countertransference often operates at the unconscious level. Therefore, the ethical psychotherapist will maintain supervisory relationships and develop personal strategies that facilitate him to bring unconscious material into conscious awareness.

We do not subscribe to theoretical orientations that define transference within the paradigm of client resistance, nor do we believe that countertransference is indicative of therapist incompetence or misjudgment. To the contrary, transference and countertransference are inherently present in all human transactions and, therefore, they are natural and expected within any therapeutic relationship. Furthermore, we believe that dealing with these complexities openly and directly—particularly when touch has become a consideration in the therapist–client relationship—is one of the most prudent strategies to ensure that the psychotherapy remains ethical. Our stance is articulately expressed by Pearlman and Saakvitne (1995): "The therapist and client's willingness to notice and name their interpersonal experience allows the transformative work with transference and countertransference dynamics in these therapies" (p. 119).

In other words, it is not necessary—and probably not possible—to avoid or eliminate erotic transference and countertransference with the therapeutic relationship. Rather, the ethical psychotherapist should seek to deepen his acceptance and understanding of the clinical dynamics of this issue for him to competently manage his client's and his own erotic feelings within the boundaries of therapeutic safety and containment. Our goal should be not to create barricades that preclude erotic energy from emerging within the context of the therapeutic relationship but instead to strive to construct safety nets that permit it to unfold in natural ways within appropriate boundaries in which the psychotherapist and client can therapeutically identify, understand, and redirect it.

Unfortunately, professionals too often approach their discussion—or nondiscussion—of this issue from a position of fear. All too frequently, considerations of this issue are approached with an overtone of judgment. For example, Dujovne (1983) commented that a heightened level of concern about sexual intimacies between therapists and clients has resulted from the emergence of "new therapies which endorse physical contact" (p. 242). To the contrary, there is no evidence to support the claim that sexual misconduct occurs because of nonerotic touch. In 1982, the Board of Professional Affairs of the American Psychological Association adopted the following statement regarding physical contact between psychologists and clients: "Permissible physical touching is defined as that conduct which is based upon the exercise of professional judgment and which, implicitly, comports with accepted standards of professional conduct" (quoted in Goodman & Teicher, 1988, p. 492). Holroyd and Brodsky's (1980) research on 375 male psychotherapists and 310 female psychotherapists reported two important findings: First, touching per se did not lead to erotic contact with clients, particularly with older and/or more experienced psychotherapists; second, those who were at risk for becoming sexually involved with clients were those therapists who had gender-restricted touch policies—meaning that they touched one gender but not the other.

In actual clinical practice, a great deal of touch occurs that is appropriate and never leads to seduction or misconduct. In this era, however, practicing psychotherapists must increasingly negotiate through the maze of prescribed treatment approaches and preauthorized clinical interventions. Within the ever-expanding milieu of managed care, ethical standards in the field of mental health are being redefined according to predetermined behavioral criteria that have little relation to therapist–client rapport. Establishing an actual therapeutic relationship, in which transference and countertransference will expectedly emerge, is increasingly defined as counterproductive within the paradigm of managed care. Lipton (1977) offered the following comment that seems quite relevant to this growing trend: "We have moved from a time when a therapist's technique was judged according to purpose, to one where the therapist is judged only by the behavior itself" (p. 332). This antiseptic and bureaucratic approach benefits from maintaining the myth that all touch falls within the dangerous zone of erotic touch. We believe that these emerging trends are antithetical to the advancement of solid psychotherapy.

If we accept the premise that transference is a natural and expected client response, we can then benefit from exploring those formations of client transference that might be predicted. Within the context of touch being present in the therapeutic relationship, any of the following transference themes may emerge.

The Therapist as Perpetrator

Perpetrator transference may emerge with the client who has been erotically abused at some previous time during his life. Because such physical violation probably occurred within the context of an abuse of power or authority, the client may have intense feelings about the inherent power differential that accompanies the structure of the therapist–client relationship.

The Therapist as Nurturant Figure

This type of transference may emerge with the client who has never learned to distinguish intimacy from eroticism or with the client for whom the primary sources of nurturance throughout his life have been linked to erotic contact. Furthermore, sexuality and aggression are likely to have become merged for the client whose early exposure to sexuality involved exploitation and pain. Such a client may describe feelings of emotional or physical pain as the therapeutic relationship becomes increasingly nurturant, or the client may exhibit responses that are sadistic in nature as the therapist attempts to reach out with interventions that have a nurturing quality.

The Therapist as an Ideal Figure

This transference may emerge with the client for whom the therapist becomes such an intensely idealized figure that the client seeks to merge or fuse with him to become like the therapist. This is the same type of energy that frequently exists during intensely passionate moments when two lovers experience the desire to become like one.

The Therapist as the "Good" Partner

This type of transference may emerge during couples therapy. It involves the dynamics of triangulation and/or splitting, in which the client begins to perceive the therapist as a more desirable mate than his current partner.

The Therapist as the Object of Developmental Transference

Developmental transference may emerge at various times and with contrasting presentations as the client moves through the developmental stages that accompany the normal process of growth and maturity. For example, the client who embraces his adolescent energy may develop a "crush" on his therapist, or the client who gains access to midlife feelings of loneliness or alienation may seek to bond with the therapist in ways that can diminish his painful feelings.

Developmental transference is affected by the same types of variables that are present in the process of socialization within the larger culture. Consequently, it is not unusual for a client to struggle with homophobia if he experiences feelings of intimacy with a same-sex therapist or to exhibit sexist prejudices in an other-gender therapeutic relationship.

Assessing whether a client's response is transference based may not always be directly obvious. Frequently, transference is revealed only through close attention to context. The observant therapist tracks the ways in which a client responds to issues and interactions that occur as the therapeutic relationship evolves. In this way, he can become acutely sensitive to unique or unfamiliar client responses, which are generally clues to the development of transference.

A clinical dilemma commonly emerges when working with survivors of childhood abuse and neglect, for whom early attachments existed within a context of interpersonal trauma. These clients often exhibit transference double binds in which the positive aspects of relatedness are accompanied by pain. Because so many clients who seek therapy have experienced some form of attachment trauma (as children or as adults), this clinical phenomenon is extremely relevant to practitioners who use touch within the therapeutic relationship.

> [Waites, 1993] identifies four classic double bind frameworks in which the transference develops: (1) contact is necessary for survival/contact is dangerous, (2) attachment is desirable/attachment is disappointing, (3) attachment is pleasurable/love means hurting, and (4) attachment is good/love means total surrender. These early templates for attachment and dependence are often at the root of the intense conflicts evoked by the invitation to intimacy in the therapeutic relationship. (Pearlman & Saakvitne, 1995, p. 103)

In a stance similar to ours on transference, we subscribe to the premise that countertransference is a natural and expected part of the therapist's experience. Therefore, we can also benefit from elaborating the primary formations of countertransference that can be predicted for those therapeutic relationships in which touch is an active variable.

Perpetrator Countertransference

Because most therapists engage with their clients from a stance of altruism and genuine caring, it can be exceedingly difficult to withstand perpetrator transference from a client. It is common for this type of countertransference to be exhibited through therapist responses that include anger, defensiveness, distancing, or feeling personally hurt that the client fails to notice the ways he is trying to be empathic and helpful. The dynamics of the therapeutic relationship reflect more distinct overtones of attack and seizure when the client has learned to eroticize fear and/or pain. In such circumstances, countertransference may emerge in therapist responses that are more punitive, self-protective, or acting out in their tone. Therapists must be alert to notice transference themes in which the client is developing feelings of being special to the therapist, as this may be a precursor to the emergence of a perpetrator transference. The use of touch during such times is inappropriate.

Victim Countertransference

A high level of stress in a therapist's personal or professional life or an intense or sustained atmosphere in which the therapist is under siege by one or several clients can leave the therapist feeling victimized. In such situations, the therapist may increasingly demonstrate appeasement-based behaviors, in which he finds himself capitulating to client demands, especially demands for a clear demonstration of caring. The therapist may feel coerced into abandoning therapeutic boundaries, or he may find himself negotiating boundaries and ground rules to a degree that he recognizes as counterproductive. It is not uncommon for a therapist who encounters victim countertransference to be experiencing a more global existential dilemma involving a loss of confidence in his abilities as a therapist.

The emergence of victim countertransference within the context of physical contact between therapist and client is extremely dangerous. Such circumstances are ripe for a therapist to misjudge the level of self-disclosure that is appropriate or to minimize the negative impact of revealing personal shortcomings. Therapists must attend to the ever-present tasks of maintaining solid supervisory relationships and to sustaining a healthy quality of life that includes significant relationships outside the therapy environment.

Authoritarian Countertransference

This type of countertransference may emerge in response to transference in which the therapist is experienced as either a nurturant or an idealized figure or when the therapist has become the transference object of the client's developmental dynamics. As the therapist seeks to reparent the client or to help him overcome the injuries from his childhood, caution must be exercised that the client does not become so important that the professional boundaries inherent to the therapist–client relationship become diluted.

The therapist who operates from a godlike stance may eroticize a client's repeated expressions of adoration, especially if that therapist's sexual fantasies or practices condone the linkage of power and sex. The therapist who comes to feel a deep sense of mutual love and caring with a client must also exercise caution to ensure that the intensity of that relationship stays within the confines of the prescribed therapeutic roles, making the use of touch inappropriate.

Therapist as Client Countertransference

Providing clinical services to clients can be extremely taxing when a therapist is experiencing emotional distress in his own life or when a client's issues too closely parallel the personal issues with which the therapist is grappling. Every therapist encounters periods in his life in which it feels like a difficult stretch to sustain his energy and attention for the clinical service of his clients. Under such circumstances, it is possible that the therapist may begin to wish (consciously or unconsciously) to be healed or helped by the client. Or the therapist may seek to resolve his own issues and feelings vicariously through the client's work in therapy.

A therapist should be alert to this countertransference if he finds himself encouraging the client to give him positive feedback, if self-disclosure is prompted by his own need to share content with a client rather than for a defined therapeutic purpose, or if he finds himself anticipating opportunities for physical contact with a client. A therapist's lapse in judgment about maintaining his role as the helper is a dangerous precursor for the occurrence of an inappropriate and unethical reversal of roles.

Sexual and Voyeuristic Countertransference

It is undeniable that some client material can become acutely provocative or that some clients may deliver content in a way that is intentionally seductive. In such cases, it may be hard for the therapist to contain his own sense of arousal. The therapist may find himself having frequent nighttime dreams involving a client or having sexualized daydreams or fantasies about a client. The therapist who is unprepared for such intense emotional and/or physiological responses may experience considerable embarrassment, shame, anxiety, and discomfort. Consequently, the therapist may be inclined to isolate himself from supervisory contact at just the time when collegial support is most necessary. The therapist who is experiencing intimacy deficits in his own life is at greater risk for entering into a danger zone with a client whom he perceives as particularly attractive.

* * *

As we have stated previously, we do not believe that countertransference reflects a defect or disturbance in the therapeutic relationship. To the contrary, countertransference can provide invaluable clinical information and can be useful in helping the therapist form effective therapeutic interventions. Within the context of erotic touch, however, the effective use of countertransference requires that the therapist must be able to identify it without shame. Once countertransference has been identified and labeled by the therapist, the task at hand becomes how to work with this dynamic in a way that is clinically appropriate.

Because 95% of male and 76% of female psychologists in private practice report that they have experienced sexual attraction to at least one client and yet 91% of males and 98% of females do not go on to have sexual contact with clients (Pope et al., 1986), one might think that it would be safe to state that thinking about having sex with a client and actually having sex with a client are distinct things. Yet the helping professions behave as if to have the thought is to have done the deed. More than half (63%) of psychologists report that they felt guilty, anxious, or confused about having been attracted to a client. Although some literature does address the topic of erotic countertransference (Schoener & Gonsiorek, 1989), more attention should be devoted to this issue in clinical training programs and continuing education forums. Furthermore, practitioners would be well served if more supervisors promoted the preventive aspect of their role by fostering a safe environment in which supervisees were encouraged to explore issues of erotic transference and countertransference.

Therapists are generally undertrained and ill prepared to deal with their own erotic feelings and responses. We cannot emphasize strongly enough the need for continuing supervision as a safety net for working with erotic countertransference from its earliest stage of formation. Unfortunately, many therapists seek consultation only in an emergency, after their countertransference has evolved to an alarming magnitude.

Clinical Presentations Exhibited by Clients That Indicate the Emergence of Erotic Transference

A number of clinical presentations, if they emerge for a client during therapy, should alert the therapist to an increased likelihood that erotic transference is developing. Dujovne (1983) suggested that it is helpful for the psychotherapist to understand erotic presentations within the framework of metaphor, thereby allowing the skilled clinician to address the underlying dynamic and assisting the client in circumventing the need to act out the sexual theme of the metaphor. In other words, the therapist is responsible for helping the client identify the historical material underlying the sense of literalness that accompanies the transference.

Numerous client-based erotic presentations may need to be dealt with during the therapeutic relationship. We will briefly examine some of those that are commonly seen in clinical settings.

Acceptance

By desiring sexual contact with the therapist, the client is seeking a signal of acceptance. The underlying thinking is, "If you will have sex with me, then you must think I am an acceptable person." In such cases, the psychotherapist can best serve the client by demonstrating other nonsexual forms of acceptance and instructing the client on methods of gaining or recognizing acceptance from others outside the therapeutic relationship.

Rejection

On the other extreme, the expression of sexual interest from a client may be sending the signal that the client is rejecting the psychotherapist as an agent of change; in other words, "If you are my sex partner, you can't function as my psychotherapist." In such an instance, the skilled psychotherapist can make this covert message more overt, thereby taking the discussion out of the sexual arena and putting the focus on the client's fear and anger about the psychotherapist's role.

Becoming the Special Client

In this case, the erotic energy is a result of the client's interest in being special, not "just another client." Sexual contact is viewed as proof of this special status. With such a client, the psychotherapist's task is to discuss the client's urge to be different from others and the role this desire to be unique has in his other relationships.

Testing the Therapist

The client may test the trustworthiness of the therapeutic boundaries by tempting the psychotherapist with the promise of sexual favors. It is the responsibility of the psychotherapist to pass this ethics test by maintaining appropriate limits and by exploring with the client how other relationships in the past may not have been safe.

Self-Image Problem

Some clients, particularly those who were sexually abused early in life, come to view themselves as nothing more than sex objects. When they enter into relationships as adults, even therapeutic relationships, they believe that all they have to offer other people are sexual favors. The psychotherapist's task is to facilitate these clients in the process of identifying personal attributes other than the body and/or sexual performance.

Repetition Compulsion

This dynamic is also frequently found in the client with an early history of sexual abuse. The client unconsciously re-creates the sexual abuse dynamic within the psychotherapy relationship. The psychotherapist can best serve this client by noting the similarities to the past while also pointing out the important differences between the present and the past.

Fear of Being Alone

The client who cannot tolerate being separated from others will sometimes sexualize that terror of isolation and see sex as a way to fuse with the therapist. The therapeutic task with this client is to help him develop a support system with others and to teach techniques for the containment of anxiety and loneliness.

Envy

Dujovne (1993) described this dynamic as follows:

The contrast between the client's experienced badness and the therapist's goodness may become so intolerable that the client becomes envious and attempts to correct the apparent imbalance via sexual acting out. When envy is at work the attempt is at corrupting, degrading, and making the therapist worthless. (p. 247)

This sexualized shame/rage response by the client may be difficult for the psychotherapist to respond to without lashing out. Therefore, in such cases, the use of consultation with colleagues is strongly recommended. Once the psychotherapist is confident he will not respond in an inappropriate manner, he can interpret the client's erotic expression as a shame response worthy of being carefully examined.

A Sign of the Client's Increased Maturity

Of all the client-based themes, this is the most hopeful clinical area to deal with because it is, in effect, an outcome of the client's becoming a more mature adult who is now able to fantasize about another mature, well-adjusted adult—the psychotherapist—as the type of person who would make a good sexual partner. In no way, however, does the increased maturity level make sexual contact between the therapist and this client any more appropriate than it is for the client who exhibits the other forms of erotic energy.

We acknowledge that it is sometimes difficult to distinguish whether a sexual innuendo or overture genuinely represents increased maturity or if it is more accurately another type of transference response. Unfortunately, there is no simple answer to this dilemma, nor is there any generic formula by which to decode this level of a client's message. As a general guideline, however, the therapist has the best chance to decipher this dynamic by attending to context. It is to be expected that sexual feelings may begin to emerge for a client as the therapy experience facilitates his movement through life developmental stages, while corresponding progress with maturation predicts that he would internalize an accompanying ability to distinguish the inappropriateness of acting out sexual feelings when they involve the therapist. In other words, viewing maturity as a process allows the therapist to evaluate the meaning of a client's response in relationship to the context of previous behavior: Erotic behavior that is more regressive in its quality or direction is more suggestive of transference dynamics than reflective of an increase in maturity.

▨ Conclusions and Recommendations

We suggest that therapists incorporate into the intake and assessment stage of therapy a standard procedure whereby it is directly stated to clients that under no circumstances will erotic touch be a part of the therapeutic relationship. This statement should be communicated in a language and a manner that can be understood and retained by the client. For example, merely stating that no unethical touch will take place or that boundaries will be maintained may not be clear to a client who is not already familiar with ethical codes or those terms. Rather, it is more useful to use a phrase such as "I never have any sexual contact with any of my clients for any reason. I assume complete responsibility to maintain this boundary." Stating the prohibition against erotic and other forms of inappropriate touch at the formation of the relationship facilitates the client's sense of safety and ought to be restated later in the therapy process if the use of touch is being considered. It is often useful to provide clients with a written set of guidelines to clarify this and other issues that define the boundaries of the therapy relationship (e.g., a comprehensive set of guidelines might also address confidentiality, client responsibilities, therapist responsibilities, fees, attendance at appointments, legal concerns, and therapist availability between sessions).

Practicing psychotherapists will never be able to handle issues related to erotic transference and countertransference in a mature and responsible manner if there continues to be a vacuum about this topic in clinical training programs and continued education forums. Although common sexual attraction to clients is stressful for therapists—and particularly for graduate students and interns (Rodolfa, Kraft, & Reilley, 1987)—only 9% of the psychologists surveyed thought that their training was adequate concerning the clinical issue of how to cope with sexual attraction in a therapeutic relationship. More than half (55%) the respondents had no training at all on the issue (Pope et al., 1986). As Pope noted,

> The long-standing absence of systematic research on this topic might well give the impression that psychologists—unlike other human beings—are incapable of experiencing sexual attraction to those they serve, or that the phenomenon is at most a strange and regrettable aberration, limited mostly to those relative few who engage in sexual intimacies with their clients. (p. 155)

▓ Summary

In this chapter, we have attempted to promote an open discussion of issues related to erotic dynamics in psychotherapy. We suggested that such discussions must occur more frequently within professional settings for mental health providers. Our position is that rigid taboos that discourage the discussions of issues related to erotic transference and countertransference will do little to improve the field of psychotherapy.

Appendix 13.1
Prohibitions to Erotic Contact in Professional Codes

■ American Association for Counseling and Development

In the counseling relationship, the counselor is aware of the intimacy of the relationship and maintains respect for the client and avoids engaging in activities that seek to meet the counselor's personal needs at the expense of that client.

Members do not condone or engage in sexual harassment which is defined as deliberate or repeated comments, gestures, or physical contacts of a sexual nature.
(From *Ethical Standards* in Gorlin, 1986, p. 226)

The member will avoid any type of sexual intimacies with clients. Sexual relationships with clients are unethical.
(From *Ethical Standards* in Gorlin, 1986, p. 228)

■ American Association for Marriage and Family Therapists

Marriage and family therapists maintain high standards of professional competence and integrity.

Marriage and family therapists do not engage in sexual or other harassment or exploitation of clients, students, trainees, supervisees, employees, colleagues, research subjects, or actual or potential witnesses or complainants in investigations and ethical proceedings.

> (American Association for Marriage
> and Family Therapy, *A.A.M.F.T. Code
> of Ethics*, 1991, Sec. 3, 3.5, pp. 4-5)

▨ American Group Psychotherapy Association

The group psychotherapist acts to safeguard the patient/client and the public from the incompetent, unethical, illegal practice of any group psychotherapist.

Sexual intimacy with patients/clients is unethical.
> (American Group Psychotherapy Association,
> *Guidelines of Group Psychotherapy Practice*,
> 1991, Sec. 3, 3.3, p. 3)

▨ American Psychiatric Association

The requirement that the physician conduct himself or herself with propriety in his/her profession and in all the actions of his/her life is especially important in the case of the psychiatrist because the patient tends to model his/her behavior after that of his/her therapist by identification. Further, the necessary intensity of the therapeutic relationship may tend to activate sexual and other needs and fantasies on the part of both patient and therapist, while weakening the objectivity necessary for control. Sexual activity with a patient is unethical.

> (*Principles of Medical Ethics With Annotations Especially
> Applicable to Psychiatry*, in Gorlin, 1986, p. 240)

▪ American Psychological Association

Sexual Intimacies With Current Patients or Clients

Psychologists do not engage in sexual intimacies with current patients or clients.
(American Psychological Association, 1992, p. 1605)

Therapy With Former Sexual Partners

Psychologists do not accept as therapy patients or clients persons with whom they have engaged in sexual intimacies.
(American Psychological Association, 1992, p. 1605)

Sexual Intimacies With Former Therapy Patients

Psychologists do not engage in sexual intimacies with a former therapy patient or client for at least two years after cessation or termination of professional services.
(American Psychological Association, 1992, p. 1605)

▪ National Association of Social Workers

The Social Worker's Ethical Responsibility to Clients

The social worker should avoid relationships or commitments that conflict with the interests of clients.

The social worker should under no circumstances engage in sexual activities with clients.
(National Association of Social Workers,
Code of Ethics, 1979, Sec. II.4-5, pp. 4-5)

Chapter 14

Examining Personal Views on the Use of Touch in Psychotherapy

In earlier chapters, we examined factors to consider prior to using touch in psychotherapy. Now that you have read the remainder of the chapters, we again return to that topic. In this chapter, we will ask you to individualize the material by evaluating how your personal and professional experiences with touch have affected your view of the use of touch in psychotherapy. Knowledge of yourself and your internal process is vital when making ethical decisions.

▪ Actions That Could Be Misinterpreted by a Client

One of the objections to the use of touch in psychotherapy is the fear that the client may misinterpret the meaning of the touch. You will now be asked to imagine how a client may misinterpret various actions within the psychotherapy setting. Developing the ability to imagine the therapeutic setting from the client's viewpoint increases the psychotherapist's ability to be empathic and to address transference and countertransference dynamics as they occur. Please read the statements below and determine for each the following:

1. Is there a possibility of a therapist's ethical intent being misinterpreted?
2. If there is a possibility of misinterpretation, what is the probability that a misinterpretation will take place? In other words, how likely is it that the client will negatively respond?
3. In your assessment, what is the most likely misinterpretation that would take place?
4. If such a misinterpretation took place, what action, if any, would you take?

The therapist hugs the client.
The therapist holds the client.
The therapist places an arm around the client's shoulder.
The therapist places a hand on the client's shoulder.
The therapist offers the client a stuffed animal (e.g., a teddy bear).
The therapist discloses to the client that the therapist is gay, lesbian, or bisexual.
The therapist discloses having been a psychotherapy client in the past.
The client witnesses the therapist hug another client.
The therapist glances at the clock while engaged in some type of touch with the client.
The client asks the meaning of the diagnostic code number on the bill, and the therapist tells the client the diagnostic term that the number represents.

After examining each of these situations, what have you learned that will be of use as a psychotherapist?

▓ Examining Personal Experiences

Reflection on how a client's history is affecting presenting situations is common in psychotherapy. In this section, however, you will be asked to examine how *your* individual history has shaped your view of touch. In Chapters 6, 8, and 13, the concept of countertransference was discussed. The reactions of the psychotherapist to the client can be better understood if the psychotherapist has examined the personal impact of early life experiences. Some of the questions are of a personal nature and may trigger unpleasant memories. It is important that these triggers be identified, however, to reduce their impact within the therapeutic relationship.

1. In your childhood, how were you touched?

2. As a child, were you ever pressured by your family to hug, kiss, or otherwise touch someone with whom you did not wish to have physical contact? (e.g., "Here, meet your Grandpa for the very first time. Go give him a kiss.") How did this experience affect your view of touch?

3. In your family of origin, did touch between you and your parent(s) drop off when you reached puberty? If so, how did this experience affect your view of touch?

4. As an *adult*, were you ever pressured by your partner or family to hug, kiss, or otherwise touch someone with whom you did not wish to have physical contact? How did this experience affect your view of touch?

5. What is your most pleasant memory related to touch as a child? As an adolescent? As an adult? How do these experiences affect your use of touch with clients?

6. What is your most *un*pleasant memory related to touch as a child? As an adolescent? As an adult? How do these experiences affect your use of touch with clients?

7. At what age do you think it is inappropriate for a daughter to kiss her father? Her mother?

8. At what age do you think it is inappropriate for a son to kiss his father? His mother?

9. How does your history of touch within your family of origin affect your use of touch in relationship with your
   Romantic partner
   Friends
   Coworkers
   People you are meeting for the first time
   Clients

10. Have you ever been touched, appropriately or inappropriately, by the following authority figures? If so, how did that experience affect you? If they did not touch you, how did that affect your relationship?
    Elementary schoolteacher
    Coach
    High school teacher
    Religious representative (e.g., minister, priest, rabbi, deacon, or organist)
    Camp counselor
    College professor
    Graduate school adviser
    Graduate school instructor
    Internship/practicum supervisor
    Clinical supervisor
    Employer

11. Have you ever been in any of the above-listed roles? If so, did you ever use touch while functioning within the authority of that role? If so, was your use of touch appropriate, respectful, and consensual of your own and other people's boundaries, or did you ever engage in touch that was disrespectful, inappropriate, or nonconsensual? How did your experiences of using or not using touch affect you and your relationships?

12. Have you ever been a psychotherapy client? If so, did your therapist(s) make use of touch in your psychotherapy? If you were touched, was the touch appropriate and consensual? How did the use of touch affect your progress on your treatment goals? If touch was not used, how did that affect your progress on your treatment goals? How has your experience as a consumer of psychotherapy services affected your use of touch with your clients?

13. At the next consultation group or staff meeting you attend, be aware of whether the members of that group touch one another. If they do touch one another, how do they touch, what are the reasons they touch, and how does it seem to affect their relationships? What can you determine about the dynamics of this group on the basis of the way touch is used or avoided? What role does touch play in your relationship with these people?

Now that you have taken time to examine your personal history with touch, write a statement that summarizes how your past is affecting your present view of touch.

▪ Clarifying Personal Views: Questions to Consider

In their book on ethics, Corney, Corney, and Callanan (1994) suggested that clinicians consider a number of questions prior to using any technique in psychotherapy. With that material as a foundation, we have formulated the following questions for you to think about carefully before any use of touch in psychotherapy.

1. What criteria do you use to determine if touching a client is likely to be therapeutic?
2. What criteria do you use to determine if touching a client is likely to be countertherapeutic?
3. How would you know if you were touching a client to meet your own needs rather than the client's?
4. What training do you have in the use of touch in psychotherapy? Are you adequately prepared?
5. How would you defend your use of touch in psychotherapy to a licensing board or in a courtroom?
6. How do you feel when a client declines your offer of touch?
7. Do you touch same-gender clients in the same manner, on the same parts of the body, and with the same frequency that you touch other-gender clients? If not, how do you justify this gender-related difference in the treatment of your clients?

8. Does knowledge of a client's affectional/sexual preference change your use of touch with that client? For example, do you have more or less comfort hugging a gay male or lesbian client than hugging a heterosexual client?

9. Have you thought about how you would respond if you found yourself becoming sexually aroused during a touch interaction with a client? Do you trust your ability to think and act clearly if you were in a physical interaction with a client that generated highly charged sexual feelings?

10. How long would you have to work with a client before you would consider the use of touch as a part of the client's treatment?

11. How would you feel touching a client with cancer? With a positive HIV status? With diagnosed AIDS?

12. Are there any diagnostic groups (e.g., depression, anxiety, borderline personality organization, and dissociative identity constellation) that you think ought never to be touched as a part of their psychotherapy? If so, on what do you base your decision?

13. When was the most recent time you touched a client? What factors did you take into account before using touch? What was your goal in using touch? Did you obtain that goal? Given the opportunity, would you change your use of touch with this client in any way? If so, how and what are your reasons?

14. What is the best experience you have had related to the use of touch with a client? Describe what factors played a role in making it a positive event.

15. What is the worst experience you have had related to the use of touch with a client? Describe what factors played a role in making it a negative event.

16. Go to your active client file and make a list of each client. Once you have compiled this list, ask yourself if it would be appropriate to touch each client in the following manner (pay attention to *how* you decide, not merely *what* you decide).

Handshake at the beginning of a session
Handshake at the termination of a session

Handshake at a moment of success in therapy
Handshake at a moment of great sadness or loss
Handshake at the termination of the therapeutic relationship
Hugging at the beginning of a session
Hugging at the termination of a session
Hugging at a moment of success in therapy
Hugging at a moment of great sadness or loss
Hugging at the termination of the therapeutic relationship
Holding at the beginning of a session
Holding at the termination of a session
Holding at a moment of success in therapy
Holding at a moment of great sadness or loss
Holding at the termination of the therapeutic relationship

Now that you have responded to the earlier questions, return to those sections in which you determined touch would not be appropriate. Ask yourself how a client's psychotherapy might be *negatively* affected by *not* receiving these types of touch as an adjunct to psychotherapy.

By completing the previous exercise, you have consciously practiced the process of decision making that has likely taken place subconsciously, or even unconsciously, in the past. The more you are aware of how you decide whether to, or how to, touch a client, the less likely you are to take action impulsively and the less likely you are to make potentially harmful decisions.

▓ Questions to Identify Signs
of Boundary Violations

In Chapter 13, we noted that certain nonerotic behaviors usually precede erotic contact between therapist and client. Be alert for these behaviors in supervisees, coworkers, and yourself to avoid the development of an erotic or a romantic relationship with a client. These problematic behaviors are repeated here so that you can examine your own behavior, and the behavior of others, to be vigilant for signs of boundary confusion that may put the therapeutic relationship at risk, endangering both the client and the psychotherapist.

1. Does the therapist in question have a particular client or clients who are usually scheduled at the end of a workday or when other staff are unlikely to be in the area?

2. Does the therapist in question frequently allow sessions to extend 10 minutes or more beyond the scheduled end?

3. Does the therapist in question discuss current unresolved personal problems with any clients?

4. Does the therapist in question eliminate usual and customary fees for therapy services with any clients?

(The above four are based on Gabbard in Slovut, 1992.)

5. Does the therapist in question meet clients for coffee, meals, or other forms of socialization outside therapy sessions?

6. During sessions, does the therapist in question take off jewelry or shoes or loosen clothing—such as a tie—or unbutton a shirt or blouse?

7. Does the therapist in question accept expensive gifts or numerous gifts from any clients?

8. Does the therapist in question become sexually stimulated by clients' descriptions of sexual behaviors or thoughts?

9. Does the therapist in question make comments about the attractiveness of any clients or make remarks about the bodies of any clients?

(The above five are based on Brock, n.d.)

10. Are sessions offered in nontraditional settings, such as the client's home, or in an automobile? (Keith-Spiegel & Koocher, 1985)

11. Is the office furnished in a manner that is not "businesslike" but rather has a "too-cozy ambiance"? (Keith-Spiegel & Koocher, 1985, p. 260)

12. Has the therapist in question avoided bringing a particular client's case to supervision or consultation because "others would not understand this client as I do"?

13. Does the therapist in question refer to a client by pet names?

14. Has the therapist in question sexually or romantically fantasized about any clients during sessions or after sessions?

15. If the therapist in question is male, has he gotten an erection during a session?

16. If the therapist in question is female, has she begun to lubricate during a session?

17. Has the therapist in question masturbated while thinking about any clients?

If you responded to the questions related to a coworker or supervisee, did you have concerns about their behavior? If so, what action do you plan to take? If you responded to the questions related to your own behavior, did your responses cause you any concern? If so, what action will you take to correct these ethical shortcomings?

▓ Examining Beliefs That Can Lead to Inappropriate Touch Within Psychotherapy

Sanderson (1995) described nine common types of relationships within psychotherapy that can lead to inappropriate touch. To identify if you have attitudes that lead to these types of relationships, respond to the following statements:

1. If a client's presenting problem is the result of sexual inhibitions, it is appropriate for a psychotherapist to prescribe sexual contact with the therapist as a part of the treatment.

2. If a client is going to learn to become a mature, loving person, the therapist must be viewed as a love/sexual object by that client. As a part of this dynamic, it may become necessary for erotic contact to take place between a client and the psychotherapist.

3. It is possible to cure a client of homosexuality by having the psychotherapist engage in sexual contact with that client.

4. A psychotherapist who is treating a client who is having difficulty accepting being a gay male or lesbian or who is just "coming out" as a gay male or lesbian can facilitate that client's progress by initiating sexual contact with that client.

5. Unlike sexual contact between men and women, sexual contact between people of the same gender is not exploitative.

6. It is common for a therapist and a client to develop an intense sexual attraction at the initial session.

7. Psychotherapists and clients frequently fall in love, and it is appropriate for such relationships to lead to marriage or other long-term relationships.

8. A client with developmental issues requires the use of regressive techniques so that the client can be reparented. As a part of this regression, it is often necessary for the client to sit on the psychotherapist's lap or to pretend to breast-feed. Contact with a client's genitals is sometimes necessary.

9. Sex between a feminist psychotherapist and a client does not have the patriarchal dynamics that usually exist in more traditional psychotherapeutic relationships and, therefore, is not harmful to a client and may empower a client.

If you found yourself agreeing with any of these statements, it is inadvisable for you to engage in the use of touch as an adjunct to talk therapy. Rather, participating in supervision/consultation is called for and ought to be sought immediately.

▓ Experiential Learning

Experiential learning is perhaps the best way to learn about personal attitudes and the effects of touch. Therefore, we have provided guidelines for exercises that make use of touch. These exercises can be done with seasoned psychotherapists, trainees, or, in some cases, clients.

Round 1

Instructions. This is a nonverbal exercise. The participants are strongly encouraged to remain silent until asked to process their experience. It will involve touching one another's hands. Participants are free to choose to end their involvement at any time during the exercise.

1. Take a few moments to become aware of being in this room. Pay attention to your breathing.
2. At this point, you are free to wander silently around the room or remain where you are standing.
3. As you pass people or they pass you, notice how you feel and what you are thinking.
4. If you are so inclined, offer to shake the hand of a passerby. If you choose to shake someone's hand, shake it as you would at any normal social function.
5. Notice how you decide whether to shake someone's hand.
6. If you or someone else declines a handshake, notice how you feel and what you think.
7. If you shake someone's hand, notice what you learn about this person and yourself. Is there fear, warmth, joy, or tension? Where are your eyes focused?
8. Notice who initiates the separation and how it is done.
9. Form a circle and discuss what you have learned about yourself.

Round 2

Round 2 is a more threatening exercise for many people because it involves not only the use of touch but also having one's eyes closed.

Instructions. This second exercise is similar to the first exercise in that it involves shaking hands; this time, however, participants are asked to keep their eyes closed whenever touching anyone. As before, any participant may cease taking part in the exercise at any time.

1. Close your eyes, and take a few moments to pay attention to breathing deeply.
2. Now you are free to move about the room or remain where you are standing.
3. You may offer your hand to anyone. Remember that each of you is free to accept or decline an offer of a handshake. In the event that you both choose to shake hands, you are both asked to close your eyes and keep them closed for the remainder of the physi-

cal contact. Once the physical contact has ended, you are free to open your eyes.

4. Pay attention to how this experience is similar to and different from the previous exercise.

5. Form a circle and discuss what you learned about yourself by closing your eyes during any handshakes in which you took part.

Round 3

Round 3 involves extended touch and can be more anxiety producing for some individuals.

Instructions. This exercise is similar to the previous two experiences in that it involves hand-to-hand contact. It is different in that participants will be asked to extend the duration of the touch longer than in the first two exercises. As always, participants are free to cease participation at any time.

1. Take a moment to become consciously aware of your breathing.

2. You are now free to silently move about the room or remain where you are standing.

3. If you are so inclined, offer your hand to someone nearby. If that person takes your hand, rather than shaking it as before, simply grasp one another's hand and hold it still.

4. What do you notice about this experience? How is it different from shaking hands? What are you thinking and feeling?

5. Decide if you want to experience this contact with your eyes open or closed.

6. Notice how long you are comfortable having this contact with another person. Can you remain in contact for a few seconds longer than you are comfortable? What do you think and feel when you do this?

7. Form a circle and discuss what you have learned about yourself.

▩ Summary

As we have stressed when discussing the use of touch with clients, it is vital that the participants in these exercises, whether trainees or practicing psychotherapists, have the freedom to participate at the level at which they are comfortable. Participants must know that they can stop the process at any time and be given adequate time and attention to process the impact of the experience.

References

Adorno, T. W., Frenkel-Brunswick, E., Levinson, D. L., & Sanford, R. N. (1950). *The authoritarian personality*. New York: Harper.

Aguilera, D. (1967) Relationships between physical contact and verbal interactions between nurses and patients. *Journal of Psychiatric Nursing, 5*, 5-21.

Ainsworth, M. S. (1978). *Patterns of attachment: A psychological study of the strange situation*. Hillsdale, NJ: Lawrence Erlbaum.

Ainsworth, M. S. (1982, Fall). Effects of illuminating changes on infant monkey contacts with surrogates. *Psychological Record, 32*(4), 513-518.

Ainsworth, M. S. (1984, December). Contact comfort: A reconsideration of the original work. *Psychological Reports, 55*(3), 943-949.

Alagna, F. J., Whitcher, S. J., Fisher, J. D., & Wicas, E. A. (1979). Evaluative reaction to interpersonal touch in a counseling interview. *Journal of Counseling Psychology, 26*, 465-472.

Alyn, J. H. (1988, March). The politics of touch in therapy: A response to Wilison & Masson. *Journal of Counseling and Development, 66*(9), 432-433.

American Association for Counseling and Development. (1988). *Ethical standards*. Alexandria, VA: Author.

American Association of Marriage and Family Therapists. (1991). *A.A.M.F.T. code of ethics*. Washington, DC: Author.

American Group Psychotherapy Association. (1991). *Guidelines of group psychotherapy practice*. New York: Author.

American Medical Association Council on Scientific Affairs. (1994). *Memories of childhood abuse* (CSA Report No. 5-A-94).Chicago: Author.

275

American Psychiatric Association. (1986). *Principles of medical ethics with annotations especially applicable to psychiatry.* Washington, DC: Author.

American Psychiatric Association. (1994a). *Diagnostic and statistical manual of mental disorders* (4th ed.). Washington, DC: Author.

American Psychiatric Association. (1994b). *Statement on memories of sexual abuse.* Washington, DC: Author.

American Psychoanalytic Association. (1983). *Principles of ethics for psychoanalysis and provisions for implementation of the principles of ethics for psychoanalysts* (Rev. April 1983, approved December 1983, by the Board of Professional Standards and Executive Council). New York: Author.

American Psychological Association. (1981). *Ethical principles of psychologists.* Washington, DC: Author.

American Psychological Association. (1982). *Ethical principles in the conduct of research with human participants.* Washington, DC: Author.

American Psychological Association. (1992). Ethical principles of psychologists and code of conduct. *American Psychologist, 47,* 1597-1661.

Andersen, J. F., Andersen, P. A., & Lustig, M. W. (1987). Opposite sex touch avoidance: A national replication and extension. *Journal of Nonverbal Behavior, 11,* 89-109.

Andersen, P. A., & Leibowitz, K. (1978). The development and nature of the construct touch avoidance. *Environmental Psychology and Nonverbal Behavior, 3,* 89-106.

Ansbacher, H., & Ansbacher, R. (1964). *The individual psychology of Alfred Adler: A systematic presentation in selections.* New York: Harper & Row.

Argyle, M. (1988). *Bodily communication.* New York: Methuen.

Bacorn, C., & Dixon, D. (1984). The effects of touch on depressed and vocationally undecided clients. *Journal of Counseling Psychology, 31,* 488-496.

Bailey, K. (1992, Summer). Therapeutic massage with survivors of abuse. *Massage Therapy Journal,* 79-85, 116-120.

Barnett, K. (1972). A theoretical construct of the concepts of touch as they relate to nursing. *Nursing Research, 21*(2), 106-107.

Barnlund, D. (1975). Communication styles in two cultures: Japan and the United States. In A. Kendon, R. Harris, & M. Keys (Eds.), *Organization of behaviour in face-to-face interaction.* Chicago: The Hague.

Bauer, B. (1977a). Tactile sensitivity: Development of a behavioral response checklist. *American Journal of Occupational Therapy, 31*(6), 357-361.

Bauer, B. (1977b). Tactile-sensitive behavior in hyperactive and non-hyperactive children. *American Journal of Occupational Therapy, 31*(7), 447-453.

Bear, E., & Dimock, P. (1988). *Adults molested as children: A survivor's manual for women and men.* Orwell, VT: Safer Society Press.

Beck, A. T. (1976). *Cognitive therapy and the emotional disorders.* New York: International Universities Press.

Benjamin, B. E. (1995a, Summer). Massage and bodywork with survivors of abuse, part I. *Massage Therapy Journal,* 23-32.

Benjamin, B. E. (1995b, Fall). Massage and bodywork with survivors of abuse, part II. *Massage Therapy Journal,* 23-30.

Berkowitz, S. R. (1980, October 1). *Opinion on potential legal liability with respect to the use of sexual surrogates for therapy.* Paper prepared for the Massachusetts Psychological Association by its legal counsel, Boston.

Biggar, M. L. (1984). Maternal aversion to mother–infant contact. In C. C. Brown (Ed.), *The many facets of touch.* Skillman, NJ: Johnson & Johnson Baby Products.

Bisbing, S. B., Jorgenson, L. M., & Sutherland, P. K. (1995). *Sexual abuse by professionals: A legal guide.* Charlottesville, VA: The Michie Co.

Boderman, A., Freed, D. W., & Kinnucan, M. T. (1972). Touch like me: Testing an encounter group assumption. *Journal of Applied Behavioral Science, 8*(5), 527-533.

Boguslawski, M. (1979). The use of therapeutic touch in nursing. *Journal of Continuing Education in Nursing, 10*(4), 9-15.

Borys, D. S., & Pope, K. S. (1989). Dual relationships between therapist and client: A national survey of psychologists, psychiatrists and social workers. *Professional Psychology: Research and Practice, 20,* 283-293.

Bouhoutsos, J. C. (1984). Sexual intimacy between psychotherapists and clients. In L. Walker (Ed.), *Women and mental health policy* (pp. 207-227). Beverly Hills, CA: Sage.

Bowlby, J. (1952). *Maternal care and mental health: A report on behalf of the World Health Organization.* Geneva, Switzerland: World Health Organization.

Brazelton, T. B., & Cramer, B. (1990). *The earliest relationship: Parents, infants, and the drama of early attachment.* Reading, MA: Addison-Wesley.

Breuer, J., & Freud, S. (1955). Studies in hysteria. In *The standard edition of the complete psychological works of Sigmund Freud: Vol. 2.* London: Hogarth.

Breuer, J., & Freud, S. (1957). *Studies in hysteria (1893-1895).* New York: Basic Books.

Brock, G. W. (n.d.). *Ethics "at risk" test for marriage and family therapists.* Unpublished form available from author at 315 Funkhourser Building, University of Kentucky, Lexington, KY 40506-0054.

Brown, C. C. (Ed.). (1984). *The many facets of touch* [Proceedings from conference chaired by K. F. Barnard & T. B. Brazelton]. Skillman, NJ: Johnson & Johnson Baby Products.

Brown, R., & Gilman, A. (1960). The pronouns of power and solidarity. In T. A. Sebeok (Ed.), *Style in language.* Cambridge, MA: Technology Press.

California Department of Consumer Affairs. (1990). *Professional therapy never includes sex.* (Available from Board of Psychology, 1430 Howe Ave., Sacramento, CA 95825)

Cohen, S. S. (1987). *The magic of touch.* New York: Harper & Row.

Collard, R. R. (1967). Fear of strangers and play behavior in kittens with varied social experience. *Child Development, 38,* 877-891.

Collier, G. (1985). *Emotional expression.* Hillsdale, NJ: Lawrence Erlbaum.

Committee on Women in Psychology. (1989). If sex enters into the psychotherapy relationship. *Professional Psychology: Research and Practice, 20*(2), 112-115.

Corney, G., Corney, M. S., & Callanan, P. (1994). *Issues and ethics in the helping professions* (4th ed.). Monterey, CA: Brooks/Cole.

Cousins, N. (1989). *Head first: The biology of hope.* New York: Dutton.

Cowen, E. L., Weissberg, R. P., & Lotyczeuski, B. S. (1982). Physical contact in helping interactions with young children. *Journal of Consulting and Clinical Psychology, 50*(2), 219-225.

Cowen, E. L., Weissberg, R. P., & Lotyczeuski, B. S. (1983). Physical contact in interactions between clinicians and young children. *Journal of Consulting and Clinical Psychology, 51,* 132-138.

Crawford, C. B. (1994). Effects of sex and sex roles on avoidance of same- and opposite-sex touch. *Perceptual and Motor Skills, 79*(1), 107-112.

Derlega, V. J., Lewis, R. J., Harrison, S., Winstead, B. A., & Costanza, R. (1989, Summer). Gender differences in the initiation and attribution of tactile intimacy. *Journal of Nonverbal Behavior, 13*(2), 83-96.

Dies, R. R., & Greenberg, B. (1976). Effects of physical contact in an encounter group context. *Journal of Consulting and Clinical Psychology, 44*(3), 400-405.

Diocese of Minnesota. (1990, May). What is sexual exploitation? *Soundings, 13*(4), 7.

Dixon, S., Yogman, M., Tronick, E., Als, H., Adamson, L., & Brazelton, T. B. (1981). Early social interactions with parents and strangers. *Journal of the American Academy of Child Psychiatry, 20,* 32-52.

Dobson, K. S., & Craig, K. D. (Eds.). (1996). *Advances in cognitive-behavioral therapy.* Thousand Oaks, CA: Sage.

Dorland's medical dictionary (25th ed.). (1974). Philadelphia: Saunders.

Dujovne, B. E. (1983). Sexual feelings, fantasies, and acting out in psychotherapy. *Psychotherapy: Theory, Research, and Practice, 20*(2), 242-250.

Dunne, C., Bruggen, P., & O'Brien, C. (1982). Touch and action in group therapy of younger adolescents. *Journal of Adolescence, 5,* 31-38.

Edwards, D. J. A. (1984). The experience of interpersonal touch during a personal growth program: A factor analytic approach. *Human Relations, 37*(2), 769-780.

Ekman, P., & Friesen, W. V. (1977). Hand movements. *Journal of Communication, 22,* 353-374.

Ellis, A. (1962). *Reason and emotion in psychotherapy.* New York: Lyle Stuart.

Ellis, A., & Bernard, M. E. (Eds.). (1985). *Clinical applications of rational-emotive therapy.* New York: Plenum Press.

Feldman-Summers, S., & Jones, G. (1984). Psychological impacts of sexual contact between therapists or other health care practitioners and their clients. *Journal of Consulting and Clinical Psychology, 52,* 1054-1061.

Ferber, A., Mendelsohn, M., & Napier, G. (Eds.). (1972). *The book of family therapy.* New York: Science House.

Ferenczi, S. (1952). *First contributions to psychoanalysis.* New York: Brunner/Mazel.

Field, T., Schanberg, S., Scafidi, F., Bauer, C., Vega-Lahr, N., Garcis, R., Nystrom, J., & Kuhn, C. (1986). Tactile/kinesthetic stimulation effects on preterm neonates. *Pediatrics, 77,* 654-658.

Fisher, J. D., Rytting, M., & Heslin, R. (1976). Hands touching hands: Affective and evaluative effects of an interpersonal touch. *Sociometry, 39,* 416-421.

Flores, A. (Ed.). (1988). *Professional ideal.* Belmont, CA: Wadsworth.

Ford, C. W. (1989). *Where healing waters meet: Touching mind and emotion through the body.* Barrytown, NY: Station Hill Press.

Forer, B. (1969). The taboo against touching in psychotherapy. *Psychotherapy: Theory, Research, and Practice, 6*(4), 229-231.

Frank, J. D. (1973). *Persuasion and healing* (2nd ed.). Baltimore: Johns Hopkins University Press.

Frank, L. (1957). Tactile communication. *General Psychological Monographs, 56,* 209-255.

Freeman, T., McGhie, A., & Cameron, J. (1957). The state of the ego in chronic schizophrenia. *British Journal of Medical Psychology, 30*(1), 9-19.

Freud, S. (1960). *The ego and the id.* New York: Norton.

Freud, S. (1983). Further recommendations in the technique of psychoanalysis: Observations on transference-love. In P. Rieff (Ed.), *Freud: Therapy and technique* (pp. 167-180). New York: Collier. (Original work published 1915)

Fromm-Reichmann, F. (1959). *Psychoanalysis and psychotherapy.* Chicago: University of Chicago Press.

Fromme, D. K., Jayness, W. E., Taylor, D. K., Hanold, E. G., Daniell, J., Rountree, R., & Fromme, M. L. (1989, Spring). Nonverbal behavior and attitudes toward touch. *Journal of Nonverbal Behavior, 13*(1), 8-14.

Fuchs, L. L. (1975). Reflections on touching and transference in psychotherapy. *Clinical Social Work Journal, 3*(3), 167-176.

Gabbard, G. O. (1994). Teetering on the precipice: A commentary on Lazarus's "How certain boundaries and ethics diminish therapeutic effectiveness." *Ethics and Behavior 4(3)*, 283-286.

Gabbard, G. O., & Lester, E. P. (1995). *Boundaries and boundary violations in psychoanalysis.* New York: Basic Books.

Gechtman, L. (1989). Sexual contact between social workers and their clients. In G. O. Gabbard (Ed.), *Sexual exploitation in professional relationships* (pp. 27-38). Washington, DC: American Psychiatric Press.

Geib, P. G. (1982). The experience of nonerotic physical contact in traditional psychotherapy: A critical investigation of the taboo against touch. *Dissertation Abstracts International, 43,* 248B.

Geldard, F. (1972). *The human senses* (2nd ed.). New York: John Wiley.

Goffman, E. (1956). The nature of deference and demeanor. *American Anthropologist, 58,* 473-502.

Goffman, E. (1971). *Relations in public: Microstudies in the public order.* New York: Basic Books.

Goldberg, S., & Lewis, M. (1969). Play behavior in the year-old infant: Early sex differences. *Child Development, 40,* 21-31.

Goldberg, S., & Rosenthal, R. (1986). Self-touching behavior in the job interview: Antecedents and consequences. *Journal of Nonverbal Behavior, 10*(1), 65-80.

Goldman, A. H. (1980). *The moral foundations of professional ethics.* Totowa, NJ: Rowman and Littlefield.

Goldman, M., & Fordyce, J. (1983). Prosocial behavior as affected by eye contact, touch, and voice expression. *Journal of Social Psychology, 121,* 125-129.

Gonsiorek, J. C. (1995). *Breach of trust: Sexual exploitation by health care professionals and clergy.* Thousand Oaks, CA: Sage.

Goodman, M., & Teicher, A. (1988, Winter). To touch or not to touch. *Psychotherapy, 25*(4), 492-500.

Gorlin, R. A. (Ed.). (1990). *Codes of Professional Responsibility, 2nd ed.* Washington, DC: The Bureau of National Affairs, Inc.

Guntrip, H. (1971). *Psychoanalytic theory, therapy, and the self.* New York: Basic Books.

Gutheil, T. G., & Gabbard, G. O. (1993). The concept of boundaries in clinical practice: Theoretical and risk-management dimensions. *American Journal of Psychiatry, 150*(2), 188-196.

Halberstadt, A. (1985). Race, socioeconomic status, and nonverbal behavior. In A. Siegman & S. Felstein (Eds.), *Multichannel integrations of nonverbal behavior.* Hillsdale, NJ: Lawrence Erlbaum.

Hall, E. (1966). *The hidden dimension.* Garden City, NY: Doubleday.

Hall, E. T. (1963). A system for the notation of proxemic behavior. *American Anthropologist, 65,* 1003-1026.

Hall, J. (1984). *Nonverbal sex differences: Communication accuracy and expressive style.* Baltimore: Johns Hopkins University Press.

Hall, J. A., & Veccia, E. M. (1990). More "touching" observations: New insights on men, women, and interpersonal touch. *Journal of Personality and Social Psychology, 59*(6), 1155-1162.

Hall, K. R. L. (1962). The sexual, agonistic, and derived social behaviour patterns of the wild chacma baboon, Papio ursinus. *Proceedings of the Zoological Society of London, 139*(2), 283-327.

Hammond, C. D., Mutter, C. B., Frischholz, E., Hibler, N. S., Scheflin, A., & Wester, W. (1995). *Clinical hypnosis and memory: Guidelines for clinicians and for forensic hypnosis.* Des Plaines, IL: American Society of Clinical Hypnosis Press.

Harlow, H. (1971). *Learning to love.* New York: Albion.

Harlow, H., & Harlow, M. K. (1962). The effect of rearing conditions on behavior. *Bulletin of the Menninger Clinic, 26,* 213-224.

Henley, N. W. (1973a). The politics of touch. In P. Brown (Ed.), *Radical psychology.* New York: Harper & Row.

Henley, N. W. (1973b). Status and sex: Some touching observations. *Bulletin of the Psychonomic Society, 2*(2), 91-93.

Henley, N. W. (1977). *Body politics: Power, sex, and nonverbal communication.* Englewood Cliffs, NJ: Prentice Hall.

Herman, J. L. (1992). *Trauma and recovery.* New York: HarperCollins.

Heslin, R., & Alper, T. (1983). Touching: A bonding gesture. In J. Wiemann & R. Harrison (Eds.), *Nonverbal interaction.* Beverly Hills, CA: Sage.

Heslin, R., & Boss, D. (1980). Nonverbal intimacy in airport arrival and departure. *Personality and Social Psychology Bulletin, 6,* 248-252.

Hollender, M. (1970). The need or wish to be held. *Archives of General Psychiatry, 22,* 445-453.

Hollender, M., & Mercer, A. (1976). The wish to be held and wish to hold in men and women. *Archives of General Psychiatry, 33,* 49-51.

Hollinger, L. (1986). Communicating with the elderly. *Journal of Gerontological Nursing, 12*(3), 8-13.

Holroyd, J. C., & Brodsky, A. (1977). Psychologists' attitudes and practices regarding erotic and nonerotic physical contact with patients. *American Psychologist, 32,* 843-849.

Holroyd, J. C., & Brodsky, A. (1980, October). Does touching patients lead to sexual intercourse? *Professional Psychology: Research and Practice, 11*(5), 807-811.

Holroyd, J. C., & Brodsky, A. (1985). Biased reporting of therapist-patient sexual intimacy. *Professional Psychology: Research and Practice, 16*(5), 701-709.

Horton, J., Clance, P., & Sterk-Elifson, E. J. (1995). Touch psychotherapy: A survey of patients' experiences. *Psychotherapy, 32*(3), 457.

Hubble, M. A., Noble, F. C., & Robinson, E. E. (1981). The effect of counselor touch in an initial counseling session. *Journal of Counseling Psychology, 28,* 533-535.

Hunter, M. (1990). *Abused boys: The neglected victims of sexual abuse.* Lexington, MA: Lexington Books.

Huss, A. J. (1977). Touch with care or a caring touch? *American Journal of Occupational Therapy, 31*(1), 11-18.

Itakura, S., & Imamizu, H. (1994). An exploratory study of mirror-image shape discrimination in young children: Vision and touch. *Perceptual and Motor Skills, 78*(1), 83-88.

Jones, S. E., & Yarbrough, A. E. (1985). A naturalistic study of the meaning of touch. *Communication Monographs, 52,* 19-56.

Jourard, S. M. (1966). An exploratory study of body accessibility. *British Journal of Social and Clinical Psychology, 5*, 221-231.

Jourard, S. (1968). *Disclosing man to himself.* Princeton, NJ: Van Nostrand.

Jourard, S. M., & Rubin, J. (1968). Self-disclosure and touching: A study of two modes of interpersonal encounter and their interrelation. *Journal of Humanistic Psychology, 8*, 39-48.

Kadohata, C. (1989). *The floating world.* New York: Viking.

Kaplan, B., & Johnson, D. (1964). The social meaning of Navaho psychopathology and psychotherapy. In A. Kiev (Ed.), *Magic, faith, and healing: Studies in primitive psychiatry today.* New York: Free Press.

Kaplan, H. S. (1974). *The new sex therapy: Active treatment of sexual dysfunctions.* New York: Brunner/Mazel.

Kardener, S. H., Fuller, M., & Mensh, I. N. (1973). A survey of physicians' attitudes and practices regarding erotic and nonerotic contact with patients. *American Journal of Psychiatry, 130*(10), 1077-1081.

Katz, D. (1989). *The world of touch.* Hillsdale, NJ: Lawrence Erlbaum.

Keith-Spiegel, P., & Koocher, G. R. (1985). *Ethics in psychology: Professional standard and cases.* New York: Random House.

Knable, J. (1981). Handholding: One means of transcending barriers of communication. *Heart and Lung, 10*(6), 1106-1110.

Knaster, M. (1996). *Discovering the body's wisdom.* New York: Bantam.

Kolb, L. (1987). Neurophysiological hypotheses explaining post-traumatic stress disorder. *American Journal of Psychiatry, 144*, 989-995.

Krieger, D. (1975). Therapeutic touch: The imprimatur of nursing. *American Journal of Nursing, 75*(5), 784-787.

Krieger, D. (1979). *The therapeutic touch: How to use your hands to help or to heal.* Englewood Cliffs, NJ: Prentice Hall.

Krystal, H. (1988). *Integration and self-healing: Affect, trauma, alexithymia.* Hillsdale, NJ: Analytic Press.

L'Abate, L., Ganahl, G., & Hansen, J. C. (1986). *Methods of family therapy.* Englewood Cliffs, NJ: Prentice-Hall.

LaCrosse, M. B. (1980). Perceived counselor social influence and counseling outcomes: Validity of the Counselor Rating Form. *Journal of Counseling Psychology, 27*, 320-327.

Lamb, M. (1977). Father-infant and mother-infant interaction in the first year of life. *Child Development, 48*, 167-181.

Lamb, M. (1981). The development of father-infant relationships. In M. Lamb (Ed.), *The role of the father in child development.* New York: John Wiley.

Langland, R., & Panicucci, C. (1982). Effects of touch on communication with elderly confused clients. *Journal of Gerontological Nursing, 8*(3), 152-155.

Langs, R. (1987, January). Clarifying a new model of the mind. *Contemporary Psychoanalysis, 23*(1), 162-180.

Larsen, K. S., & LeRoux, J. (1984). A study of same sex touching attitudes: Scale development and personality predictors. *Journal of Sex Research, 20*(3), 264-278.

Lazarus, A. A. (1994). How certain boundaries and ethics diminish therapeutic effectiveness. *Ethics and Behavior 4*(3), 255-261.

Lazarus, R. S. (1976). *Patterns of adjustment* (3rd ed). New York: McGraw-Hill.

Leboyer, F. (1975). *Birth without violence.* New York: Knopf.

Levitan, A., & Johnson, J. (1986). The role of touch in healing and hypnotherapy. *American Journal of Clinical Hypnosis, 28*(4), 218-223.

Lipton, S. D. (1977). The advantages of Freud's techniques as shown in his analysis of the Rat Man. *International Journal of Psychoanalysis, 58,* 255-333.

Lowen, A. (1958). *Physical dynamics of character structure.* New York: Grune and Stratton.

Lowen, A. (1976). *Bioenergetics.* New York: Penguin.

Lubin, A. W. (Ed.). (1988). *Family therapy: A bibliography, 1937-1986.* New York: Greenwood.

Lutz, T., & Willcox, B. (1994). [Policy on teaching appropriate touch]. Unpublished materials from the Personal/Social Awareness Program, Lutheran Social Service, Minneapolis, MN. (Used with permission)

Lynch, J., Thomas, S., Mills, M., Malinow, K., & Katcher, A. (1974). The effect of human contact on cardiac arrhythmia in coronary care patients. *Journal of Nervous and Mental Disease, 158*(2), 88-99.

Lynch, M. A. (1978, April). The prognosis of child abuse. *Journal of Child Psychology and Psychiatry and Allied Disciplines, 19*(2), 175-180.

Major, B. (1981). Gender patterns in touching behavior. In C. Mayo & M. Henley (Eds.), *Gender and nonverbal behavior* (pp. 15-37). New York: Springer-Verlag.

Major, B., & Heslin, R. (1982). Perception of cross-sex and same-sex nonreciprocal touch: It is better to give than to receive. *Journal of Nonverbal Behavior, 6,* 148-162.

Major, B., Schmidlin, A., & Williams, L. (1990). Gender patterns in social touch: The impact of setting and age. *Journal of Personality and Social Psychology, 58*(4), 634-643.

Malmquist, C., Kiresuk, T., & Spano, R. (1966). Personality characteristics of women with repeated illegitimacies: Descriptive aspects. *American Journal of Orthopsychiatry, 36,* 476-484.

Marshall, M. (1992, February). Unpublished memorandum from the Minnesota Department of Health, Saint Paul.

Mason, W. A. (1967). Motivational aspects of social responsiveness in young chimpanzees. In H. Stevenson, E. Hess, & H. Rheingold (Eds.), *Early behavior: Comparative and developmental approaches.* New York: John Wiley.

Masson, J. M. (1988). *Against therapy: Emotional tyranny and the myth of psychological healing.* New York: Atheneum.

Masters, W., & Johnson, V. (1970a). *Human sexual inadequacy.* Boston: Little, Brown.

Masters, W. & Johnson, V. (1970b). *Human sexual response.* Boston: Little, Brown.

Masters, W. H., & Johnson, V. E. (1976). Principles of the new sex therapy. *American Journal of Psychiatry, 110,* 3370-3373.

McCartney, J. (1966). Overt transference. *Journal of Sex Research, 2*(3), 227-237.

McCorkle, R. (1974). Effects of touch on severely ill patients. *Nursing Research, 23*(2), 126-132.

McKechnie, J. L. (Ed.). (1983). *Webster's new universal unabridged dictionary* (2nd ed.). New York: Dorset & Baber.

McNeely, D. A. (1987). *Touching: Body therapy and depth psychology.* Toronto, Ontario, Canada: Inner City Books.

Mead, M., & MacGregor, F. (1951). *Growth and culture.* New York: Putnam.

Mehrabian, A. (1971). *The silent language: Implicit communication of emotions and attitudes.* Belmont, CA: Wadsworth.

Menninger, K. (1958). *Theory of psychoanalytic technique.* New York: Basic Books.

Menninger, K., & Holzman, P. (1973). *Theory of psychoanalytic technique.* New York: Basic Books.

Milakovich, J. C. (1993). Touching is psychotherapy: The differences between therapists who touch and those who do not. *Dissertation Abstracts International, 54*(6-B), 3347.

Miller, L. A. (1979). An explanation of therapeutic touch using the science of unitary man. *Nursing Forum, 18*(3), 278-287.

Mintz, E. E. (1969a). On the rationale of touch in psychotherapy. *Psychotherapy: Theory, Research, and Practice, 6*, 232-234.

Mintz, E. E. (1969b). Touch and the psychoanalytic tradition. *Psychoanalytic Review, 56*, 365-376.

Mitchell, G. (1979). *Behavioral sex differences in nonhuman primates.* New York: Van Nostrand Rienhold.

Moitoza, E. (1982). Portuguese families. In M. McGoldrick & J. Giordano (Eds.), *Ethnicity and family therapy.* New York: Guilford.

Money, J., Anneaille, C., & Werlwas, J. (1976). Hormonal and behavioral reversals in hyposomatotropic dwarfism. In E. Sacher (Ed.), *Hormones, behavior, and psychopathology.* New York: Raven.

Montagu, A. (1971). *Touching: The significance of the human skin.* New York: Columbia University Press.

Morgan, M. (1991). *Mutant message down under.* New York: HarperCollins.

Morris, D. (1971). *Intimate behavior.* New York: Random House.

Moursund, J. (1985). *The processing of counseling and therapy.* Englewood Cliffs, NJ: Prentice Hall.

Murphy, J. (1964). Psychotherapeutic aspects of shamanism on St. Lawrence Island, Alaska. In A. Kiev (Ed.), *Magic, faith, and healing: Studies in primitive psychology today.* New York: Free Press.

National Association of Social Workers. (1979). *Code of ethics.* Silver Springs, MD: Author.

Nelson, J. B. (1978). *Embodiment.* New York: Pilgrim.

Nguyen, M. L., Heslin, R., & Nguyen, R. (1975). The meaning of touch: Sex differences. *Journal of Communication, 25*, 92-103.

Noller, P. (1978). Sex differences in the socialization of affectionate expression. *Developmental Psychology, 14*(3), 317-319.

Offit, A. (1977). *The sexual self.* New York: J. B. Lippincott.

O'Hearne, J. J. (1972). How can we reach patients most effectively? *International Journal of Group Psychotherapy, 27*, 446-454.

Older, J. (1977, August). Four taboos that may limit the success of psychotherapy. *Psychiatry, 40*, 197-204.

Older, J. (1982). *Touching is healing.* New York: Stein & Day.

Ornstein, R. (1991). *Evolution of consciousness: The origins of the way we think.* New York: Simon & Schuster.

Parkes, C. M., Stevenson-Hinde, J., & Marris, P. (Eds.). (1991). *Attachment across the life cycle.* New York: Tavistock/Routledge.

Patterson, J. E. (1973). Effects of touch on self-exploration and the therapeutic relationship. *Journal of Consulting and Clinical Psychology, 40*, 170-175.

Pearlman, L. A., & Saakvitne, K. W. (1995). *Trauma and the therapist: Countertransference and vicarious traumatization in psychotherapy with incest survivors.* New York: Norton.

Peloquin, S. M. (1989, Winter). Helping through touch: The embodiment of caring. *Journal of Religion and Health, 8*(4), 299-322.

Perls, F. (1969). *Gestalt Therapy Verbatim.* Moab, UT: Real People Press.

Peterson, M. R. (1992). *At personal risk: Boundary violations in professional–client relationships.* New York: W. W. Norton.

Pisano, M. D., Wall, S. M., & Foster, A. (1986). Perceptions of nonreciprocal touch in romantic relationships. *Journal of Nonverbal Behavior, 10*(1), 29-40.

Polster, E., & Polster, M. (1973). *Gestalt therapy integrated: Contours of theory and practice.* New York: Vintage Books.

Pope, K. S. (1989). Therapists who become sexually intimate with a patient: Classifications, dynamics, recidivism, and rehabilitation. *Independent Practitioner, 9*(3), 28-34.

Pope, K. S. (1990a). Response to Williams's comment. *Professional Psychology: Research and Practice, 21,* 421-423.

Pope, K. S. (1990b). Therapist–patient sex as sex abuse: Six scientific, professional, and practical dilemmas in addressing victimization and rehabilitation. *Professional Psychology: Research and Practice, 21,* 227-239.

Pope, K. S., & Bouhoutsos, J. C. (1986). *Sexual intimacy between therapist and patients.* New York: Praeger.

Pope, K. S., Keith-Spiegel, P., & Tabachnick, B. G. (1986). Sexual attraction to clients: The human therapist and the (sometimes) inhuman training system. *American Psychologist, 41*(2), 147-158.

Pope, K. S., Tabachnick, B. G., & Keith-Spiegel, P. (1987). Ethics of practice: The beliefs and behaviors of psychologists as therapists. *American Psychologist, 42*(11), 993-1006.

Prescott, J. (1975, April). Body pleasure and the origins of violence. *The Futurist, 9,* 64-74.

Prescott, J. (1976). Somatosensory deprivation and its relationship to the blind. In Z. Jastrzembska (Ed.), *The effects of blindness and other impairments on early development.* New York: American Foundation for the Blind.

Prince, M. (1995). Theory of memory as a process. *Treating Abuse Today, 5*(2), 29-30. (Original work published in *The unconscious,* by M. Prince, 1914, New York: Macmillan)

Reeck, D. (1982). *Ethics for the professions: A Christian perspective.* Minneapolis: Augsburg.

Reich, W. (1972). *Character analysis.* New York: Simon & Schuster.

Reite, M., & Field, T. (Eds.). (1985). *The psychobiology of attachment and separation.* New York: Academic Press.

Rodolfa, E. R., Kraft, W., & Reilley, R. (1987). Stressors of professionals and trainees at APA-approved VA and counseling center internship sites. *Professional Psychology: Research and Practice, 19,* 31-40.

Rogers, C. (1970). *Carl Rogers on encounter groups.* New York: Harper & Row.

Ross, J. M. (1994). In search of fathering: A review. In S. Cath, A. Gurwitt, & J. M. Ross (Eds.), *Father and child: Developmental and clinical perspectives.* Hillsdale, NJ: Analytic Press.

Rubin, R. (1963). Maternal touch. *Nursing Outlook, 2,* 828-831.

Samovar, L., Porter, R., & Jain, N. (1981). *Understanding intercultural communication.* Belmont, CA: Wadsworth.

Sanderson, B. A. (1995). *It's never OK: A handbook for professionals on sexual exploitation by counselors and therapists.* Saint Paul: Minnesota Department of Corrections.

Satir, V. (1967). *Conjoint family therapy.* Palo Alto, CA: Science & Behavior Books.

Satir, V. (1972). *Peoplemaking.* Palo Alto, CA: Science & Behavior Books.

Schaffer, H. R., & Emerson, P. (1964). Patterns of response to physical contact in early human development. *Journal of Child Psychology and Psychiatry, 5,* 1-13.

Scheflen, A. E. (1973). *Body language and social order.* Englewood Cliffs, NJ: Prentice Hall.

Schoener, G. R. (1997). Personal communication, March 27th.

Schoener, G. R., & Gonsiorek, J. (1989, December). Assessment and development of rehabilitation plans for counselors who have sexually exploited their clients. *Journal of Counseling and Development, 67*(4), 227-232.

Schoener, G. R., & Luepker, E. T. (1996). Boundaries in group therapy: Ethical and practice issues. In B. DeChant (Ed.), *Women and group psychotherapy: Theory and practice* (pp. 373-388). New York: Guilford Press.

Schoener, G. R., Milgrom, J. M., Gonesiorek, J. C., Luepker, E. T., & Conroe, R. M. (Eds.). (1989). *Psychotherapists' sexual involvement with clients: Intervention and prevention.* Minneapolis, MN: Walk-In Counseling Center.

Schreber, D. (1955). *Memoirs of my illness.* London: W. Dawson.

Schultz, B. (1992). The body, touch, and psychotherapy: A brief orientation. *Body psychotherapy ethics.* Unpublished handout.

Schultz, L. G. (1975). A survey of social workers' attitudes and use of body and sex psychotherapies. *Clinical Social Work Journal, 3*(2), 90-99.

Seagull, A. (1968). Doctor don't touch me. *Voices, 4,* 86.

Shapiro, A. K., & Morris, L. A. (1978). Placebo effects in medical and psychological therapies. In S. Garfield & A. E. Bergin (Eds.), *Handbook of psychotherapy and behavioral change.* New York: John Wiley.

Shepard, M. (1972). *A psychiatrist's head.* New York: Peter H. Syden.

Shepard, M. (1975). *Fritz.* New York: E. P. Dutton.

Shepherd, I. (1979). Intimacy in psychotherapy. *Voices, 15*(1), 9-14.

Silverman, A. F., Pressman, M. E., & Bartel, H. W. (1973). Self-esteem and tactile communication. *Journal of Humanistic Psychology, 13,* 73-77.

Simon, R. I. (1989). Sexual exploitation of patients: How it begins before it happens. *Psychological Annals, 19,* 104-122.

Sivik, T. (1992). The thematic apperception test as an aid in understanding the psychodynamics of development of chronic idiopathic pain syndrome. *Psychotherapy and Psychosomatics, 57,* 57-60.

Sivik, T. (1993). Alexithymia and hypersensitivity to touch and palpation. *Integrative Physiological and Behavioral Science, 28*(2), 130-136.

Skinner, B. F. (1938). *The behavior of organisms: An experimental analysis.* New York: Appleton.

Skinner, B. F. (1969). *Contingencies of reinforcement: A theoretical analysis.* New York: Appleton-Century-Crofts.

Skinner, B. F. (1971). *Beyond freedom and dignity.* New York: Alfred A. Knopf.

Skinner, B. F. (1974). *About behaviorism.* New York: Alfred A. Knopf.

Slovut, G. (1992, October 15). Therapists who have sex with patients betray a trust. *Minneapolis Star Tribune,* pp. 1-2.

Smith, E. W. L. (1985). *The body in psychotherapy.* Jefferson, NC: McFarland.

Smith, J. (1989). *Senses and sensibilities.* New York: John Wiley.

Sonne, J., Meyer, B., Borys, D., & Marshall, V. (1985, April). Clients' reactions to sexual intimacy in therapy. *American Journal of Orthopsychiatry, 55*(2), 183-189.

Sonne, J., & Pope, K. S. (1991, Spring). Treating victims of therapist–patient sexual involvement [Special issue: Psychotherapy with victims]. *Psychotherapy, 28*(1), 174-187.

Spiegel, H., & Spiegel, D. (1978). *Trance and treatment: Clinical uses of hypnosis.* New York: Basic Books.

Spotnitz, H. (1972). Touch countertransference in group psychotherapy. *International Journal of Group Psychotherapy, 22,* 455-463.

Steele, K., & Colrain, J. (1990). Abreactive work with sexual abuse survivors: Concepts and techniques. In M. Hunter (Ed.), *The sexually abused male: Volume II* (pp. 1-55). Lexington, MA: Lexington Books.

Stier, D. S., & Hall, J. A. (1984). Gender differences in touch: An empirical and theoretical review. *Journal of Personality and Social Psychology, 47*(2), 440-459.

Stockwell, S. R., & Dye, A. (1980). Effects of counselor touch on counseling outcome. *Journal of Counseling Psychology, 27*(5), 433-446.

Strong, S. R. (1978). Social psychological approach to psychotherapy research. In S. Garfield & A. E. Bergin (Eds.), *Handbook of psychotherapy and behavioral change.* New York: John Wiley.

Strupp, H. H. (1973). On the basic ingredients of psychotherapy. *Journal of Consulting and Clinical Psychology, 41,* 1-8.

Strupp, H. H. (1978). Psychotherapy research and practice: An overview. In S. Garfield & A. E. Bergin (Eds.), *Handbook of psychotherapy and behavioral change.* New York: John Wiley.

Sue, D. W., & Sue, D. (1981). *Counseling the culturally different: Theory and practice* (2nd ed.). New York: John Wiley.

Summerhayes, D., & Suchner, R. (1978). Power implications of touch in male–female relationships. *Sex Roles, 4*(1), 103-110.

Suomi, S. J., & Harlow, H. F. (1972). Social rehabilitation of isolate reared monkeys. *Developmental Psychology, 6*(3), 487-496.

Sussman, N. M, & Rosenfeld, H. M. (1978, December). Touch, justification, and sex: Influences on the aversiveness of spatial violations. *Journal of Social Psychology, 106*(2), 215-225.

Taylor, B., & Wagner, N. (1976, November). Sex between therapist and clients: A review and analysis. *Professional Psychology: Research and Practice, 7*(4), 593-601.

Taylor, G., Bagby, R. M., & Parker, J. (1991). The alexithymia construct: A potential paradigm for psychosomatic medicine. *Psychosomatics, 32*(2), 153-164.

Thayer, S. (1982). Social touching. In W. Schiff & E. Foulke (Eds.), *Tactile perception: A source book.* New York: Cambridge University Press.

Thomas, Z. (1994). *Healing touch: The church's forgotten language.* Louisville, KY: Westminster/John Knox.

Thompson, E., Jr., & Pleck, J. (1987). The structure of male role norms. In M. Kimmel (Ed.), *Changing men.* Newbury Park, CA: Sage.

Timms, R., & Connors, P. (1990). Integrating psychotherapy and body work for abuse survivors: A psychological model. In M. Hunter (Ed.), *The sexually abused male: Volume II* (pp. 117-136). Lexington, MA: Lexington Books.

Timms, R., & Connors, P. (1992). *Embodying healing: Integrating bodywork and psychotherapy in recovery from childhood sexual abuse.* Orwell, VT: Safer Society Press.

Van der Kolk, B. (1994, January/February). The body keeps the score: Memory and the evolving psychology of post-traumatic stress. *Harvard Review of Psychiatry,* 253-265.

Van der Kolk, B., & Van der Hart, O. (1989). Pierre Janet and the breakdown of adaptation in psychological trauma. *American Journal of Psychiatry, 146,* 1530-1540.

Van der Kolk, B., & Van der Hart, O. (1991). The intrusive past: The flexibility of memory and the engraving of trauma. *American Imago, 48,* 425-454.

Wagner, N. (1972). *Ethical concerns of medical students.* Paper presented at the 1972 Western Workshop of the Center for the Study of Sex Education in Medicine, Santa Barbara, CA.

Waites, E. (1993). *Trauma and survival: Post-traumatic and dissociative disorders in women.* New York: Norton.

Watson, J. (1928). *Psychological care of infant and child.* New York: Norton.

Watson, W. (1975). The meaning of touch: Geriatric nursing. *Journal of Communication, 25*(3), 104-112.

Watson, W. H., & Graves, T. D. (1966). Quantitative research in proxemic behavior. *American Anthropologist, 68,* 971-985.

Weeks, G. R., & Treat, S. (1992). *Couples in treatment.* New York: Brunner/Mazel.

Weiss, S. (1966). The language of touch. *Nursing Research, 28*(2), 76-79.

Weiss, S. (1984). Parental touch and the child's body image. In C. C. Brown (Ed.), *The many facets of touch* (pp. 130-138). Skillman, NJ: Johnson & Johnson Baby Products.

Weiss, S. (1986). Psychophysiologic effects of caregiver touch on incidence of cardiac dysrhythmia. *Heart and Lung, 15*(5), 495-505.

Whitehurst, T., & Derlega, V. (1985). Influence of touch and preferences for control on visual behavior and subjective responses. In S. Ellyson & J. Dovidio (Eds.), *Power, dominance, and nonverbal behavior.* New York: Springer-Verlag.

Wilison, B. G., & Masson, R. L. (1986, April). The role of touch in therapy: An adjunct to communication. *Journal of Counseling and Development, 64,* 497-500.

Williams, M. H. (1990). Comment on Pope (1990). *Professional Psychology: Research and Practice, 21*(6), 420-421.

Willis, F. R., & Hamm, H. K. (1980). The use of interpersonal touch in securing compliance. *Journal of Nonverbal Behavior, 5*(1), 49-55.

Willis, F. R., Rinck, C. M., & Dean, L. M. (1978). Interpersonal touch among adults in cafeteria lines. *Perceptual and Motor Skills, 47,* 1147-1152.

Wilson, J. M. (1982, January). The value of touch in psychotherapy. *American Journal of Orthopsychiatry, 52*(1), 65-72.

Wilson, J. P., & Lindy, J. D. (Eds.). (1994). *Countertransference in the treatment of PTSD.* New York: Guilford.

Winnicott, D. (1965). *The maturational processes and the facilitating environment: Studies in the theory of emotional development.* New York: International Universities Press.

Wolberg, L. R. (1954). *The technique of psychotherapy.* New York: Grune & Stratton.

Wolpe, J. (1990). *The practice of behavior therapy, 4th ed.* New York: Pergamon.

Woodall, W. G., & Folger, J. P. (1985). Nonverbal cue context and episodic memory: On the availability and endurance of nonverbal behaviors as retrieval cues. *Communication Monographs, 52,* 319-333.

Woodard, K. (1993). The relationship between skin compliance, age, gender, and tactile discriminative thresholds in humans. *Somatosensory and Motor Research, 10*(1), 63-67.

Wright, R. H. (1985). The Wright way: Who needs enemies? *Psychotherapy in Private Practice, 3,* 111-118.

Wright, R. W. (1981). Psychologists and professional liability (malpractice) insurance: A retrospective review. *American Psychologist, 36,* 1485-1493.

Yankura, J., & Dryden, W. (1994). *Albert Ellis.* London: Sage.

Yehuda, R., Giller, E., Southwick, S., Lowy, M., & Masson, J. (1991). Hypothalamic-pituitary-adrenal dysfunction in post-traumatic stress disorder. *Biological Psychiatry, 30,* 1031-1048.

Index

About the Authors

Mic Hunter, Psy. D., is a clinical psychologist in private practice in Saint Paul, Minnesota. Previously, he was employed in several chemical dependency treatment programs and mental health centers in Minnesota. His educational background includes a bachelor's degree in psychology from Macalester College, a master of arts degree in human development from Saint Mary's University, Winona, a master of science degree in education-psychological services from the University of Wisconsin–Superior, and a doctoral degree in clinical psychology from the Minnesota School of Professional Psychology. He has completed the 2-year intensive postgraduate program at the Gestalt Institute of the Twin Cities and the University of Minnesota's Alcohol/Drug Counseling Education Program and Chemical Dependency and Family Intimacy Training Project. He was first licensed as a psychologist in 1988, and as a marriage and family therapist in 1989. He first received certification as a chemical dependency practitioner in 1980, and is now internationally certified as an alcohol and drug counselor.

He speaks throughout North America to both professional audiences and the general public. He has presented workshops at the annual meetings of the American Association of Sex Educators, Counselors and Therapists; the American Psychological Association; the Society for the Scientific Study of Sex; and the American Orthopsychiatric Association. He has presented at all five National Conferences on Male Sexual Abuse Survivors, including giving a keynote address at the conference in Tucson in 1990. He has been sought out by the print and broadcast media for interviews more than 100 times. He serves on the editorial boards of the *Journal of Child Sexual Abuse*, *Violence Against Women*, and the *Journal of Men's Studies*. He has been a member of the M.A.L.E., Inc. Advisory Board and the Board of the National Organization on Male Sexual Victimization.

He is the author of *Abused Boys: The Neglected Victims of Sexual Abuse* and *Joyous Sexuality: Healing From Family Sexual Dysfunction*. He is the editor of *The Sexually Abused Male: Volume I. Prevalence, Impact, and Treatment* and *Volume II. Application of Treatment Strategies*, *Adult Survivors of Sexual Abuse: Treatment Innovations*, and *Child Survivors and Perpetrators of Sexual Abuse: Treatment Innovations*. His most recent publication is a photographic documentary focusing on the disappearance of the traditional male barbershop titled *The American Barbershop: A Closer Look at a Disappearing Place*, which was nominated for the Minnesota Book Award for nonfiction. His current writing project is *Emotions: The Language of Intimacy*.

He can be reached at 2469 University Ave. West, Saint Paul, MN 55114.

Jim Struve, L. C. S. W., is in full-time private practice with Metropolitan Psychotherapy Associates in Atlanta, Georgia. He provides specialized services related to trauma (including sexual abuse), dissociation, sexual identity, gay and lesbian concerns, and men's issues. He is also certified as a Diplomate in Clinical Social Work by the National Association of Social Workers and is a member of the National Registry of Certified Group Psychotherapists. His educationalbackgroundincludesanundergraduate degree in communication arts from the University of Wisconsin–Madison and a master's degree in social work from Atlanta University.

Prior to his move to private practice, he worked with a variety of social service agencies in both the public and private sectors. He has extensive clinical and administrative experience with child protective services, residential treatment for children and adolescents, and inpatient psychiatric treatment, and he previously served as Clinical Department Head for Social Work Services in two private psychiatric hospitals.

As a conference speaker and workshop presenter in North America, Canada, and Europe, he is frequently invited to address clinical issues concerning the treatment of sexual abuse survivors, sociopolitical issues related to patriarchy, and alternative roles for men in society. He regularly speaks to both professional audiences and the general public. He has presented at all five National Conferences on Male Sexual Abuse Survivors, and he was Chairperson for the Second National Conference on Male Survivors of Sexual Abuse in Atlanta in September 1989. He is frequently sought out by local and national print and broadcast media for interviews.

He is the author of "Dancing With the Patriarchy: The Politics of Sexual Abuse" in *The Sexually Abused Male: Volume I. Prevalence, Impact, and Treatment* (1990) edited by Mic Hunter. He is a Board Member of the National Organization on Male Sexual Victimization, a position he has held since the organization's inception. In addition to his work as a therapist, he is an active volunteer in a variety of social services projects in the community. He has a particular interest in activities that are focused toward social change and the creation of alternatives to patriarchy. He has served on the Board of Directors for Men Stopping Violence (Atlanta, Georgia) and has been a member of the Georgia Council on Child Abuse Sexual Advisory Committee (on which he was instrumental in expanding services to include male survivors of sexual abuse). His current project is a book that will focus on patriarchy and the politics of psychotherapy.

He can be reached at Metropolitan Psychotherapy Associates, 2801 Buford Highway, N.E., Suite 400, Atlanta, GA 30329.

Printed in the United States
979900005B